THE
GERMAN
GENERALS
TALK-

BY THE SAME AUTHOR:

REPUTATIONS TEN YEARS AFTER
SHERMAN, GENIUS OF CIVIL WAR
WAR IN OUTLINE 1914-1918

THE
GERMAN
GENERALS
TALK -

B. H. LIDDELL HART

QUILL
NEW YORK 1979

To my son, Adrian,
and to all who helped in this effort
to be of service to history

CONTENTS

PART III—THROUGH GERMAN EYES

MAPS

PREFACE

WHEN THE WAR ENDED, I WAS FORTUNATE IN HAVING AN early opportunity of exploring the inside of "the enemy camp"—to find out what had gone on behind the opposing front, and in the opponent's mind. Some work I was doing for official quarters brought me in contact with the German generals and admirals over a lengthy period. In the course of many discussions with them I was able to gather their evidence on the events of the war before memories had begun to fade or become increasingly coloured by after-thoughts. It brought to light many secrets of the German command and its workings.

Understanding of what happened was helped by studying the German generals, as well as hearing their accounts. Few of them resembled the typical picture of an iron "Prussian" soldier. Rundstedt came nearest it, but in his case the impression was offset by his natural courtesy and light touch of humour. His quiet dignity in adversity and uncomplaining acceptance of hard conditions—that were no credit to his captors —won the respect of most British officers who encountered him. In contrast to him were a number of aggressive young generals, blustering and boorish, who owed their rise to Nazi favour. But the majority were of a different type to both, and by no means a dominating one. Many would have looked in their natural place at any conference of bank managers or civil engineers.

They were essentially technicians, intent on their professional job, and with little idea of things outside it. It is easy to see how Hitler hoodwinked and handled them, and found them good instruments up to a point.

In sifting and piecing together their evidence it was useful to have a background knowledge of the military situation in the pre-war period. It was a guide not only in saving time but in avoiding misconceptions that were still widely prevalent at the end of the war.

Between the wars, my work as a military correspondent required me to keep a watchful eye on developments in Europe, and I always sought to keep touch with the trends in Germany. This task was eased, directly and indirectly, by the extent to which my own military books were read in Germany, some of the leading soldiers themselves undertaking the translation.

The warnings I gave about the Nazi menace, and the emphatic line I took in opposing the policy of "appeasement" will be known to most of those who, in America as well as in Europe, followed my pre-war writings. I pointed out the ominous signs even before Hitler came into power. At the same time it was evident to me that the German General Staff had little influence with Hitler compared with what it had exercised in the Kaiser's time, and that it tended to be more of a brake upon his aggressive plans than an impetus to them.

But the idea that the General Staff had played a dominant part in Germany's aggressive course, as it did before 1918, still coloured the prosecution proceedings at the Nuremberg trial. Earlier, that fixed idea had hindered the British and American governments from giving timely and effective encouragement to the underground movement in Germany which, with military backing, had long been planning Hitler's overthrow. That still prevailing conception of the General Staff's influence on policy was a long out-of-date notion. But legends are persistent, and delusions tenacious. They had the unfortunate effect of postponing Hitler's downfall and prolonging the war months, and probably years, after it would otherwise have ended. The ill-consequences for Europe are now beginning to be realised.

I would like to acknowledge my indebtedness to the help and historical sense of those who facilitated the early exploration of events. Also, to Captain F. S. Kingston, whose mastery of the German language and intuitive teamwork were of great assistance in the discussions. At the same time I would express my appreciation of the ready help given by so many of those in the other camp in contributing to this piece of historical research, and of the objective attitude most of them showed in discussing events. Finally, I wish to thank Major-General Sir Percy Hobart, Chester Wilmot, G. R. Atkinson and Desmond Flower for valuable comments and suggestions while the book was in preparation.

B. H. LIDDELL HART

PART I

HITLER'S GENERALS

I

THE SUICIDAL SCHISM

EVERYTHING IN WAR LOOKS DIFFERENT AT THE TIME FROM WHAT it looks in the clearer light that comes after the war. Nothing looks so different as the form of the leaders. The public picture of them at the time is not only an unreal one, but changes with the tide of success.

Before the war, and still more during the conquest of the West, Hitler came to appear a gigantic figure, combining the strategy of a Napoleon with the cunning of a Machiavelli and the fanatical fervour of a Mahomet. After his first check in Russia, his figure began to shrink, and towards the end he was regarded as a blundering amateur in the military field, whose crazy orders and crass ignorance had been the Allies' greatest asset. All the disasters of the German Army were attributed to Hitler; all its successes were credited to the German General Staff.

That picture is not true, though there is some truth in it. Hitler was far from being a stupid strategist. Rather, he was too brilliant—and suffered from the natural faults that tend to accompany such brilliance.

He had a deeply subtle sense of surprise, and was a master of the psychological side of strategy, which he raised to a new pitch. Long before the war he had described to his associates

3

how the daring coup that captured Norway might be carried out, and how the French could be manœuvred out of the Maginot Line. He had also seen, better than any general, how the bloodless conquests that preceded the war might be achieved by undermining resistance beforehand. No strategist in history has been more clever in playing on the minds of his opponents—which is the supreme art of strategy.

It was the very fact that he had so often proved right, contrary to the opinion of his professional advisers, which helped him to gain influence at their expense. Those results weakened their arguments in later situations which they gauged more correctly. For in the Russian campaign his defects became more potent than his gifts, and the debit balance accumulated to the point of bankruptcy. Even so, it has to be remembered that Napoleon, who was a professional strategist, had been just as badly dazzled by his own success, and made the same fatal mistakes in the same place.

Hitler's worst fault here was the way he refused to "cut his loss" and insisted on pressing the attack when the chances of success were fading. But that was the very fault which had been most conspicuous in Foch and Haig, the Allied commanders of the last war, as well as in Hindenburg and Ludendorff, who then held the German Supreme Command. All these had been professional soldiers. Hitler also did much to produce the German armies' collapse in France by his reluctance to sanction any timely withdrawal. But, here again, his attitude was exactly the same as that of Foch. The vital difference was that in 1918 the commanders on the spot did not obey Foch more than they deemed wise, whereas in 1944-45 the German generals were afraid to disobey Hitler's orders.

It is the cause of that fear, and the internal conflict in the High Command, that we have to probe in order to find the real explanation why the German plans miscarried. Hitler's strategic intuition and the General Staff's strategic calculation might have been an all-conquering combination. Instead, they produced a suicidal schism that became the salvation of their opponents.

The older school of generals, products of the General Staff system, had been the chief executants of German strategy throughout the war, but in the days of success their part had not received full recognition. After the tide turned, they filled an increasing part in the public picture, and came to be regarded by the Allied peoples as the really formidable element on the opposing side. During the last year the spotlight was largely focused on Rundstedt, their leading representative. The constant question became, not what Hitler would do, but what Rundstedt would do—both in the military field and in a political coup to wrest power from the Nazis.

The German generals have been regarded as such a closely-knit body, and so much of one mind, as to be capable of wielding tremendous political power. That impression accounts for the persistent expectation, on the Allies' side, that the generals would overthrow Hitler—an expectation that was never fulfilled. It also accounts for the popular conviction that they were as great a menace as he was, and shared the responsibility for Germany's aggressions. That picture was true of the last war, but was now out of date. The German generals had little effect on the start of the Second World War—except as an ineffectual brake.

Once the war had started, their executive efficiency contributed a lot to Hitler's success, but their achievement was overshadowed by his triumph. When they came into more prominence in the eyes of the outside world, as Hitler's star waned, they had become more impotent inside their own country.

That was due to a combination of factors. They stood for a conservative order and tradition which had little appeal to a generation brought up in the revolutionary spirit and fanatical faith of National Socialism. They could not count on the loyalty of their own troops in any move against the régime—and especially its faith-inspiring Führer. They were handicapped by the way they had isolated themselves from public affairs, and by the way Hitler cunningly isolated them from sources of knowledge. Another factor was their ingrained discipline and profound sense of the importance of the oath of loyalty which they had sworn to the Head of the State. Ludicrous as this may seem in regard to one who was himself so outstanding as a promise-breaker, it was a genuine feeling on their part, and the most honourable of the factors which hampered them. But along with it often ran a sense of personal interest which undercut their loyalty to their fellows, and their country's best interests, in face of a common threat. The play of individual ambitions and the cleavage of personal interests constituted a fatal weakness in their prolonged struggle to maintain their professional claim in the military field, and to preserve it from outside interference. This struggle went on throughout the twelve years from Hitler's rise to Germany's fall.

The first phase ended in a definite advantage to the professionals that was indirectly gained when Himmler played on Hitler's fears so effectively as to prompt him to carry out a murderous purge of Captain Roehm and other Brownshirt leaders. It is by no means clear whether the latter designed to overthrow Hitler, but there is no doubt that they were aspiring to fill a big place in the military system. Once they were killed off, Hitler became more dependent on the generals' support, and the latter were able to re-establish their own supremacy in the Army.

The second phase reached a climax in January, 1938, when the professionals themselves were caught in another of Himmler's traps. In 1933 Hitler had chosen General von Blomberg as his War Minister. His fellow-generals became increasingly disturbed at his susceptibility to Hitler's influence, and were then shocked to hear that he was marrying a typist in his office. That alienated their sympathies still further. But Hitler gave this "democratic" marriage his blessing and graced the wedding. Soon after it, Himmler produced a police dossier purporting to show that the bride was a prostitute. Thereupon Hitler, in real or simulated fury, dismissed Blomberg from office. Himmler followed this up by producing another dossier in which homosexual charges had been fabricated against General von Fritsch, the Commander-in-Chief of the Army, whereupon he in turn was removed from his post by Hitler —and never reinstated, though subsequently vindicated after a court of inquiry. (A fuller account of this crisis is given in Chapter III.)

Hitler exploited the moral shock that the officers' corps had suffered by seizing the opportunity to assume supreme command of the German armed forces. This paved the way for his ultimate control of strategy, while enabling Himmler to strengthen his own influence. General Keitel, whose wire-pulling had weakened the united front of the generals in their protest against Fritsch's treatment, was appointed to succeed Blomberg, but with a lower status, and henceforth only kept that place by subservience to Hitler. A more reputable soldier, General von Brauchitsch, who belonged neither to the reactionary nor the Nazi school, was made head of the Army. By this shrewd step, Hitler sought to placate the Army, while assuring himself of an executive commander who would be easier to handle than Fritsch.

Brauchitsch, however, made a stronger rally in defence of the professional class than had been expected. He also sought to slow down the pace of Nazi foreign policy by a warning that the German Army was not ready for war and that Hitler must not push his aggressive moves so far as to produce a fight. He was stiffened in his protests by the Chief of the General Staff, General Beck, who came out with such open condemnation of Hitler's warlike policy as to spur Hitler to dismiss him. Even then, Brauchitsch and Halder, Beck's successor, made a stand when Hitler looked like proceeding to extremes against Czecho-Slovakia, but the ground was cut away beneath their feet when the French and British Governments bowed to Hitler's threat of war.

With the added prestige of his bloodless conquest of Czecho-Slovakia Hitler was able to force the pace over Poland. The generals were little check on him here beyond helping to convince him that no risk of war on that issue must be taken unless he first secured Russia's neutrality. On the other hand, once he had done that, he was able to persuade most of them that Britain and France would stand aside, and that a stroke against Poland would carry no serious risk of involving Germany in a major war.

A fresh strain developed between Hitler and his generals when, after the conquest of Poland, they found that he was intent on precipitating the wider conflict they feared by taking the offensive in the West. Apart from the long-term risks, they did not believe that it was even possible to overcome France. But once again their protests were overruled, and their subsequent talk of a concerted move to overturn Hitler came to nothing. It would be unjust to blame them for their ineffectiveness at this stage, for it is clear that they had good reason to doubt whether their troops would have followed them in turning against Hitler, and they had a natural repugnance to appearing as traitors to their country when at war.

The invasion of France was ordered by Hitler in face of their doubts. Its success was due partly to new tactics and weapons which he had fostered when the older generals were still conservatively sceptical; partly to an audacious new plan, suggested by a junior, which he had pushed them into adopting; partly to blunders by their fellow-professionals in France on which they had not reckoned.

Nevertheless, their executive skill was an indispensable factor in Hitler's conquest of France. Indeed, it was through his sudden and strange hesitation, not through theirs, that the full fruits of the swift cut through to the Channel were not reaped. But their great contribution to victory resulted, ironically, in a further weakening of their own position. It was Hitler who filled the world's eye after that triumph, and the laurels crowned his brow, not theirs. He took care to crown himself.

In his mind, too, he now became convinced that he was the greatest of all strategists, and henceforth interfered increasingly in the generals' sphere of activity, while becoming even less willing to listen to any arguments from them that ran counter to his desires.

Most of them were fearful when they found that he was intending to plunge into Russia. But, like so many specialists, they were rather naïve outside their own sphere, and Hitler was able to overcome their doubts about his Russian adventure with the aid of political "information" designed to convince them of its necessity, and that Russia's internal weakness would affect her military strength. When the invasion began to go wrong, Brauchitsch and Halder wanted to pull back, but Hitler had come too close to Moscow to resist its temptation. He insisted on pressing the attack at all cost, though the chances were fading. When his failure could no longer be concealed, he cleverly shifted the blame by a public dismissal of Brauchitsch, and himself assumed supreme command of the Army as well as of the forces as a whole.

For the rest of the war, he was able to brush aside the generals' views on policy, and even to override their judgment in their own field. If one of them made a protest, he could always find another one ambitious to fill the vacancy, and ready to express faith in continued attack—as most soldiers are, by instinct, always inclined to do. At the same time, the way was now open for ever increasing infiltration of S.S. leaders into the Army, and of Nazi spies to keep watch on all suspected commanders. The possibility of a successful revolt of the generals progressively diminished. All the latter could do was to make the best of their orders—or to make the worst of them. For there is reason to suspect that some of the generals became ready to carry out orders that they considered hopelessly rash, simply as a way of sabotaging Hitler's designs and hastening the end of the war.

II

THE MOULD OF SEECKT

THE GERMAN GENERAL WHO HAD THE GREATEST INFLUENCE ON the First World War died the year before it began—and had retired seven years before it. This was Alfred von Schlieffen, who came from Mecklenburg on the Baltic coast. It was he who designed the master-plan for the invasion of France, prepared the "tin-openers" to pierce the fortress barrier, and trained the staff to handle them. That plan embraced the violation of Belgium's neutrality—for the sake of outflanking France—and thus brought Britain into the war. Although its execution was bungled by Schlieffen's successor, it came dangerously close to winning the war within a month.

The German general who had the greatest influence on the Second World War died three years before the war—and retired ten years earlier still. This was Hans von Seeckt, who came from Schleswig-Holstein, the land between Mecklenburg and Denmark. He was the man who contrived to rebuild an effective German Army after the last war, and laid the foundations on which a much greater structure could arise. His plans had to be designed and carried out under the extremely hampering conditions of the victors' peace settlement —itself designed to frustrate any serious rebuilding of the German Army. Those restrictions make his performance the more significant. Most of the achievements of the Wehrmacht, especially in the victorious early phase of this war, were cast in Seeckt's mould. Its later failures were foreshadowed in his warning words.

No attempt to assess Hitler's generals in the Second World War can be of adequate value unless it first assesses the influence of Seeckt—so important for the future was the reconstruction period of the German Army. Having treated it at length, the individual treatment of the military leaders who rose to fame in 1939-45 can be correspondingly condensed. For here we have a background common to all, and can see the mould in which their doctrine was cast. Naturally, there were differences of interpretation, but these were less important than the broad foundation that had been built up afresh in the days when the General Staff, banned by the Versailles Treaty, was working underground.

Seeckt, then a lieutenant-colonel, had begun the 1914-18 war as chief of staff of a corps in Kluck's First Army, and thus had a close view of the steps by which a masterly design went wrong in the execution, and decisive victory was forfeited just as it appeared within reach. Seeckt made his own mark a year later, in 1915, as the cool brain that guided a dashing Hussar general, the *beau sabreur* Field-Marshal von Mackensen, in the deadly break-through at Gorlice in Poland, which split the Russian armies—a stroke from which they never fully recovered. It was here that Seeckt introduced a method of attack that contained the germ of modern infiltration tactics—pushing in reserves at the soft spots, and thrusting on as deep as possible, instead of the former method of trying to advance uniformly and using the reserves to break down the tough spots.

Seeckt not only made his mark but also his name. For the concealed brain behind Mackensen became known more and more widely, so that the saying spread through the German Army—"Where Mackensen is, Seeckt is; where Seeckt is, victory is." He continued to play an important part in the

Eastern campaign, but it was his misfortune to be outside of, and unpopular with, the Hindenburg-Ludendorff ring which acquired supreme control of the German Army from 1916 to the end of the war. That, however, saved his reputation from being involved in the final collapse in the West, and he became adviser to the German delegation at the Peace Conference. From this it was a natural step for him to become Commander-in-Chief of the Reichswehr, the small army of 100,000 officers and men to which Germany was restricted under the terms of peace.

It was even more natural that he should have dedicated himself to the task of stretching these bonds and preparing the way for Germany to regain her military strength—as any soldier of any country would have done in similar circumstances. As a guide, he had the example of how Scharnhorst had managed to evade the disarmament of the Prussian Army that France had imposed after 1806, and had built up a camouflaged army that turned the tables on Napoleon seven years later. But Seeckt and his pupils in some ways improved on Scharnhorst's process, under more difficult conditions.

The first obstacle that Seeckt had to overcome was the natural mistrust of the leaders of the new Republic for the military caste that had treated civilians with disdain, and then led the nation to a crushing defeat. Here Seeckt was helped by the impression that his polished manner, diplomatic tact, and apparent understanding of their problems made upon men who had been accustomed to the domineering brusqueness of Hindenburg and Ludendorff. Seeckt was a pleasing contrast to the browbeating Prussian general of whom they had bitter experience. His elegance, artistic interests, and knowledge of the world added a subtle flavour to the self-contained personality that had gained him the nickname of the "Sphinx." While his somewhat cynical attitude and ironical comments had been distasteful in higher military circles, they appealed to the politicians as evidence of a lack of fanaticism, and an assurance that he blended military efficiency with moderation in militarism.

Seeckt kept the army as a whole out of politics, and by his apparent loyalty to the new republican régime at an awkward time, he was the better able to cloak his military development schemes, as well as the half-veiled political activities in which numerous officers of the older school indulged. So far as vested interests allowed, he ensured that the cadres of the new Reichswehr should represent the pick of the officers and N.C.O.s who had undergone the test of war. He aimed to make this small force of 4,000 officers and 96,000 men a corps of qualified instructors and leaders, capable of serving as the framework for rapid expansion—when this might become possible. Their training was developed to a high pitch and on new lines, so that they should become more intensely professional in spirit and skill than the unlimited army of the past had been.

He supplemented this framework with a variety of underground schemes by which officers could gain wider experience than was practicable in an army compulsorily deprived of the major modern weapons, and by which ex-officers could be kept from getting rusty. Many staff officers and technicians found temporary employment in Japan, China, the South American countries, the Baltic States and Soviet Russia—where they could have some practical experience with tanks. Other officers gained flying experience with civil airways. A considerable proportion of the demobilized army was able to get some continued military practice in unofficial organizations that were running inside Germany, and many subterfuges were used to preserve extra weapons for their training.

These devices were testimony to the ingenuity of a keen soldier and his assistants in evading a network of restrictions. They were also a constant worry to the Allied officers responsible for seeing that the peace terms were fulfilled. But it is an historical mistake to overrate their importance in making possible Germany's renewed burst of aggression. The total effect was very slight, compared with the weight that Germany had to regain before she could again become a serious danger. The bulk of the material developments that really mattered was only achieved after Hitler had come into power, in 1933, and launched the large-scale re-armament with which the former Allies did not attempt to interfere.

Seeckt's more real achievement was in starting a train of ideas which revitalized the German Army, turned it into a new line of progress, and enabled it to add a qualitative superiority to the quantitative recovery that the victors' inertia permitted it to carry out. He gave the Reichswehr a gospel of mobility, based on the view that a quick-moving, quick-hitting army of picked troops could, under modern conditions, make rings round an old-fashioned mass army. That view was in no small measure due to his experience on the Eastern Front, where the wide spaces had allowed far more room for manœuvre than had been possible on the Western Front. The first post-war manuals of the Reichswehr laid down that "every action ought to be based on surprise. Without surprise it would be difficult to obtain great results." Flexibility was another keynote—"reserves should, above all, be pushed in to exploit where a success is gained, even though it becomes necessary, by so doing, to shift the original centre of gravity." To promote such flexibility the Reichswehr was quick to develop new means of intercommunication, and devoted a larger proportion of its limited strength to this service than any other post-war army. It also insisted on commanders of all grades being further forward than was then the custom, so that they could keep their fingers on the pulse of battle and exert a quicker influence.

In the exaltation of manœuvre, these post-war German manuals offered a striking contrast with those of the French Army, which drew the conclusion that "of the two elements, fire and movement, fire is preponderant." The French doctrine obviously visualized the repetition in any future war of the slow-motion tactics of 1918. That difference was ominous. But the German view was not merely governed by the necessity of making the most of their handicaps under the peace treaty. For Seeckt, in his preface to the new manual, wrote with remarkable frankness—"These regulations are based on the strength, armament, and equipment of the army of a modern great military power, and not only on the German Army of 100,000 men formed in accordance with the Peace Treaty."

Seeckt's active work came to an end in 1926, when he made a slip and was forced to resign following the political storm that arose through his action in permitting the eldest son of the German Crown Prince to take part in the Army manœuvres. The limitations of his outlook—which had appeared broad by comparison with other generals—were still more clearly brought out by his subsequent venture into politics, as a spokesman of the half-baked ideas of the German People's Party. But the influence of his own military ideas continued to grow.

His vision of the future emerged clearly from the book he wrote soon after he left office—*Thoughts of a Soldier* (1928). He there questioned the value of the huge conscript armies of the past, suggesting that the effort and sacrifice was disproportionate to their effect, and merely led to a slow-grinding war of exhaustion. "Mass becomes immobile; it cannot manœuvre and therefore cannot win victories, it can only crush by sheer weight." Moreover, in peace-time, it was important "to limit as far as possible the unproductive retention of male labour in military service." Technical science and tactical skill were the keys to the future. "A conscript mass, whose training has been brief and superficial, is 'cannon fodder' in the worst sense of the word, if pitted against a small number of practised technicians on the other side." That prediction was fulfilled in 1940 when a handful of *panzer* divisions, striking in combination with dive-bombers, paralyzed and pulverized the ill-equipped conscript mass of the French Army.

In Seeckt's view, "the operating army" should consist of "professional, long-term soldiers, volunteers as far as possible." The bulk of the nation's manpower would be better employed during peace-time in helping to expand the industry required to provide the professional army with an ample equipment of up-to-date weapons. The type of weapons must be settled well in advance, and arrangements for rapid mass production developed.

At the same time a brief period of compulsory military training should be given to all fit young men in the country, "preceded by a training of the young, which would lay less emphasis on the military side than on a general physical and mental discipline." Such a system would help to link the army with the people, and ensure national unity. "In this way a military mass is constituted which, though unsuited to take part in a war of movement and seek a decision in formal battle, is well able to fulfil the duty of home defence, and at the same time to provide from its best elements a continuous reinforcement of the regular, combatant army in the field." It was a conscript levy of this kind which filled the bulk of the Germany infantry divisions in 1940. They merely followed up the decisive armoured spearheads, and occupied the conquered regions. Later, as their own training improved, they were available to expand and replenish the striking forces in the way that Seeckt had foreseen.

"In brief, the whole future of warfare appears to me to lie in the employment of mobile armies, relatively small but of high quality, and rendered distinctly more effective by the addition of aircraft, and in the simultaneous mobilization of the whole forces, either to feed the attack or for home defence."

Curiously, Seeckt's book scarcely touched on the subject of tanks, but dwelt at length on the value of cavalry, as well as of motor transport, in the mobile operations he pictured. He even wrote lyrically that "the days of cavalry, if trained, equipped and led on modern lines, are not numbered," and that "its lances may still flaunt their pennants with confidence in the wind of the future." It has been suggested in later years that Seeckt's neglect of armoured warfare was prompted purely by political discretion, and that the word "tank" should be read into his sentences wherever he used the word "cavalry." Such a view is contradicted by the undisguised way in which he advocated conscription and aircraft, both of which were forbidden to Germany by the peace terms.

For all his dynamism, Seeckt was a man of his generation, rather than a forerunner of the next. His military vision was clear enough to see the necessity of mobile warfare for any offensive purpose, but did not reach far enough to see that *armoured* mobility was the only way to make it possible. It was left for others to develop that possibility—and aggressive necessity.

The old military battle-picture also coloured Seeckt's vision when he argued that the immediate object of the air force's attack should be to destroy the opposing air force. The Luftwaffe did that in Poland, and to a lesser extent in France. But when it tried that way of preparing the invasion of Britain, it suffered crippling losses on meeting, for the first time, a strong defending air force.

On the wider issues of war and life his outlook was patchy. With some truth he contended that direct experience of the horrors of war made soldiers more chary than political leaders of becoming involved in a war, but he went too far in trying to show they were really "pacifists" in the best sense of the word. That characteristic professional apologia, familiar in every country, does not find much support in cases where the archives of a war-making country have been opened to examination. High soldiers have too often failed to show that "pacifism established on knowledge and born of a sense of responsibility" which Seeckt claimed for them.

He was rather weak in his argument that "militarism" and "aggression" were merely catchwords. At the same time he was shrewdly prophetic in his remarks that whenever policy aimed at the acquisition of power, "the statesman will soon find himself thwarted in some way or other, will deduce from this opposition a menace first to his plans, then to national prestige, and finally to the existence of the state itself—and so, regarding his country as the party attacked, will engage in a war of defence."

A sense of humanity, as well as of prophecy, gleamed through his ironical comment on the modern psychological tendency to reverse the moral judgments of the past—"I find it very inconvenient that I may no longer regard Nero simply as the imperial monster who used to go to bed by the light of a burning Christian, but rather as a wise if somewhat peculiar modern dictator." Was he hinting a doubt of the new morality that men like the Nazis were starting to proclaim? Again, in emphasizing the value of "action," there is a significant qualification conveyed in his epigrammatic judgment —"Intellect without will is worthless, will without intellect is dangerous." There was a wise warning, too, in another of his wider reflections—"The statement that war is a continuation of policy by other means has become a catch-phrase, and is therefore dangerous. We can say with equal truth—war is the bankruptcy of policy."

At the same time, Seeckt's care to keep his army out of politics carried a danger of its own. His attitude of professional detachment, and the sharp dividing line he drew between the military and political spheres, tended towards a renunciation of the soldier's potential restraining influence on adventurous statesmen.

The Seeckt-pattern professional became a modern Pontius Pilate, washing his hands of all responsibility for the orders he executed. Pure military theory deals in extremes that are hard to combine with wise policy. When soldiers concentrate on the absolute military aim, and do not learn to think of grand strategy, they are more apt to accept political arguments that, while seeming right in pure strategy, commit policy beyond the point where it can halt. Extreme military ends are difficult to reconcile with moderation of policy.

That danger would grow because professional opinion, as embodied in a General Staff, is never so united in practice as it should be in principle. It is split by its own "politics" and personal ambitions. Seeckt himself not only recalled the past but foreshadowed the future when he wrote—"A history of the General Staff . . . would be a history of quiet positive work; it would tell of arrogance and haughty acquiescence, of vanity and envy, of all human weaknesses, of the fight between genius and bureaucracy, and of the hidden causes of victory and defeat. It would take the radiance from many a halo, and it would not be lacking in tragedy."

The General Staff was essentially intended to form a collective substitute for genius, which no army can count on producing at need. Of its very nature it tended to cramp the growth of genius, being a bureaucracy as well as a hierarchy, but in compensation it sought to raise the general standard of competence to a high level. The unevenness of its performance was due less to differences of individual talent than to the underlying differences of personal interest, as well as to conflicting personal views. The chance of promotion tended to make any general swallow his doubts for the moment, long enough to enable Hitler to split the solidity of professional opinion. That applies to all armies, but is particularly marked under a dictatorship. A newly-promoted general is always confident that the situation is better than it appeared to his predecessor, and that he can succeed where the latter failed. Such a disposition is a powerful lever in the hands of any ruler.

III

THE BLOMBERG-FRITSCH ERA

SEECKT WAS SUCCEEDED BY HEYE, AND THE LATTER, IN 1930, by Hammerstein. Neither was quite of Seeckt's calibre, but both on the whole continued to develop his policy. Hammerstein was deeply perturbed by the growing strength of the Nazi movement, finding both its creed and its methods repugnant, and he was led to depart from Seeckt's principle of political detachment to the extent of considering the possibilities of taking forcible measures to check Hitler's accession to power. The ground was cut away beneath his feet, however, by the decision of the senile President of the Republic, Field-Marshal von Hindenburg, to appoint Hitler to be Chancellor —thus making his position constitutionally valid. Moreover, Hammerstein's apprehensions were not shared by other leading generals who were soldiers "pure and simple."

The next important step came when Hitler, almost immediately after entering office, appointed General von Blomberg as War Minister. That choice was inspired by the ambitious Colonel von Reichenau, who had been Blomberg's Chief of Staff in East Prussia, and was in close contact with Hitler. Blomberg himself did not know Hitler, and his character was in many ways the antithesis of Hitler's. His acceptance of the appointment, as well as his performance in it, was an illustration of how simple the pure soldier can be.

BLOMBERG

During the previous year, Blomberg had been chief military adviser to the German delegation at the Disarmament Conference. He was only just over fifty—young by comparison with the average age of the High Command in the German and other armies. This fact in itself naturally excited envy of his sudden elevation. That hostile feeling was increased by the German generals' attitude of disdain for the "Bohemian Corporal." Many of them had been ready to welcome Hitler's rise to power in so far as it seemed likely to favour their own schemes of military expansion, but they scoffed at the idea that an ex-corporal could be credited with any military judgment, and were thus the more quick to question any preference he showed in making military appointments.

This attitude among the senior officers of the Reichswehr prejudiced Blomberg's position from the outset. By becoming suspect in the eyes of his fellows he was thrown back on Hitler's support, and so was forced to follow Hitler's line further than his own judgment would have led him. Ironically, the natural pleasantness of his personality, refreshingly different from the "Prussian" type, became a handicap in such circumstances of dependence. This combination went far to account for the nickname of the "Rubber Lion" that was bestowed on him by other soldiers.

For Werner von Blomberg was of a different type from the violent and unscrupulous leaders of the new régime. If he was more in sympathy with the Nazis than other generals, it was partly because he was more idealistic—while his romantic enthusiasm easily blinded him to aspects he did not care to see. The Nazi movement for a time attracted quite a number of such idealists, though most of them were much younger than Blomberg. Soldiers, however, are slow to grow up. Blomberg was a natural enthusiast, and looked on the profession of arms in the spirit of a knight-errant. This was evident to me when I met him at Geneva in 1932. He showed an eager interest in new military ideas, especially those that promised a new artistry in tactics as a game of skill, but was still more enthusiastic about the possibilities of resuscitating the code of chivalry. He became almost lyrical in discoursing upon the appeal of "gentlemanliness" in war. Close observation of the higher military levels over a long period makes for scepticism, but Blomberg impressed me as exceptionally genuine, if boyish, in his profession of faith. Tall and broad physically, he was neither overbearing nor grim in his manner, but showed a natural courtesy combined with a refreshingly frank way of talking. It was his hard fate to be called on to deal with two rival groups, and to become a buffer between them. In a better environment he might have proved a greater figure.

Yet in one important respect his influence may have been more effective than it seemed. One of the surprising features of the Second World War was that the German Army in the field on the whole observed the rules of war better than it did in 1914-18—at any rate in fighting its western opponents— whereas it was reasonable to expect that the addition of "Nazism" to "Prussianism" would make its behaviour worse than before. The relative improvement in behaviour, and the greater care shown to avoid stains on its record, may be traced to the more refined conception of soldierly conduct which Blomberg and a number of others who shared his views had striven to instil in the Reichswehr. The restraint shown in 1940 by the troops that invaded Belgium and France, compared with their predecessors of 1914, was also a wise policy. It went quite a long way to soften the sting of defeat and conciliate the people of the conquered countries, and might have had a more lasting effect but for the contrasting behaviour of the Gestapo and the S.S. forces.

In the tactical sphere Blomberg helped to give an important turn to the trend of development. Hammerstein had perpetu-

ated the German Army's old doctrine of the offensive, without the material means to practise it or a new technique to
sharpen its edge. But, in East Prussia, Blomberg had experi-
mented with new forms of tactics which more realistically
recognized the existing superiority of modern defence, and
sought to turn this to advantage the other way, as an offensive
aid. Instead of attacking a strongly defended position, one
might lure the enemy out of position, draw him into making
a rash advance or hurried assault, catch him in a trap, and
then exploit his disorder by delivering one's own real stroke—
in the more deadly form of a riposte. The bait might be created
by luring withdrawal or by a sudden swoop that threatened
the enemy's communications. The potentialities of this "baited
move" combining offensive strategy with defensive tactics—
like sword and shield—had struck me in the course of my
study of Sherman's campaign in Georgia, and in subsequent
books I had elaborated its application to modern warfare. It
was Blomberg's particular interest in this idea which first
brought us into contact.[1]

Blomberg also showed more appreciation than most generals at that date of the new conception of mobile warfare,
with tanks fulfilling the historic rôle of cavalry—a conception
which had met with a half-hearted response in the British
Army, except in the circle of the Royal Tank Corps. Reichenau
was still keener, and had himself translated some of my books,
though even he did not embrace the concept of armoured
warfare quite so fully as men like Guderian and Thoma who

[1] Sherman's methods also fired General Patton's imagination—particularly
with regard to the way that they exploited the indirect approach and the
value of cutting down impedimenta in order to gain mobility. When I met
Patton in 1944, shortly before he took his army across to Normandy, he told
me how he had earlier spent a long leave studying Sherman's campaigns on
the ground with my book in hand, and we discussed the possibilities of applying such methods in modern warfare. They were demonstrated in his subsequent sweep from Normandy to the Moselle. General Wood, who commanded his spearhead, the 4th Armoured Division, was another enthusiast for
these ideas, and on reaching the Seine wrote to tell me how successful their
application had proved.

took a more direct hand in creating Germany's armoured forces from 1934 onwards.

The triumphs of German tactics and of the German armoured forces in the first two years of the war cast an ironical reflection on the measures taken to disarm the defeated country after the previous war. Materially, they proved effective. For the numerous evasions that German military chiefs practised were on a petty scale, and in themselves amounted to no considerable recovery of strength. Germany's actual progress in material rearmament constituted no serious danger up to the time when the Nazi Government openly threw off the restrictions of the peace treaty. It was the hesitancy of the victors after that time which allowed Germany again to become formidable. Moreover, an important result of her enforced disarmament was to give her a clear start, by freeing her army from such an accumulation of 1914-1918 weapons as the victorious nations had preserved—a load of obsolescence that tended to bind them to old methods, and led them to overrate their own strength. When the German Army began large-scale re-armament, it benefited by having more room for the development of the newer weapons suggested by a fresher current of ideas.

The development of such fresh ideas was, in turn, helped by another of the measures imposed by the victors—the suppression of the General Staff. If it had been left to carry on in its old form, and its old cumbersome shell, it might have remained as routinely inert and overwhelmed by its offices as other General Staffs. Driven underground, its members were largely exempted from administrative routine, and impelled to concentrate on constructive thinking about the future—thus becoming more efficient for war. Any such military organization can be destroyed in so far as it is a physical substance, but not in respect of its activities as a thinking organ—thought cannot be suppressed.

Thus the net effect of the sweeping disarmament of Germany after the First World War was to clear the path for the more efficient modernization of her forces when a political opportunity for re-armament developed. Limitations in the degree of modernization were due more to internal conservatism and conflicting interests than to the external restrictions that had been placed upon her.

FRITSCH

Blomberg's position as War Minister enabled him to foster the growth of the new tactics he favoured, and to overcome the resistance which the more orthodox generals had shown— as in other countries, especially France. But the weakness of his own position, as a "buffer-state," handicapped him in hastening their spread and development at the pace that might otherwise have been possible. When he tried, at the end of 1933, to secure the appointment of Reichenau as Chief of the Army Command in place of Hammerstein, he was foiled by the concerted opposition of the senior generals. Acting on their advice, Hindenburg chose General von Fritsch, a soldier of great all-round ability, who represented the more conservative school, both politically and militarily. He had grasped the value of tanks and aircraft up to a point, but regarded the new arms as "upstarts," and was intent to keep them in their place —a subordinate place, in his view. Moreover, General Beck, who subsequently became Chief of the General Staff, was almost as critical of the tank "revolutionaries" as he was of the Nazi revolution. Thus German military organization, though it forged ahead of other countries in developing mechanized forces, remained a compromise between the old and new patterns.

Werner von Fritsch, as a comparatively young staff officer, had worked under General von Seeckt at the Reichswehr Ministry from 1920 to 1922, in preparing the new organization. Then he went to regimental duty in command of a battery, and subsequently became chief of staff in East Prussia. In 1927, he returned to the Reichswehr Ministry as assistant to Blomberg, who was head of the operations branch. Here he was largely responsible for devising the plan, in case of war, for a swift offensive against Poland combined with a defensive in the West to hold France in check. It was the embryo of the plan that was actually executed in 1939, although then amplified in scale and resources.

During the pre-Nazi period Fritsch showed a diplomatic talent, unusual among German officers of the old school, in dealing with democratic deputies who were inclined to ask awkward questions regarding increases in the military budget, and the reasons why an army limited in size required such a disproportionately large framework of staff and instructional cadres. Fritsch was adept in explaining away such curious points, and in persuading critics not to press their inquiries. He knew how to gag them in subtle ways—by appealing to their patriotism, playing on their weaknesses, or cultivating their friendship. Normally he had an ice-cold manner, and nature, but he could turn on a warm-tap of charm, when it served a purpose.

When the Nazis arrived in power the generals realized that they would need a chief who combined determination with diplomacy in order to hold their own. It was Fritsch's possession of these qualities, in addition to his reputation as a strategist, that led to his appointment early in 1934. His first moves were directed to curb the ambition of the amateur soldiers of the Nazi party, headed by Captain Roehm, and to counter the threat that their advancement might carry to the authority and interests of the professional army. He provided Hitler with evidence that their plans for arming the storm troopers as a supplement to the army were designed to pave the way for a *coup d'état,* aimed at Hitler himself. Himmler was working on the same line—from a different motive. They succeeded in convincing Hitler so well as to produce the bloody purge of June 30th, 1934.

This had the double effect of strengthening Fritsch's position with Hitler and with all the elements in Germany that for diverse reasons, feared the growth of the Nazi influence. For a time, he established the supremacy of the Army Command upon the internal balance of power, and was able to outmanœuvre Himmler. Over such issues as the reintroduction of conscription and the reoccupation of the Rhineland, Fritsch marched in step with Hitler. But he insisted on testing the ground before each step was taken, and was careful to restrain the pace of developments, so that the German Army should not be committed to a dangerous trial of strength while it was still growing.

Emboldened by the submissive way in which these defiant steps were taken by the French and British Governments, the Nazi leaders next made the more far-reaching move of intervening in the Spanish Civil War—in order to ensure the success of General Franco's revolt, and thus establish a Fascist power athwart the sea-communications of France and Britain. Fritsch was keen to use the Spanish battlefield as an experimental practice-ground for the German Army's new weapons and tactics, employed by sample units sent out for the purpose, but he was shrewd enough to see that Spain was an awkward place strategically at which to risk an open challenge to France and Britain. His caution was resented by the Nazi leaders, flushed with their recent successes in defiance. At the same time his diplomatic efforts to foster better relations with the Red Army excited violent complaint on their part. Hitler's anti-Bolshevist obsession provided Fritsch's enemies with fruitful soil in which to sow suspicion. Friction was increased by Fritsch's efforts to maintain the old spirit in the new officer corps, and keep it free from permeation by Nazi ideology.

Meanwhile the rift between Fritsch and Blomberg was growing. Fritsch and his fellows felt that Blomberg was hypnotized by Hitler, and was not standing up for the Army's interests as he should have done. It seemed to them that Blomberg's spirit of subservience was symbolized in the way he wore Nazi emblems on his uniform, and they nicknamed

him Hitler-Youth-Quex, after an idealistic boy portrayed in a
Nazi film.

THE DOUBLE DISMISSAL

A crisis came in January, 1938, arising out of an affair that
was very remote in appearance from its real causes. Blomberg
had fallen in love with a typist in his office, and married her.
Hitler expressed approval of Blomberg's intention, as a public
proof that the military leaders of National-Socialist Germany
were broadening their social outlook and identifying themselves with the people, instead of marrying only into their own
caste. He graced the wedding, as a witness. Blomberg's fellow-
generals regarded the marriage as unseemly, but—contrary to
what was widely reported at the time—it is not true that they
made a concerted protest and caused Blomberg's removal from
office. For any protest they might have made was forestalled—
by Himmler.

After Blomberg's marriage had taken place Himmler presented to Hitler a police dossier purporting to show that the
bride was a prostitute. It has been suggested by American in-
vestigators since the war, that Himmler had planted her in
Blomberg's office as part of a trap. Hitler's reaction to the revelation was violent, for by his own presence at this wedding of
"a woman of the streets" he had been made to look ridiculous.
He dismissed Blomberg from his post, and even crossed his
name off the list of the officers' corps.

That news did not disturb the other generals. But they were
shaken to their roots by a second stroke that immediately followed. For now that the question of appointing a new War
Minister had to be considered Himmler brought out a further
dossier to show that Fritsch was under police watch for homosexual offences. It was, actually, a dossier about another bearer
of the same name. But when Hitler sent for the Commander-
in-Chief, Himmler produced a witness who formally identi-

fied him as the man in the case. Hitler thereupon removed him from his post.

According to General Röhricht, the reason for this move of Himmler's was to prevent Fritsch succeeding to Blomberg's position and power, which carried with it supreme command of the Wehrmacht—the armed forces as a whole. "Anyone succeeding to that post would become the superior of Goering who was now Commander-in-Chief of the Luftwaffe. It would have been very difficult to appoint any fresh soldier over his head. Fritsch was the only possible one, because of his existing seniority to Goering as a Commander-in-Chief. Himmler's intervention was not for Goering's sake, but for his own ends. All his moves had the aim of paving the way for his ambition of replacing the army by the S.S., step by step."

Fritsch demanded a Court of Inquiry, but it was only with much difficulty that he was granted one—after energetic representations by Rundstedt, as representative of the senior generals. When it was conceded, Himmler wanted to preside over it himself, but the Minister of Justice then came to Fritsch's help by declaring that a military court was necessary. Himmler next tried to get at the witnesses for the defence. To ensure their attendance, and their safety, the generals arranged for them to be guarded by soldiers. At the inquiry Himmler's chief witness recanted his evidence—and paid for this with his life. But Fritsch was completely acquitted.

Meanwhile, Hitler had taken the opportunity to assume supreme command of the Wehrmacht himself, declaring that he had lost confidence in the generals. Blomberg's former post was reduced to a lower status, and filled by General Keitel, who appeared to Hitler to have the qualities of a good lackey. At the same time General von Brauchitsch was appointed to command the Army in place of Fritsch, so no room was left for the latter by the time he was cleared of the charges that had been framed against him. Thus the outcome of the crisis that had been so deliberately engineered was to pave the way

for Hitler's ultimate control of strategy, while strengthening
Himmler's influence.

By making himself actual Commander-in-Chief of the
Wehrmacht (the armed forces as a whole), Hitler naturally
increased the importance of its executive organ, the Oberkommando der Wehrmacht—a title commonly shortened to
O.K.W. In this were centralized the political and administrative matters common to all three services. It included a small
"national defence" section (Landesverteidigung) which dealt
with matters on the borderline between policy and strategy,
and with the co-ordination of the three services. There was
soon a move to develop this into a Wehrmacht General Staff
—a development equally desired by Hitler and Keitel.

This project was strongly resisted by the Army High Command (Oberkommando das Heeres—O.K.H. for short), who
were quick to see it as an attempt to displace them as the heir
of the old Great General Staff. They argued that it was un-
sound to subordinate a long-established organization such as
theirs to a newly formed body of an amateur nature, and that
as Germany's military problems were predominantly continental the Army High Command ought to have the decisive
influence. Their opposition prevailed for the moment, helped
by the Naval High Command's inherent dislike of being directed by land-lubbers, and the more personal objections that
arose from Goering's position as Commander-in-Chief of the
Air Force. So the issue remained in abeyance, and the General
Staff of the Army remained in control of strategy, subject to
Hitler's broad direction. He had still a long way to go before
he could fulfil his ambition of playing the part of executive
strategist—and actually handling the pieces on the board.

I V

THE BRAUCHITSCH-HALDER ERA

A T FIRST SIGHT IT MAY SEEM CURIOUS THAT SUCH A MAN AS
Walther von Brauchitsch was appointed to replace Fritsch,
and that he accepted the appointment. For he had shown himself conspicuously loyal to the former republican régime, and
inclined to take a liberal view of political and economic issues,
while outspokenly critical of Nazi policies. Neither Junker
narrowness nor Nazi fanaticism appealed to him. At the same
time he was generally regarded as a man who had a keen
sense of honour and was by no means self-seeking. For these
reasons, coupled with his strong sense of justice and consideration for others, he was trusted both by his fellows and his
juniors to an exceptional degree. Was his acceptance of Hitler's
offer in February, 1938, due to a sudden yielding to personal
ambition—when the prize was so big—or to a feeling that he
might be able to serve the Service by stepping into the breach?
The second, and better, explanation tends to be supported by
the fact that Brauchitsch continued on good terms with Fritsch
after the latter had been shelved, and took more than one
opportunity of paying tribute to him, in a way distasteful to
the Nazi leaders. Events soon showed, however, that Brauchitsch had stepped on to a slippery slope where he would find
it hard to keep upright.

31

The reasons for his appointment are simpler to understand. Hitler was shrewd enough to realize the importance of making a choice that would inspire general confidence, even though it meant taking a man who was not in sympathy with the Nazi party. Brauchitsch was generally regarded as a sound yet progressive soldier—although primarily an "artillerist" he had a better appreciation of tank potentialities than most of the senior generals. In other respects, too, he was less conservative than the school that Fritsch had represented. His popularity with all sections was an obvious asset, which would help to offset suspicion of the political motives behind the changes and of the internal struggle that had preceded them. His unassuming manner fostered the hope that he would prove easier to handle than Fritsch.

Hitler soon found, however, that Brauchitsch—though more polite in his manner—was no more disposed than Fritsch had been to allow a political infiltration in the army. His first steps were to introduce a number of welfare measures for improving the condition and post-service prospects of the ordinary soldier, but he insisted on keeping these clear of Nazi organization. At the same time, he tightened discipline. He sought to quicken up the process of equipping the forces, but also to put a brake on the tendency of Nazi foreign policy to precipitate an early conflict. His stand was reinforced by General Beck, then Chief of the General Staff. Beck, though a soldier of great ability and strong character, tended towards the "anti-tank" school, so that in his opposition to Hitler's aggressive policy he was inclined to underrate what Hitler might achieve by the use of new instruments.

After Hitler, that summer, had made his designs clear, Brauchitsch summoned all the senior generals to a conference, and told them that Beck had drafted a memorandum which, if they approved, he proposed sending to Hitler. Beck then read the memorandum. It argued that German policy ought to avoid the risk of war, especially over such "a small issue as the Sudetenland." It pointed out the weakness of the German forces, and their inferiority to the combination that might be arrayed against them. It emphasized that, even if the United States did not take a direct part, she was likely to use her resources to supply Germany's opponents with arms and equipment.

Rundstedt, giving me his account of the conference, said— "When Beck had finished reading the memorandum, Brauchitsch got up and asked whether any of those present had objections to raise before it was sent to Hitler. No one objected, so the document was delivered. It provoked Hitler to great wrath, and led to the dismissal of Beck—who was replaced by Halder."

This momentarily damped opposition, but when the Czecho-Slovakian crisis came to a head, in September, Brauchitsch told Hitler that the German Army was not prepared for war, and warned him against pressing his demands so hard as to produce a fight. Brauchitsch was buttressed by Halder, who followed his predecessor's line rather than Hitler's—showing the latter that it was still difficult to drive a wedge into the close-knit German military corporation. While Halder was more progressive than Beck in his military views, he was also a man of long views in the political field and not inclined to gamble with Germany's future. A tougher personality than Brauchitsch, he was more ready to be tough with Hitler. When it became clear that Hitler was not to be checked by counsels of caution, Halder became busy with plans for a military revolt against Hitler's policy and regime.

The French and British Governments, however, were even less prepared for war or willing to risk a fight on behalf of Czecho-Slovakia, so Hitler gained his claims for the Sudetenland with little difficulty, at Munich.

In the flush of that triumph, Hitler became harder to curb. Next spring he occupied the whole of the Czechs' territory by a sudden coup, breaking the Munich agreement. He then proceeded, without pause, to put pressure on Poland for the return of Danzig to Germany and the right to build an extraterritorial railway and road across the Polish Corridor into East Prussia. Unable to see anybody else's point of view, he could not understand that these limited demands lost their appearance of moderation in the circumstances of their proposal. When the Poles, stiffened by the British Government's hurried offer of support, refused to consider such readjustments, Hitler became so angry under his sense of injury as to press matters further and quicker than he had intended. While still hoping that the Poles would climb down, and save his face, he became more inclined to risk war—provided that the risk in a war would not be too big.

When he consulted the military chiefs on this question, Brauchitsch gave a more qualified reply than Keitel. Brauchitsch considered that Germany could "probably" reckon on a favourable result if the opposition were confined to Poland, France and Britain. But he emphatically declared that Germany would not have much chance of winning if she had also to fight Russia. The French Ambassador in Berlin, M. Coulondre, heard of the arguments and reported them to his government early in June.

Brauchitsch's doubts, coupled with his disparaging comments on the value of Italy as an ally, annoyed the more violent Nazis, who had already been complaining of the way he had checked the Nazification of the Army. They developed a campaign against him. This may explain why he was led at this time to make a public declaration of confidence in the Führer, and also to express sentiments in a speech at Tannenberg which sounded threatening towards Poland—though they could be construed in a strictly defensive sense. But it is understandable that he should feel that there was little danger in such language, since no one who weighed the situation in military scales was likely to imagine that Britain and France would actually carry their support of Poland to the point of war in such a hopeless strategical position as would result if Russia was induced to stand aside. For Hitler was driven to meet Brauchitsch's stipulations so far as Russia was concerned and to recast his whole policy of the past in an effort to secure her neutrality. Once he accepted the necessity of a political turn-about, Hitler moved quickly to arrange a pact with Russia —in striking contrast to the hesitation and delay of the British Government in their negotiations with Russia at the same time.

Despite the announcement of the Russo-German pact, the British Government defied logical military calculation by deciding to fight, and pushed the French into the same course. But the invasion of Poland had already been launched, on Hitler's order, before the fallacy of that calculation was apparent. For the moment, Brauchitsch and Halder were fully occupied in conducting the campaign—and could drown their anxieties by immersing themselves in their professional task.

The plan was of their design, and the campaign was swiftly successful. The executive commanders were allowed a free hand, and demonstrated the value of it by showing an initiative and flexibility that were in the best vein of the old tradition. The main rôle was played by Rundstedt's Army Group in the South which, after breaking through the Polish front, sent Reichenau's mobile 10th Army—this had the bulk of the mechanized divisions—on a northward swerve to Warsaw, to cut astride the rear of the main Polish armies in the centre. That stroke, which decided the issue, was the more notable because O.K.W. had ordered that the 10th Army should be sent straight ahead over the Vistula, as the Poles were thought to be already retreating to the south-east. But Rundstedt and his Chief of Staff, Manstein, had gauged that the main Polish armies were still west of Warsaw, and could thus be trapped on the near side of the Vistula. On this occasion the commander on the spot was allowed to act on his own judgment, which the result vindicated—but when a similar crucial turn came in the next campaign Hitler imposed his own decision and thereby paid a heavy forfeit.

The effect of victory in Poland had an intoxicating effect on Hitler. But with it was mingled a fear of what might happen to him in the East if he did not soon secure peace in the West.

The intoxication and the fear, working on one another, impelled him to fresh action while making him more reckless.

To Brauchitsch and Halder the victory in Poland had brought no such intoxication. Once the dust of battle had settled they perceived more clearly the awkward consequences of that victory, and the dangers of becoming embroiled more deeply. After the campaign was over they recovered the long view so far as to oppose—even to the point of contemplating a revolt—Hitler's idea that an offensive in the West would make the Allies more inclined towards peace. But something more than a few months' inactivity would have been required to restore favourable conditions for peace, and during the winter the Allies' threats of "opening up the war," publicly voiced by Winston Churchill in broadcasts, had a natural tendency to spur Hitler into forestalling them. The dynamism of war increasingly took charge of the train of events.

The invasion of Norway in April, 1940, was the first of Hitler's aggressive moves that was not premeditated. As the evidence brought out at Nuremberg made clear, he was led into it unwillingly, more by fear than by desire, under the combined influence of persuasion and provocation. Although he achieved this conquest with ease he was no longer in control of his own course. The persuasion started from the arguments of Vidkun Quisling, the Norwegian pro-Nazi, about the likelihood of the British occupying the coast of Norway, with or without the connivance of the Norwegian Government. It was reinforced by the anxiety of the Naval High Command about the danger of such a development, both in tightening the grip of the British blockade and hampering their own submarine operations. These fears were increased, after the outbreak of the Russo-Finnish war at the end of November, by Franco-British offers of aid to Finland—which, as the Germans shrewdly suspected, concealed an aim of gaining strategic control of the Scandinavian peninsula. Hitler, however, still felt that Germany had more to gain by Norway's continued neutrality, and wanted to avoid an enlargement of the war.

After he had met Quisling in mid-December, he decided to wait and see whether Quisling could fulfil his hope of achieving a political coup in Norway.

In January, however, nervousness was accentuated when Churchill made an emphatic broadcast appeal to the neutrals to join in the fight against Hitler, while other signs of an Allied move multiplied. On February 18th the British destroyer Cossack pushed into Norwegian waters and boarded the German supply ship *Altmark* to rescue captured British seamen it was carrying. This step was taken on orders from the Admiralty, of which Churchill was then head. It not only infuriaved Hitler, but made him think that if Churchill was ready to violate Norwegian neutrality for the rescue of a handful of prisoners, he was still more likely to do so in order to cut off the iron-ore supplies from Narvik that were vital to Germany.

In this connection Rundstedt remarked to me in one of our talks: "Churchill's broadcasts used to make Hitler angry. They got under his skin—as did Roosevelt's later. Hitler repeatedly argued to the Army High Command, especially over Norway, that if he did not move first, the British would—and establish themselves in such neutral points." Admiral Voss, who was present, confirmed this account from his experience in the Naval High Command, and also said: "The British attack on the *Altmark* proved decisive, in its effect on Hitler—it was the 'fuse' that touched off the Norwegian offensive."

Immediately after this, Hitler appointed General von Falkenhorst to prepare the forces for a coup to seize the Norwegian ports. At a conference on February 23rd, Admiral Raeder, the Naval Commander-in-Chief, emphasized that: "The best thing for maintaining this (ore) traffic as well as for the situation in general is the maintenance of Norwegian neutrality." But he went on to say: "What must not be permitted, as stated earlier, is the occupation of Norway by Britain. That could not be undone."

By this time reports from Norway showed that Quisling's

party was losing ground, while reports from England indicated that some action in the Norwegian area was being planned, together with the assembly of troops and transports. On March 1st Hitler issued his directive for the expedition to Norway. On the 9th, the Naval High Command presented their plan, and dwelt on the urgency of the operation in view of the reports that a British landing was imminent. They were very worried, but their own preparations would take some time to complete, and all they could do was to send submarines to lie off the ports in case the British transports appeared.

But the Allies' plans were upset for the moment by Finland's capitulation on the 13th, which deprived them of the pretext on which they were intending to land at Narvik. When Admiral Raeder saw Hitler on the 26th, he expressed the view that the danger of a British landing in Norway was no longer acute for the moment, but considered it certain that a fresh pretext would soon be found and fresh attempts made to interrupt the iron-ore traffic. "Sooner or later Germany will be faced with the necessity of carrying out operation 'Weseruebung' "—the code name for the expedition to occupy Norway. Thus it was advisable to do this soon, rather than be too late. Hitler agreed, and fixed the date. Now that preparations had gone so far, there was an irresistible urge to put them into operation. At almost the same time the Allies decided to put fresh pressure on the governments of Norway and Sweden. A mine-belt was to be laid in Norwegian waters, on April 5th, and the first convoy of troops was to sail for Narvik on the 8th. But the mine-laying operation was delayed until the night of the 7th, and next afternoon the German invading force sailed.

Early on April 9th, small detachments of German troops, carried mostly in warships, landed at the chief ports of Norway, from Oslo to Narvik, and captured them with little difficulty. The sequel showed that the Allies' designs had outrun the efficiency of their preparations, and the collapse of their counter-moves left Germany in possession of the whole of Norway, together with Denmark. This conquest was achieved without any material subtraction from the forces on the Western front, or interference with the preparations there. Moreover, the operation was carried out under the direction of O.K.W. and not of O.K.H.

The story of how the plan for the invasion of the West took form is related in later chapters, and is too complex for brief summary here. For the moment it is more useful to trace the outline of the plan, and point out the basic factors that governed its issue—as a background to the more detailed record of personal influences and internal controversies.

While it appeared to the world as a supreme example of the shock-offensive, it was really more remarkable for its subtlety. The essential condition of its success was the way that the Allied armies of the left wing, comprising the pick of their mobile forces, were lured deep into Belgium, and even into Holland. It was only through the left wing being caught in this trap, and wrenched from its socket, that the *panzer* stroke cut through the Allied left centre deeply and quickly enough to have decisive effects. Moreover, as fast as the German armoured divisions drove towards the Channel coast, cutting a pocket in the Allied front, the motorized divisions followed them up to form a defensive lining along the whole length of the pocket. These tactics extracted a maximum advantage from a minimum use of shock, and exploited the power of tactical defence as an aid to the offensive. For the burden of attacking, at a disadvantage, was thereby thrown on the Allied armies in any attempt to force open the trap and reunite their severed parts. Such subtlety is the essence of strategy.

With the failure of the Allied left wing to break out, its fate was sealed, save for the portion that managed to escape by sea from Dunkirk, leaving all its equipment behind. None at all might have escaped but for the fact that Hitler stopped the sweeping advance of the *panzer* forces on the outskirts of Dunkirk—for reasons that are discussed further on. But this forfeit did not affect the immediate future. After the elimina-

tion of the left-wing armies, the remainder were left too weak
to hold the far-stretching front in France against a powerful
offensive, so that their collapse in turn was mathematically
probable even before the next German stroke was delivered. In
1914 the aim had been to wheel inwards and round up the
opposing armies in one vast encirclement, an effort that proved
too great for the Germans' capacity. In 1940 the German Command concentrated on cutting off a portion of the opposing
armies by an outward sweep, with the result that in this
piecemeal process it eventually succeeded in swallowing them
completely.

But it was baffled, as Napoleon had been, when it came to
dealing with the problem that remained—the continued resistance of island Britain, and the prospect of her continuous
"thorn-in-the-flesh" effects unless and until she was conquered.
The Wehrmacht had been prepared for continental warfare,
and for a more gradual development of events than had taken
place. Having been led on to attempt, and attain, much more
than had been foreseen, it was caught unprepared in shipping
and equipment for carrying out any such new technique as
was involved in a large-scale oversea invasion.

Placed in that dilemma, the sweeping success of the earlier
continental campaign encouraged the tendency, inherent in
the Nazi gospel, to follow in the footsteps of Napoleon and
repeat his invasion of Russia. Brauchitsch and Halder tried to
curb Hitler's ambition to succeed where Napoleon had failed,
but the immensity of their own successes hitherto made it more
difficult for them to impose a policy of moderation. Moreover,
while they were far from agreeing with the Nazi view that
the conquest of Russia would be easy, the relatively high estimate that they had formed of Russia's strength made them
more inclined to accept the necessity of tackling Russia before
that strength had still further increased.

The plan they framed was designed on the same principle
as 1940—that of piercing weak spots in the Red Army's front,
isolating large fractions of it, and forcing these to attack in

reverse in the endeavour to get out of the net woven round
them. They aimed to destroy Russia's armed strength in battles near to their own frontier, and wanted to avoid, above all,
being drawn deep into Russia in pursuit of a still unbroken
army that retreated before their advance. Conditions in Russia
favoured this design in so far as the vast width of the front
offered more room to manœuvre for piercing thrusts than there
had been in the West, but were unfavourable in the lack of
natural back-stops, comparable to the Channel, against which
they could hope to pin the enemy after breaking through.

The German plan achieved a series of great piecemeal victories which brought it ominously close to complete success—
helped by the initial over-confidence of the Russian leaders.
The armoured thrusts cut deep, and successively cut off large
portions of the Russian armies, including a dangerously high
proportion of their best-trained and best-equipped troops. But,
on balance, the advantage which the German offensive derived
from the *breadth of space* in Russia was outweighed by the
disadvantage of the *depth of space* through which the Russians could withdraw in evading annihilation. That balance
of disadvantage tended to increase as the campaign continued.

Another handicap which emerged was the limited scale of
the armoured forces on which the success of the German
strokes mainly depended. In 1940 the victory in the West had
been virtually decided by the thrusts of the 10 panzer divisions
used to open the way for the mass of 150 ordinary divisions
which the Germans deployed there. For the invasion of Russia
in 1941 the number of panzer divisions was raised to 21—but
only by halving the number of tanks in each. The greater
power of manœuvre provided by this increased scale of mobile
divisions was valuable on such a broad front, while the de-
creased punching power did not matter much in the earlier
phases of the invasion. Indeed, the consequent rise in the proportion of infantry in these divisions was welcomed by the
orthodox, since it provided a higher ratio of troops to hold the
ground gained. But the limited punching power became a

serious factor as the campaign continued, especially when the Germans met a more concentrated defence on approaching the great cities.

It was on those "rocks" that the German prospect of victory foundered. The nearer they came to such objectives, the more obvious became the direction of their attacks and the less room they had for deceptive manœuvre. Hitler's long-profitable instinct for the strategy of indirect approach deserted him when such great prizes loomed before his eyes. Moscow became as fatal a magnet for him as it had been for Napoleon.

When the German armies failed to fulfil their aim of a decisive victory west of the Dnieper—to destroy the Russian armies before they could retreat beyond it—Hitler wavered in a state of indecision, and then temporarily flung his weight southward into the Ukraine. But after a spectacular encirclement of the opposing forces around Kiev, he reverted to the original axis. Although autumn was now at hand, he decided to continue the advance on Moscow—as well as the southern advance through the Ukraine towards the Caucasus. Early in October he staked his prestige on the gamble by the announcement that the final stage of the offensive to capture Moscow had begun.

The opening phase was brilliantly successful, and 600,000 Russians were caught by a great encircling movement around Vyasma, carried out by the armies under Bock's command. But it was the end of October before they were rounded up, and by that time winter had set in, with the result that the exploitation of victory was bogged in the mud on the way to Moscow.

When Hitler called for fresh efforts, Brauchitsch and Halder advised that the armies should draw in their horns and consolidate a safe defensive line for the winter, where the troops could gain shelter from the weather as well as from the enemy. But Hitler would not listen to such cautious arguments. So another great effort was mounted in November. But the obviousness of its aim and the convergence of its thrusts simplified the Russians' problem in concentrating reserves to check each dangerous development. Brauchitsch ceased to be responsible except in a nominal sense for this later stage of the offensive, carried out under Hitler's orders. After its final failure early in December, coupled with the German retreat from Rostov in the south, it was officially announced that Brauchitsch had been relieved of his post, and that Hitler had decided to "follow his intuitions" and take over supreme command of the German Army, in addition to the supreme command of the forces as a whole, which he had assumed when he had parted with Blomberg in February, 1938.

Brauchitsch was fortunate in the time of his departure. For it left his military record distinguished by the most striking series of victories in modern history, and blemished merely by a check which he had not only foreseen but of which he had forewarned his superior. But his dismissal registered the final defeat of the soldiers' claim to decide questions of strategy and military policy. Henceforth the "Bohemian Corporal" would dictate to the generals in their own sphere, and their power would be limited to advice or protest. Unwilling executants do not make for good execution.

The transition was traced by Dittmar in one of our talks. "The Polish, Western and Balkan campaigns, and the first stage of the Russian campaign, were conducted by O.K.H.— with comparatively little interference from O.K.W. The battle of Kiev was the first occasion when Hitler attempted to take direct charge of operations. He justified this on the ground that it was essential to finish the Russian campaign before the winter. From then on, O.K.H. was increasingly dominated by O.K.W.—which really spelt Hitler."

Dittmar went on to emphasize the effect of another important development: "Hitler decided that O.K.H.'s sphere of responsibility should not be confined to the Russian front, and that O.K.W. should assume the exclusive direction of all other theatres of war. As a result, O.K.H. could not keep a view of the war as a whole, and this restriction of outlook progressively weakened its ability to argue the case against errors of strategy. The division of spheres, and interests, between O.K.W. and O.K.H. was a grave weakness in the German planning.

"I heard much about the effects from Halder. He said that Hitler was a mystic, who tended to discount, even where he did not disregard, all the rules of strategy.

"Hitler taught and believed that reason and knowledge are nothing, and that the unbending will to victory and the relentless pursuit of the goal are everything. Mystical speculation replaced considerations of time and space, and the careful calculation of the strength of one's own forces in relation to the enemy's. All freedom of action was eliminated. Even the highest commanders were subjected to an unbearable tutelage."

V

"SOLDIER IN THE SUN"—ROMMEL

FROM 1941 ONWARDS THE NAMES OF ALL OTHER GERMAN GEN-erals came to be overshadowed by that of Erwin Rommel. He had the most startling rise of any—from colonel to field-marshal. He was an outsider, in a double sense—as he had not qualified for high position in the hierarchy of the General Staff, while he long performed in a theatre outside Europe.

His fame was deliberately fostered—not only by his own efforts but by Hitler's calculated choice. For Hitler, recogniz-ing the public craving in wartime for glamorous military fig-ures, decided to pick two soldiers (and two only) whom he could safely turn into popular heroes—"one in the sun and one in the snow." Rommel in Africa was to be the sun-hero and Dietl in Finland was to be the snow-hero.

Both performed in the wings of the main stage, where Hitler intended to keep the limelight for himself. Both were vigorous fighting soldiers whose qualities promised well for local suc-cess, without being of the intellectual calibre that might make them competitors for the higher strategic direction. Both seemed certain to be loyal instruments of Hitler. In the out-come, Rommel did more of the two in performance to justify his selection, but Hitler's confidence in his sustained loyalty was not so well justified. When Rommel came to see that

Hitler's survival and Germany's survival were incompatible
he put his country first and turned against his patron.

While Rommel owed much to Hitler's favour, it was testimony to his own dynamic personality that he first impressed
himself on Hitler's mind, and then impressed his British opponents so deeply as to magnify his fame beyond Hitler's
calculation.

As a junior officer in the previous war Rommel gained exceptional distinction, receiving the highest German decoration,
Pour le Mérite, after the Caporetto offensive of 1917 against
the Italians. But his professional knowledge was not regarded
as equal to his fighting record, and he was given only minor
employment in the post-war army. He was not considered
suitable for the select circle of the future General Staff. The
story that in the post-war years he was a Nazi storm-troop
leader is, however, a legend invented by propagandists in the
days when he became famous, in order to associate his reputation with that of the party.

His opportunity came when, after the Nazis attained power
in 1933, he was appointed a military instructor to the S.A.
He was a good lecturer, with a gift of vivid exposition, and had
widened his horizon by studying the new "science" of geo-
politics—he was one of Professor Haushofer's disciples. Subsequently he became instructor at the Infantry School at Dres-
den, and was then appointed to the new one at Wiener-
Neustadt. Before this he had come in contact with Hitler, who
found him a refreshingly unorthodox soldier with whom to
discuss new military ideas. On the outbreak of war he was
appointed commander of Hitler's personal headquarters, which
naturally increased both the contact and the opportunity. After
the Polish campaign he asked Hitler for command of a panzer
division, and got it. This was characteristic of Rommel's keen
sense of the right opening and his opportunism in grasping it.
For, prior to the war, he had been such a keen infantryman
that he had opposed the ideas of those who preached the gos-

pel of tank warfare. He saw the light on the road to Warsaw,
and lost no time in "following the gleam."

He was appointed to command the 7th Panzer Division, and
led it in the Western offensive. His division played a dashing
part in the break-through over the Meuse and on to the Channel coast. In the next stage, it broke through the French front
on the Somme between Abbeville and Amiens, and led the
drive to the Seine near Rouen. Its brilliant performance was
still further enhanced by subsequent publicity, and it was
retrospectively christened "The Phantom Division."

Then, early in 1941, when Hitler decided to send an armoured and motorized expeditionary force to help his Italian
allies in the invasion of Egypt, he appointed Rommel to command this "Africa Corps." By the time it arrived in Tripoli
the Italians had not only been thrown back over the frontier,
but their army had been destroyed in the pursuit. Rommel was
not daunted by the disastrous situation which greeted him.
Knowing that the victorious British army was small, and
guessing that it was probably at the end of its tether, he
promptly launched an offensive with the first instalment of
his corps. He had little understanding of tank technique, but
he had a tremendous sense of mobility and a flair for surprise. He caught the British distributed piecemeal, and with
most of their tanks in need of repair. The speed of his onset
and enveloping dust-clouds magnified his strength. The British
were swept headlong out of Cyrenaica and back over the
Egyptian frontier.

In the next eighteen months Rommel's fame continually
grew, owing to the way he baffled successive British offensives,
and, above all, through his startling ripostes whenever his annihilation was prematurely announced. In the process the
troops of the British Eighth Army came to think much more
highly of him than they did of their own commanders, and
his Jack-in-the-box performance so tickled their sense of humour that their admiration became almost affectionate. He
reached the peak of his career in the summer of 1942 when

he defeated the Eighth Army piecemeal between Gazala and Tobruk, and then chased the remainder of it back through the Western Desert to the verges of the Nile delta.

General Auchinleck, the British Commander-in-Chief in the Middle East, intervened at this crisis by taking over personal charge of the battered Eighth Army and rallying the disheartened troops for a definite stand on the El Alamein position. Rommel's troops were tired and short of supplies after their long pursuit. In two successive efforts they were foiled and thrown back. That check proved fatal to the invader's prospects.

Rommel still appeared confident that he would succeed at a third attempt, but his inward hopes were fading, while time was slipping away in the process of accumulating supplies. During the interval the British were reinforced by fresh divisions from home. There was also a change of commanders. Mr. Churchill wanted the British to take the offensive as soon as the reinforcements arrived. Auchinleck, more wisely, insisted on waiting until they were accustomed to desert conditions. In the sequel, Auchinleck was replaced by Alexander as Commander-in-Chief, while Montgomery took over the Eighth Army. But Rommel struck first, at the end of August, and was again baffled by the new defence plan. Then the initiative changed sides. After a long pause for thorough preparation—longer than Auchinleck had contemplated—Montgomery launched an offensive in the last week of October that was now backed by a tremendous superiority in airpower, gun-power, and tank-power. Even then it was a tough struggle for a whole week, as there was no wide outflanking manœuvre. But the enemy, besides being overstretched, were vitally crippled by the submarine sinkings of their petrol tankers crossing the Mediterranean. That decided the issue, and once the enemy began to collapse at their extreme forward point they were not capable of any serious stand until they had reached the western end of Libya, more than a thousand miles back.

For Rommel himself the decisive blow had been the frustra‚
tion of his August attack. Following that disappointment, he
was so badly shaken that his moral depression lowered his
physical state, and he had to go sick, with desert sores, for
treatment in Vienna. On hearing of Montgomery's offensive,
he insisted on flying back to Africa at once, regardless of the
doctors' protests, but was not fit enough to do himself justice
in the months that followed. Although he conducted the long
retreat sufficiently well to evade each of Montgomery's attempts to encircle his forces, he lost opportunities to administer
a check, while his sickness may have accounted for his bad
slip in the Battle of Mareth that opened Montgomery's path
into Tunisia, and thus paved the way for the enemy's final
collapse in Africa. He himself left Africa, for further treatment, in March—over a month before that occurred. For
Hitler it was as important to preserve Rommel's prestige as
to preserve his services for the future.

Since Alamein, there has been a tendency to talk of the
"Rommel legend," and to suggest that his reputation was unduly inflated. Such disparagement is a common accompani-
ment of a change of fortune. But there was a deeper reason
for it in the first place. He had become the hero of the Eighth
Army troops before Montgomery arrived on the scene—the
scale of their respect for him was shown by the way they
coined a term "a Rommel" as a synonym for a good performance of any kind. This attitude of admiration carried a subtle
danger to morale, and when Montgomery took over command
special efforts were made to damp the "Rommel legend" as
well as to create a counter-legend around "Monty."

This propaganda gradually spread the view that Rommel
was an overrated general. Montgomery's private feelings, however, were shown in the way he collected photographs of
Rommel and pinned them up beside his desk, though he later
expressed the view that Rundstedt was the more formidable
opponent of the two. Here it must be remembered that Montgomery never met Rommel at his best, and that when they

met in battle Rommel was not only weakened by sickness but tactically crippled by a heavy inferiority of force and shortage of petrol supplies.

The outstanding feature of Rommel's successes is that they were achieved with an inferiority of force, and without any command of the air. No other generals on either side gained the victory under such conditions, except for the early British leaders under Wavell, and their successes were won against Italians. That Rommel made mistakes is clear, but when fighting superior forces any slip may result in defeat, whereas numerous mistakes can be effectively covered up by the general who enjoys a big advantage of strength.

More definite defects were his tendency to disregard the administrative side of strategy and his lack of thoroughness over detail. At the same time he did not know how to delegate authority, a defect that was very irritating to his chief subordinates. He not only tried to do everything himself but to be everywhere—so that he was often out of touch with his headquarters, and apt to be riding round the battlefield when he was wanted by his staff for some important decision. On the other hand, he had a wonderful knack of appearing at some vital spot and giving a decisive impetus to the action at a crucial moment. He also gave dynamic junior officers such opportunities to prove their value as seniority-bound generals would never have dreamt of allowing them. As a result he was worshipped by the younger men. That feeling was shared by many of the Italian soldiers who saw him in such a vital contrast to their own senile and safety-first higher commanders.

In the field of tactics, Rommel was often brilliant in ruse and bluff. In his first attack in Africa he pushed his tanks so hard that many went astray in the desert, but when he reached the main British position he cleverly concealed the scanty number that were present by utilizing trucks to raise a great cloud of dust, and create the impression that tanks were converging from all sides. This produced a collapse.

While extremely daring he was also subtle. A repeated feature of his battles was the way he used his tanks as a bait, to lure the British tanks into traps that were lined with anti-tank guns—thus skilfully blending the defensive with the offensive. These "Rommel tactics" became increasingly adopted by all armies as the war advanced.

When he left Africa his departure was almost regretted by his opponents, so big was the place he had come to fill in their lives, and in their imagination. That was partly due to his remarkably good treatment of British prisoners; indeed, the number who managed to escape and return to their own lines after a personal contact with him suggests that his chivalry was blended with strategy. Much wider still was the impression made by his swiftness of manœuvre and his startling comebacks after being apparently defeated.

As a strategist, his defects were apt to be a serious offset to his subtlety and audacity. As a tactician, his qualities tended to eclipse his defects. As a commander, his exceptional combination of leading power and driving power was accompanied by a mercurial temperament, so that he was apt to swing too violently between exaltation and depression.

In 1944 Rommel reappeared as army group commander on the Channel coast, to meet the Anglo-American invasion. Here he was under Field-Marshal von Rundstedt, the Commander-in-Chief in the West. Their views differed as to the best way to meet the invasion and also as to the place where it was to be expected. Rundstedt favoured defence in depth, trusting to the effect of a powerful counter-offensive when the invaders had fully committed themselves. Rommel had a natural disposition to favour such a form of strategy, which he had followed so often in Africa, but experience there had modified his view of its practicability against an invader superior in air-power. He was now anxious to concentrate right forward with the aim of checking the invasion before it became established ashore. Rundstedt also held the view that the main Allied offensive would come direct across the Channel at its narrower part, between the Somme and Calais, whereas Rommel became more concerned with the possibilities of an invasion of Western Normandy, between Caen and Cherbourg. Here he took the same view as Hitler.

On the latter issue Rommel's anticipation (and Hitler's) was right. Moreover, there is evidence that he had striven hard in the last four months to improve the coast defences in Normandy, which had been neglected by comparison with those in the Pas de Calais. His efforts, fortunately for the Allies, were hampered by the shortage of resources—so that both the under-water obstructions and the coast fortifications were far from complete.

On the other issue, the general opinion on the Allied side, especially among the generals, has been that Rundstedt's plan —of holding the reserves back and then launching a massive stroke at a chosen moment—was a good one, and that Rommel spoilt it by using up strength in the effort to pen the Allied armies within their Normandy bridgehead. That was even more strongly the opinion of most of the German generals— those who belonged to the General Staff "caste" regarded Rommel as only less of an amateur than Hitler. They argued, also, that Rommel had had no war experience comparable to that provided by the Russian campaign, which had taught the importance of disposing forces in great depth.

Rundstedt's plan was certainly more in accord with the basic theory of strategy. But when one takes account of the size of the Allied forces, coupled with their domination of the air, and set against the wide space open for manœuvre, it looks very doubtful whether any deliberate counter-offensive by the Germans could have stopped the invading armies once they penetrated deep into France. In such circumstances the only real hope may have lain in preventing them from securing a bridgehead big enough for building up their strength on that side of the Channel. Rommel went close to depriving them of this opportunity in the first few days, and his eventual failure to hold them in check may be traced back, not to his mistakes, but to delay in switching forces from the Pas de Calais. That was due to the Higher Command's continued belief that the Normandy landings were only a prelude to larger landings between Le Havre and Calais. Beyond that there was the lack of any adequate general reserve in the West. Rundstedt had wished to create one by evacuating the southern half of France, but Hitler would not sanction such a step.

The effects were made fatal by Hitler's refusal to allow a withdrawal in Normandy when it became clear to both Rundstedt and Rommel that it was no longer possible to hold the invading forces in check. A timely withdrawal might have enabled the German forces to make a stand on the Seine, and a much longer stand subsequently on the German frontier. But Hitler insisted that there must be no general withdrawal, and would not allow the commanders in the West the freedom to carry out a local withdrawal, even of a few miles, without his approval. As a result divisions had to cling on until they were hammered to bits—a rigidity which in the end resulted in much longer retreats than Rundstedt and Rommel had proposed.

A common sense of the hopelessness of Hitler's policy had brought these two into closer accord than ever before. At the end of June Hitler came to France at their urgent request—it was the only visit he paid to the West in 1944—and they met him at Soissons. But he would not agree to their very modest proposal to withdraw behind the Orne, preparatory to an armoured counter-stroke. In the following week the strain on the front grew worse. Rundstedt now bluntly said that it was vain to continue the struggle, and that the war ought to be ended. As that solution did not appeal to Hitler, he decided to try a change of commanders, and despatched his leading general in the East, Field-Marshal von Kluge, to replace Rundstedt.

It was significant that Hitler passed over Rommel, though he did not remove him. Rommel's attitude at Soissons had not found favour with Hitler. But Rommel's view of Hitler had changed even more. He had remarked to a number of his own subordinate commanders that Germany's only hope now lay in doing away with Hitler as quickly as possible, and then trying to negotiate peace. It is certain that he was acquainted —at the least—with the plot that culminated in the attempted assassination of Hitler on July 20th.

Three days before that Rommel was driving along a road near the front when low-flying 'planes attacked it. His car capsized and he was thrown out, fracturing his skull. The scene of this crash was the aptly-named village of Sainte Foy de Montgommery. He was taken to hospital in Paris and when convalescent went to his home at Ulm. By this time the Gestapo had investigated the plot against Hitler. Two generals came to see Rommel at his home and took him out for a drive. During it they gave him a message from Hitler that he could choose between taking poison and coming to Berlin for interrogation. He chose the poison. It was then announced that he had died from the result of his accident, and he was given a state funeral.

Thus ended the career of a soldier who, though defective both in his grasp of higher strategy and in administrative detail, had a real touch of genius in the tactical field, combined with dynamic executive power. He had a flair for the vital spot and the critical moment. Exasperating to his staff officers, he was worshipped by his fighting troops.

VI

SOLDIERS IN THE SHADOW

IN CHAPTER IV THE PATTERN OF THE WAR ON GERMANY'S SIDE was traced as far as the end of 1941. The last chapter, after following the divergent thread of Rommel's career in the African field, came back along with him to the decisive reopening of the Western field in the summer of 1944. But that has left a gap in the pattern; before passing to the final stage it is desirable to pick up the thread of events in Europe from the end of 1941, and carry it through the interval. To avoid anticipating the fuller picture that emerges from the accounts of the generals, in Part III, this interim chapter will be confined to a brief indication of the course of events, still in terms of the chief military personalities concerned. They were "soldiers in the shadow," in a double sense—for the cloud of Hitler's disapproval as well as the cloud of defeat overhung their course.

HALDER'S LAST LAP

In 1942 the operations in Russia were conducted by General Franz Halder, Chief of the General Staff, but subject to over-riding *directives* from Hitler. Halder had a fine strategical brain, and the actual design of the plans which had proved so

successful earlier had been mainly his own work, rather than
the inspiration of brilliant assistants in the background. But
O.K.H., over which he presided after Brauchitsch's removal,
was henceforth more definitely under the control of O.K.W.,
which was scoffingly called "the military bureau of Corporal
Hitler."

In this difficult situation Halder missed the support that
Brauchitsch, by virtue of his authority, had formerly provided.
It had been more possible to argue with the Commander-in-
Chief of the Wehrmacht when backed by the Commander-in-
Chief of the Army than it now became when the two were
one—and when that one was a man of Hitler's temperament.
Between Brauchitsch and Halder there was a harmony rare
in high quarters, and differences of view hardly ever arose.
According to other generals who knew them, the two had
worked so closely together that their respective functions and
influence could hardly be distinguished, though Halder tended
to be the dominating mind. "What Halder thought out,
Brauchitsch presented to Hitler. Halder never saw Hitler without Brauchitsch being present to support him." But henceforth Halder had to fight his battles alone.

The summer campaign of 1942 had brilliant initial success
and bore evidence of masterly planning by Halder. An artful
delay in opening the campaign on the main front, coupled
with a startling coup against the Crimean peninsula, incited
the Russians to take the initiative with an offensive towards
Kharkov. Having got the southern Russian armies deeply
embedded here, the main German offensive was launched past
their flank, and gained a clear run down the corridor between
the Don and the Donetz rivers. But after crossing the Lower
Don the German drive split in divergent directions under
Hitler's interference. The prospects of the main advance into
the Caucasus, and of securing the oilfields there, were sacrificed
to his desire to retrieve the check suffered by the subsidiary
advance on Stalingrad, the original object of which had merely
been to secure flank cover for the avenue of advance into the

Caucasus. Worse still, Hitler's eyes became as narrowly focused on Stalingrad as they had been on Moscow the previous year. The very name of the city was a challenge to him. Once again, by the directness of his aim he helped the Russians to concentrate their reserves to frustrate him.

As soon as it became clear that the effort was losing momentum, Halder argued that it should be broken off. Hitler had grown increasingly impatient of his objections, and this time his unwelcome advice led to his dismissal, at the end of September.

ZEITZLER

Halder was replaced by Kurt Zeitzler, who had recently been Chief of Staff in the West. The fact that he had thus been out of touch with the situation in the East added to his handicap in taking over at such a critical moment—and lessened his chance of disputing Hitler's view of it.

Zeitzler, a much younger man, had been only a colonel commanding an infantry regiment before the war, but subsequently became chief of staff to Kleist's panzer army. It was he who found a way to solve the problem of supplying armoured forces during long-range advances and rapid switches. Able and energetic, he was predominantly the "man of action" type that appealed to the Nazi leaders, in contrast to the "man of reflection" represented in Halder, who was a mathematician and botanist as well as a military writer of distinction.

Less of a strategist than his predecessor, Zeitzler was an outstandingly resourceful organizer of strategic moves, with an exceptional grasp of what could be done with mechanized forces. His brilliant staffwork in organizing and maintaining the panzer drive through the Ardennes and on through France, in 1940, had been excelled in the complex series of manœuvres called for in 1941—when Kleist's panzer forces had first swerved down through the Ukraine towards the Black Sea, to block Budenny's retreat across the Bug and the Dnieper; then turned about and dashed north to meet Guderian and complete the vast encirclement round Kiev; then been switched south again, onto the rear of the fresh Russian forces that were attacking the German bridgehead over the Dnieper at Dnepropetrovsk; and, after producing a Russian collapse here, had driven down through the Donetz Basin to cut off the Russian forces near the Sea of Azov. As Kleist emphasized to me, in paying unstinted tribute to his chief of staff, the biggest problem in "throwing armies about in this way" was that of maintaining supplies.

Zeitzler's performance attracted Hitler's attention, and early in 1942 he summoned him for an interview. Hitler's impression was deepened by what Zeitzler told him of the emergency measures that had been improvised, in the 1st Panzer Army, to help the troops through the rigours of the winter. It impressed Hitler all the more because he had a deep conviction that German professional soldiers were too imbued with sealed-pattern methods, and could not improvise. Soon afterwards, Zeitzler was sent to be Chief of Staff in the West, and reorganize the defences there. In September, after the repulse of the Dieppe landing, he was called back to the East, and told by Hitler that he was to become Chief of the General Staff. It was a dazzling jump for a young major-general.

Hitler's preference for younger men who understood mechanized warfare, coupled with Zeitzler's practical record in that field, might suffice to explain his selection—but it was not the complete explanation. In placing such a junior general at the head of O.K.H., Hitler hoped he would be so grateful to his patron as to sink his professional loyalty and become Hitler's henchman as Keitel and Jodl had done. In ridding himself of Halder, Hitler counted on relief from the constant objections he had endured from that "turbulent priest" of the established military order.

Momentarily, Zeitzler was dazzled. Thus he acquiesced in the continuance of the assault on Stalingrad, as well as the advance in the Caucasus, until the bulk of the German re-

serves had been committed too far to be extricated—in so far
as they had not already been consumed in vain efforts.

But his doubts soon began to grow, and he questioned the
wisdom of Hitler's intention to hold on to an advanced position at Stalingrad during the winter. When the Russian
counter-offensive began, he wanted to withdraw Paulus's army
immediately, but Hitler angrily refused. After that, friction was
frequent, for even when Paulus's army was encircled Hitler
would not agree that it should be ordered to abandon its position and fight its way out to the west. Zeitzler was driven to
tender his resignation, but Hitler brushed that aside.

After the army at Stalingrad had been forced to surrender,
Zeitzler managed to induce Hitler to sanction withdrawals
from two dangerous salients in the north, facing Moscow and
Leningrad respectively. This eased the strain and helped to
maintain that front intact in face of subsequent assaults, besides releasing reserves for elsewhere. But Hitler was galled
by having to make such an unconcealable step-back from
Russia's two greatest cities, and he would not consider any
general strategic withdrawal. Zeitzler did not lack courage in
standing up to Hitler, but he had to fight his battles alone, for
Keitel and Jodl always backed Hitler. He was the more
handicapped in combating their influence because their offices
were at Hitler's headquarters, while his was some distance
away. But the separation was more than a matter of mileage,
for as time went on and his protests multiplied, Hitler's manner became distant when they met at the daily conferences.

All this tended to augment the influence of General Jodl,
the chief of Hitler's personal staff, and thus of Hitler's own
control over operations. For Jodl, who kept his place throughout the war, would never have lasted so long if he had not
been adept in "keeping his place" within the limits assigned
to him. He was a first-rate clerk. Zeitzler, by contrast, was
impulsive and far from subservient—he frequently lost his
temper in arguing with Hitler. But the latter seems to have
been reluctant to part with a man who was such a master of

mechanized logistics, with a practical capacity to solve movement problems that neither Keitel nor Jodl possessed.

The end came early in July, 1944, soon after the collapse of
the armies on the Upper Dnieper. Zeitzler went to see Hitler
privately and urged him to sanction the withdrawal of the
Northern Army Group, in the Baltic States, before it was
encircled. Hitler refused, and then both men flared up. Having
had his resignation rejected several times, Zeitzler went sick as
the only way out of a responsibility he was unwilling to share
any longer. Hitler took his revenge by depriving Zeitzler of
various privileges of his rank, and then by giving the humiliat-
ing order that he was to be discharged from the Army without
the normal right to wear uniform.

GUDERIAN

To fill Zeitzler s place Hitler called on an earlier and older
tank expert—Guderian. That appointment shocked many of
the members of the General Staff, who regarded Guderian as
a one-sided enthusiast for his specialty and a "bull" on the
battlefield, lacking the strategical sense and balanced view
required in a Chief of the General Staff. The choice demonstrated Hitler's instinctive preference for revolutionary ideas,
and his appreciation of what he had owed to Guderian's past
activities.[1] It appeared to set the crown on the career of the
man who had been the pioneer in creating Germany's panzer
forces, and then the spearman of Germany's run of victories.
But, in reality, it proved more in the nature of window-
dressing.

For Hitler had long since taken the direction of the war
completely into his own hands, and regarded O.K.H. as little
more than a means of transmitting his orders to, and handling
the executive details of, the Eastern Front. Even if Guderian
had been fitted by temperament and experience to be Chief
of the General Staff he would not have been allowed to play

[1] These are related in Chapter IX, "The Rise of Armour."

the part. As things were, he was doubly checked—by an atmosphere of professional mistrust around him, and by Hitler on top of him.

His subordinates on the General Staff patronizingly, and rather resentfully, spoke of him as "a fighting soldier, not a War-Academy soldier." They were suspicious of any sign of his unfamiliarity with their technique. With Hitler's backing he might have overcome such resistance, but he soon found himself clashing with Hitler as well. It was difficult enough that his entry into office came when Germany's strength was ebbing, but more difficult still that it came just after the plot of July 20th. Hitler was now in such a mood of distrust that he was apt to take any contrary opinion as a symptom of treason. Some of the younger soldiers knew how to disarm his suspicions, and could argue with him up to a point, but Guderian lacked the knack.

Guderian himself had aged, and much of his original vitality had been used up. He had partially burnt himself out in fighting continued battles against disbelievers and doubters. In the process, determination had tended to degenerate into obstinacy; and fiery energy, into irascibility—as often happens to men of his kind. The cramping circumstances of his belated opportunity aggravated these tendencies.

Nevertheless, this apostle of the new offensive gospel seems to have shown more insight than his master into the defensive requirements of the situation. Early in 1944, when he was still Inspector-General of the Panzer Forces, he had urged Hitler to carry out a strategic withdrawal in the East, and for that purpose prepare a strong rearward defensive line along the 1940 frontier. When he became Chief of the General Staff, the front north of the Pripet Marshes had just previously collapsed, but the Russian flood was eventually checked on a line not far behind what he had proposed. Some twenty divisions, however, had been lost or had sacrificed their equipment in the hasty retreat that followed the collapse, and the breach was only filled by rushing back panzer divisions from Rumania. The weakened front in that quarter soon collapsed, and the collapse was deepened by Rumania's quick change of side. This opened the way for the Russians to push up through the Carpathians into Central Europe in a wide flank march.

Guderian's autumn efforts to consolidate the new line covering East Prussia and Central Poland were hampered, not only by the drain of reserves to bolster up the Hungarian forces, but by Hitler's desire to attempt another offensive in the West. All possible reserves were collected for this dream-plan of "dunkirking" the British again by another flank thrust through the Ardennes. Yet even at this late stage, Hitler would not listen to arguments for withdrawing from the Baltic States, the Balkans and Italy in order to provide reserves for the main front in the East.

When the Ardennes stroke had ended in failure, Hitler still resisted Guderian's arguments. He allowed only a paltry reinforcement to be sent eastward, although Guderian warned him that a fresh Russian offensive was imminent there, and that the German front was not strong enough to hold out. Worse still, that small addition was more than cancelled out by Hitler's order that three of the best armoured divisions in Poland were to be sent southward in a vain offensive attempt to break the Russians' encircling grip on Budapest.

When the Russian offensive was launched on January 12th, Guderian had a mobile reserve of only twelve divisions for a front of nearly 800 miles. Moreover, three days earlier, Hitler had refused his appeal for permission to forestall the Russians by withdrawing from the threatened salients. As a result the front in Poland collapsed quickly, and the Russians' onrush could not be stemmed until they had penetrated deep into Germany and reached the Oder. Here there was a momentary chance for a riposte, as they had outrun their supplies and their flanks were exposed. Hitler had now agreed to release the 6th Panzer Army from the West, but instead of allowing it to be used for this counterstroke he sent it to Hungary for another vain bid to relieve Budapest. He was living in a world of dreams, remote from reality.

Reduced to desperation, Guderian now tackled some of the other leading Nazis about the urgency of seeking peace. His activities soon came to Hitler's ears, and he was dismissed from his post, in March, barely a month before the final collapse.

MANSTEIN

The ablest of all the German generals was probably Field-Marshal Erich von Manstein. That was the verdict of most of those with whom I discussed the war, from Rundstedt downwards. He had a superb strategic sense, combined with a greater understanding of mechanized weapons than any of the generals who did not belong to the tank school itself. Yet in contrast to some of the single-track enthusiasts he did not lose sight of the importance of improving alternative weapons, and defence. He was responsible, shortly before the war, for developing the armoured assault-gun, which proved invaluable later.

A Lewinski by birth, he had been adopted by the Manstein family as a boy. He got an infantry commission shortly before the 1914 war, and, although too young to qualify for the Staff College, he made his mark on the staff of General von Lossberg, who in 1917 produced the new system of defence in depth. By 1935 Manstein had become head of the operations section of the General Staff, and next year was made Deputy Chief under Beck. But in February, 1938, when Fritsch was ousted, Manstein was also removed from O.K.H.—as another move in eliminating opposition to O.K.W. and Nazi designs. He was sent to command a division in Silesia. However, on the eve of war in 1939 he was appointed Chief of Staff to Rundstedt's Army Group, which played the decisive rôle in the Polish campaign. After that he accompanied Rundstedt to the West.

Here he was the source of the brain-wave that produced the defeat of France—the idea of the tank-thrust through the Ardennes. But his arguments only prevailed after he had paid personal forfeit. For the top military circles felt that he was too pushing, and at the end of January, 1940, he was pushed out of the way by sending him to command an infantry corps, the 38th—his request for a panzer corps being rejected on the ground that he lacked experience. After his removal he was summoned to see Hitler and seized the chance to explain his idea. Hitler agreed with it; a week later O.K.H. issued the revised plan. Manstein's removal at least had the benefit of allaying sore feelings in Bock's Army Group, which was reduced to a secondary rôle, by showing that Manstein's advocacy of transferring the leading rôle to Rundstedt's Army Group was not for personal advantage. At the same time his "brain-wave" proved so effective in upsetting the French that his own absence from the steering-wheel was not seriously missed.

In the first stage of the campaign, Manstein had no chance to show what he could do as a commander of troops, for his corps was merely among the backers-up of the panzer drive. But in the second stage, the attack on the new French defence line along the Somme, his corps was instrumental in achieving the first break-through, west of Amiens. Rommel's tanks exploited the opening, but Manstein raced them in the pursuit, handling his infantry like mobile troops. His corps was the first to reach and cross the Seine, on June 10th—marching over forty miles that day. Then, by rapid strides, he pushed on to the Loire. After that, when it came to a question of invading England, he was allotted the formidable task of making the initial landing across the Straits of Dover, near Folkestone. But that plan was stillborn.

Before the invasion of Russia he was given command of a new panzer corps—the 56th, in East Prussia. He broke through the Russian front here, and raced on so fast that he reached the Dvina (nearly 200 miles distant) within four days—capturing the main bridges across it. But he was not allowed to pursue his drive towards Leningrad or Moscow, as he wished, and had to wait on the Dvina for a week while the other panzer corps and the 16th Army came up. He then drove as far again to reach Lake Ilmen south of Leningrad, by July

15th, but was there checked by Russian reserves that had now had time to gather. In September he was promoted to command the 11th Army, in the far south, and there opened the gateway to the Crimea, by breaking through the narrow and fortified Perekop Isthmus—a feat which proved his mastery of the technique of siege warfare.

When the invasion of Russia became stuck in the mud and snow before Moscow that winter, and Hitler sought a scapegoat in sacking Brauchitsch, many of the younger generals in the German Army hoped that Manstein would be chosen to succeed him as Commander-in-Chief. But Hitler wanted to assume the post himself. He thought of appointing Manstein Chief of the General Staff, but felt he might prove even more difficult than Halder.

In the summer of 1942, Manstein was responsible for the attack on the famous fortress of Sevastopol, which preceded the main offensive. His success in that task deprived the Russians of their chief naval base in the Black Sea. After that, he was chosen to command the attack on Leningrad, with forces transferred for the purpose from one extreme flank to the other. It looked as though his scope was to be continually limited by the skill he had shown in this specialized rôle of siege tactics.

Manstein's mission went unfulfilled, however, for by the time the forces were being moved to Leningrad, a call came for them to go to Stalingrad, where Hitler's advance had become stuck. Soon that impasse developed into a crisis, and the army there was surrounded. In the emergency Manstein was given an improvised force, called Army Group "Don," and sent to the rescue.

It was too late and the effort failed—after some of the most breathless cut-and-thrust in the war. In the subsequent retreat he rallied the cracking line and prevented the Russians crossing the Dnieper. A dazzling counter-stroke threw them back a long way and recaptured Kharkov, in March, 1943. Manstein now commanded Army Group "South." That summer, in combination with Kluge (Army Group "Centre"), he delivered Germany's last offensive in the East.

He had proposed alternative courses. One was to strike early in May before the Russians were ready, and dislocate their preparations by a pincer-stroke against the Kursk salient. The other—which he thought better—was to wait for the Russians' offensive, recoil before it, and then launch a flank stroke from the Kiev area to roll up their line. Hitler rejected the latter, fearing to run the risks involved in such a daring strategic gambit. But after choosing the former he postponed the attack—just as it was about to be launched—with the idea that by waiting until his own strength had increased he would re-insure his chances. In the end he waited until July before striking—and the Russians profited more by the delay. Although the southern pincer (Manstein's) penetrated fairly deep, the northern one was blunted by the combined tenacity and elasticity of the Russian defence, and then broken by a flank counter-stroke on the part of the Russians. This developed into a general counter-offensive, which the Germans no longer had the strength to resist.

Manstein showed great skill, against heavy odds, in conducting the step-by-step retreat to the Polish frontier. But Hitler would not listen to his arguments for shaking off the Russian pressure by a long step-back. The vigour with which he argued became an increasing annoyance to Hitler, who finally shelved him in March, 1944, in favor of Model—saying that stubborn resistance yard by yard was more needed than skill in manœuvre. An underlying factor in the change was Hitler's and Himmler's political distrust of Manstein. That ended the military career of the Allies' most formidable military opponent —a man who combined modern ideas of mobility with a classical sense of manœuvre, a mastery of technical detail, and great driving power.

Dwelling regretfully on Manstein's disappearance from the field, Blumentritt said to me: "He was not only the most brilliant strategist of all our generals, but he had a good political sense. A man of that quality was too difficult for Hitler to swallow for long. At conferences Manstein often differed from Hitler, in front of others, and would go so far as to declare that some of the ideas which Hitler put forward were nonsense."

KLUGE

Hitler had lost his other best-known commander in the East a few months earlier, when Kluge was injured in an air crash. But in the summer of 1944, when he was fit again, Hitler found fresh room for him—in the West. He was sent to supersede Rundstedt as Commander-in-Chief there.

Field-Marshal Guenther von Kluge was the only survivor of the original army commanders with whom Hitler embarked on war in 1939. In the Polish campaign, the French campaign, and the 1941 campaign in Russia he commanded the Fourth Army. In the first and the third he had been in Bock's Army Group, and had been entrusted with the offensive against Moscow, even though he did not share the optimism of Hitler and Bock. While he was a strong personality, it was testimony to his forbearing temperament that he endured Bock so long—for Bock was a very difficult man to serve. In the same way Kluge had sufficient moral courage to express his views frankly to Hitler, yet he also refrained from pressing his views to the point of being troublesome. After Bock was put on the shelf early in 1942, Kluge succeeded him in command of the Central Army Group. There he created a well-woven defence that withstood successive Russian assaults during the next two years.

His defensive successes, together with his temperament and loyalty, naturally recommended him to Hitler when Rundstedt and Rommel failed to give satisfaction by achieving the impossible—and caused Hitler further annoyance by pointing out the inevitable. By the time Kluge took over, the Allies had poured such a volume of force into their enlarged Normandy bridgehead that the sheer weight of it was soon bound to burst the too extensive dam with which the Germans were trying to contain it. Three weeks later it collapsed at the western end under the fresh impact of Patton's American Third Army. But Hitler still forbade any withdrawal.

Kluge was too obedient to disregard such definite instructions. One effect was seen in the attempted counter-stroke on August 6th against the bottleneck at Avranches through which Patton's forces had poured out. Shrewdly aimed, this stroke could have been deadly if the panzer divisions there employed had been strong in tanks; but in their diminished state its chances were desperately small, even before it was broken up by concentrated air attack. Worse still, the German forces were not permitted to break away from the clinch when this forlorn hope miscarried. Although retreat was now inevitable, every withdrawal was fatally late and short. In consequence, the battle ended in a general collapse of the German armies in France. When this developed, Hitler sacked Kluge and appointed Field-Marshal Model to replace him.

Kluge took his dismissal with apparent calm, spent a day and a half explaining the situation to his successor, then quietly set off for home and swallowed a capsule of poison on the way. That action was due, not to his chagrin at the ending of his career, but to his anticipation that he would be arrested on arriving home. For he had been in close contact, and sympathy, as early as 1942 with the conspiracy that culminated on July 20th, 1944, in the attempt to overthrow Hitler. Characteristically, he had refrained from committing himself, but he knew that his name had been found in the documents when the plot was investigated after the attempt had failed.

MODEL

Walter Model was fifty-four, a decade younger than most of the German higher commanders—whose average age had remained much higher than in the opposing armies. Nor did he come from the same social level. In this as in other repects he had many similarities to Rommel though he had profited by a more thorough professional grounding. When the big expansion of the army began, with the Hitler régime, Model worked under Brauchitsch in the training department of the War Ministry, and there established close touch with the Nazi leaders. He made a strong impression on Goebbels, who introduced him to Hitler. Later he was put in charge of the inventions department. His technical knowledge was scanty, but he made up for it by imagination and energy, so that, although his enthusiasm was apt to mislead him as to the practicability of various ideas, he did a lot towards developing new forms of equipment.

After being chief of staff of the 4th Corps in the Polish campaign, and then of the 16th Army in the French campaign, he was given command of the 3rd Panzer Division. In the invasion of Russia he distinguished himself by his thrusting power, and led the way in the race to the Dnieper. His extreme energy won quick promotion—first to a panzer corps and then, in the winter, to command of an army, the 9th. He showed much ability here in a defensive rôle under difficult conditions and was among the first to demonstrate the value of tanks in defence, notably by digging them in as miniature movable "hedgehogs."

In 1943 he was cast for a leading rôle in the summer offensive—as the northern arm of the pincer-stroke against the Kursk salient. Here he lost the best chance by persuading Hitler—contrary to the opinion of Kluge and Manstein—to postpone the stroke so as to accumulate more tanks and strengthen the punch. The delay gave the Russians time to prepare, and Model's eventual attack failed, at heavy cost, to break through their well-knit elastic defence. But he did well in checking the dangerous Russian offensive that followed, and in October was promoted to command Army Group "North," where he conducted the withdrawal from Leningrad and stabilized the front on the line Narva-Pskov. In April, 1944, he was transferred to Army Group "South," in place of Manstein, and parried the Russian thrust towards the Carpathian passes. In late June the Russians' summer offensive was launched against Army Group "Centre," which speedily collapsed. Model was sent to take it over. Just as he had checked the Russians along the line of the Vistula, he was despatched to deal with the crisis in the West.

After the failure of the July 20th attempt on Hitler's life, Model had given a lead in reproclaiming his faith in the Führer, and had sent the first telegram of loyalty received from the Eastern front. That assurance reinforced Hitler's confidence in his military gifts. But Model was also one of the few who ventured to disregard Hitler's instructions and act on his own judgment.

In talking to a number of generals who had served under him, I found that all paid tribute to his power of command while emphasizing that he was difficult both as a superior and subordinate. Manteuffel said of him: "Model was a very good tactician, and better in defence than in attack. He had a knack of gauging what troops could do, and what they could not do. His manner was rough, and his methods were not always acceptable in the higher quarters of the German Army, but they were both to Hitler's liking. Model stood up to Hitler in a way that hardly anyone else dared, and even refused to carry out orders with which he did not agree."

In the West it was mainly owing to his efforts and his extraordinary capacity for scraping up reserves, from an almost bare cupboard, that the shattered German forces succeeded in achieving their astonishing rally on the German frontier and frustrating the Allies' expectation of complete victory in the autumn of 1944. He also played the principal executive part in checking the Allies' later offensives and in the Germans' Ardennes counter-offensive of December—although the supreme direction of these final operations in the "Battle for Germany" was in the hands of Rundstedt. For Hitler had called back the "Old Guard" at the moment when Germany seemed about to fall.

VII

"THE OLD GUARD"—RUNDSTEDT

THE WHEEL HAD COME FULL CIRCLE. IN THE FRANTIC EFFORT TO restore the army's confidence Hitler was driven to put back in the chief military place the man who, above all others, represented the old Germany and the military tradition—with its devotion to duty, political conservatism, professional exclusiveness, and contempt for amateurs in strategy as represented by Hitler. Moreover, Gerd von Rundstedt was a gentleman to the core. His natural dignity and good manners inspired the respect even of those who differed widely from him in views. To such an essential aristocrat the democracy of the Weimar Republic had been unpalatable, but he had found the manners of Nazism far more distasteful.

Now close on his seventieth year, he was almost the same age as Hindenburg had been on attaining supreme command in the last war. Age and achievement had similarly combined to make him a national idol on something approaching the same scale. But he was a far abler soldier than Hindenburg— abler even than the combination of Hindenburg and Ludendorff—while his achievements were intrinsically finer. That was symbolized in the contrast that his face and figure presented to theirs. As forceful as they had been, in a more refined way, he was lean, ascetic, and thoughtful in appearance

—though his thought was confined to his profession. In his devotion to the Army, and to Germany, an overriding sense of duty had led him to swallow much that he would have liked to spit out. Here was the root of an inner conflict which revealed itself in the career and in the countenance of this military priest. He despised politics, but they kept on intruding into his seclusion.

By 1932, after successive promotions, he became Chief of the First Army Group Command, covering Berlin. Almost at once he unwittingly acquired a political smell, for it fell to him to carry out the orders of the new Chancellor, Papen, to evict the Social-Democratic Ministers of Prussia when they refused to quit office. Then Papen overreached himself and was succeeded as Chancellor by General von Schleicher. But Schleicher could not gain sufficient political support to maintain his position, and thus the way was opened for Hitler to become Chancellor and abolish all parties other than the Nazi. Rundstedt did not like the way things had turned out, and he definitely disliked both the social aims and the manners of the Nazi leaders. But he found satisfaction in the vehement campaign of the Nazis for military expansion, and was even better content when the purge of June 30th, 1934, curbed the power of the storm-troopers. It seemed a healthy sign to his simple soldierly mind that so many military pretenders were wiped off the slate and the professional army freed from the menace of such "brown dirt," as he described them.

He was now able to devote his attention to the development of the Army. In the military sphere he was primarily concerned to revive the power of the infantry, and their confidence in themselves, by modernizing their equipment as well as their training. For while he was receptive to the new ideas of mechanized warfare, and followed with keen interest the British theories and experiments, he was not one of those who fervently embraced them. Rather, he was one of the more progressive leaders of the school that regarded tanks as useful servants, not as the future masters, of the battlefield.

He believed that there was more value in motorization and multiplied fire-power to improve the capacity of the existing arms than in producing completely mechanized forces. Besides his practical steps to overcome the "machine-gun paralysis" that the infantry had suffered in the last war, he initiated a propaganda campaign to cure their inferiority complex. But he was too nearly a scientific soldier to go so far as the British generals who in 1934 contrived that the big exercise of the season should show that an infantry division could paralyze an armoured division—and thereby helped to postpone the formation of Britain's first armoured division for three years more. Rundstedt favoured the creation of armoured divisions in the German Army, provided that the proportion was not unduly high and did not hinder the re-equipment of the infantry mass. In sum, the extent of his vision and that of his school accounts for the superiority which the German Army enjoyed against France in 1940, while the limitations of their vision explain why it fell short of the technical superiority that was needed for victory over Russia in 1941.

At the start of 1938 his concentration was disturbed by another political shock, when Himmler's machinations provided Hitler with an excuse to turn out Fritsch, the head of the Army, at the same time as Blomberg, the head of the whole armed forces, and himself assume the supreme command. Rundstedt protested to Hitler against Fritsch's treatment, but, although Fritsch was acquitted of the moral charge framed against him, such acquittal did not alter the fact that his post had already been filled. A few months later Rundstedt endorsed the warning memorandum drafted by Beck, the Chief of the General Staff, in an attempt to put a brake on Hitler's war-risking policy—but that protest merely led to Beck's removal. In the autumn, after the occupation of the Sudetenland, Rundstedt asked and obtained permission to retire, on the plea of age.

In August, 1939, he was called back to take command of an army group on the Polish front. His obedience to that summons may seem hard to explain, since he had long insisted that a primary principle of German policy must be to avoid another war with England. It was a questionable conception of patriotism which required him to take a leading part in the kind of war which he had predicted as likely to prove fatal to Germany in the end. To account for it, we need to understand the extremely strait rule of soldierly duty and obedience in which he had been brought up. Beyond that may have been the psychological factor that any ardent soldier finds it hard to resist a professional opportunity.

That opportunity he certainly fulfilled, for it was the army group he commanded which brilliantly carried out the decisive moves in the conquest, first of Poland, and then of France. Yet there were signs that the glory and the pleasure were spoilt for him by an underlying disquietude. In the Russian campaign of 1941 he again proved the outstanding figure, by his direction of the sweeping operations that overturned the Russian armies in the south and gave Germany possession of the mineral and agricultural riches of the Ukraine. But this time even the victories fell short of being a complete success, and in that falling short presaged ultimate disaster. Rundstedt was quick to see confirmation of the apprehensions which had impelled him, beforehand, to offer Hitler unwelcome advice against attacking Russia. When the question of continuing the advance on Moscow was discussed in the autumn, Rundstedt argued in favour not merely of a halt but of a withdrawal to the original starting-line. That advice was still more unwelcome to the Führer. At the same time Rundstedt was growing more and more impatient of "Corporal" Hitler's interference in operational details. Eventually, at the end of November, Rundstedt replied to one of Hitler's orders by telegraphing back that, if the Führer did not trust him to carry out the operation as he judged best, the Führer should find someone else to take command. The offer of resignation was accepted by Hitler with equal alacrity; Rundstedt's doubts and protests had been getting on his nerves, which were already strained by the way that victory was eluding his grasp.

But Rundstedt was not left long on the shelf. Early in 1942 Hitler asked him to take charge in the West, and overcame his hesitation by emphasizing the note of national duty. The entry of the United States into the war created the possibility that American armies might eventually jump off from Britain to invade the Continent, and Rundstedt was very conscious of that risk. He spent the next two years in preparation for the danger he feared, as well as in wrestling with the civil problems arising out of the German occupation of France and the Low Countries. In June, 1944, the danger matured. That part of the story has already been outlined.

Rundstedt was in retirement on the fatal July 20th, so that he had no chance of giving the army a lead against the Nazi régime when the first telegraphic message of the conspirators —saying that Hitler had been killed—reached the higher headquarters in the East and the West. It is thus impossible to say whether he would have acted differently from most of the other high commanders—who, whatever their intentions, became paralyzed as soon as second reports indicated that Hitler was still alive. Rundstedt was not associated with the plot, and that is significant.

While many soldiers, knowing his repugnance to Nazism, had been looking to him to give them a lead against Hitler, those who knew him best do not seem to have had any such idea. In the first place, he was regarded as a man so straightforward, so strict in his conception of the soldierly code of honour, as to be unsuitable to participate in a conspiracy which required subtlety. Secondly, because of the symbolical value of his reputation, they wanted to keep it clear of the inevitable taint that any plot carries, even though its object may be good. Beyond that he was more closely watched than others, because of his eminence, by the network of Nazi spies in which all the generals were enveloped.

At the same time a number of the generals had hoped that Rundstedt would bring about an armistice with the British and Americans, or at least allow them an unopposed entry into Germany, in order to check the Russians. That hope was quenched by his removal early in July, though it revived with his recall in September. In the meantime Kluge had contemplated a similar step on July 20th, but had hesitated to attempt it. The reasons for his hesitation were, first, that it would be a breach of the oath of loyalty to Hitler; second, that the German people had been kept so much in the dark that they would not support such an action; third, that the soldiers on the East front would reproach the West front for betraying them; fourth, the fear of going down to history as a traitor to his country. It was natural that such restraining considerations should have even more influence on a man like Rundstedt when he was summoned back in the September crisis—apart from the practical difficulties of taking such a step when under close surveillance. As a result of that psychological conflict between his judgment and his sense of duty, as well as Hitler's continued interference at every turn, he was virtually in a state of impotence during the autumn months when the Allies imagined him to be conducting the German defence in the West.

His connection with the so-called "Rundstedt offensive" of December in the Ardennes was hardly more than that of a distant and doubting observer. The project was purely Hitler's in respect of aim, timing, and place—though improved by the technical suggestions of Manteuffel, commanding the Fifth Panzer Army. The execution was in the hands of Model and his two principal subordinates, Manteuffel and Sepp Dietrich, commander of the Sixth Panzer Army.

Late in October Hitler sent his plan to Rundstedt. It had the same basic pattern as the 1940 masterpiece. It was designed to profit by the way that the Allies had committed their strength to the push through the Belgian plain towards Aachen and Cologne, and were unlikely to expect a German counter-offensive at this time, particularly in the Ardennes—a psychological calculation that again proved correct. The main effort was to be a double-pronged thrust by the Fifth and Sixth Panzer Armies, with the aim of breaking through the weak American front in the Ardennes, then wheeling north to cross the Meuse and converge on Antwerp. The Sixth Panzer Army was to move on the inner arc of the wheel, past Liege, and the Fifth Panzer on the outer arc, past Namur. The Fifteenth Army was to help the Sixth Panzer Army by a flank thrust north of Liege, while the Seventh Army was to provide flank cover for the Fifth Panzer Army as it wheeled north.

By this scythe-like sweep Hitler hoped to cut off Montgomery's Twenty-first Army Group from its bases and from its American allies, driving it to a Dutch "Dunkirk" even if he could not annihilate it. Britain was now out of reach, but her armies were not—and they were the chosen target of his final fling. But Hitler's executive commanders all regarded the aim as far too ambitious for the resources.

Realizing that a direct protest was hopeless, Rundstedt, Model, and Manteuffel agreed in proposing a more modest alternative plan—to pinch off the American salient east of the Meuse, around Aachen. But Hitler rejected any such limitation of aim, though Manteuffel persuaded him to accept certain changes of timing and method—for Hitler was always more receptive to the arguments of the younger generals than to those of the older generals, and ready to listen to original ideas when he was deaf to counsels of caution. The changes increased the chances of initial surprise, but they could not increase the ultimate chances.

The offensive was a gamble—at long odds. All the higher executants realized that Germany was playing her last trump, and that she had not the resources to provide more than a slender chance of success—unless the offensive was accompanied by extraordinary luck or the Allied commanders were extraordinarily inept. That realization was not a good foundation for an offensive. In the event, the stroke threw the Allies off their balance sufficiently to put them in serious difficulties and undue danger. But the German forces were so diminished in strength that they could not afford anything like the normal proportion of checks and slips that occur in the run of any offensive. Manteuffel almost reached the Meuse, but Sepp Dietrich, who had a larger strength and a shorter distance to go, ran into trouble sooner; and when the reserves were switched to back up Manteuffel it was too late for any great results in the face of the Allies' prompt counter-measures. The offensive fell far short of its aims, and when it ended it had fatally impoverished Germany's reserves, leaving her no chance of long-continued defence.

PART II

PRELIMINARIES TO WAR

VIII

THE RISE OF HITLER

THE STORY OF HITLER'S ENTRY INTO POWER HAS BEEN TOLD from many angles, but not from that of the Reichswehr. Its chiefs have been charged with aiding and abetting his entry, but remarkably little evidence has been produced to support this accusation.

It is obvious that the officers of the Reichswehr were beneficiaries, in their professional prospects, from the expansion of the forces that followed Hitler's advent. Moreover, Blomberg and other generals have admitted that they originally welcomed his régime because it released Germany and the Army from the shackles of the Versailles Treaty. That was a very natural attitude on the part of keen professional soldiers, though one that many of them lived to regret. Others, with more foresight, were apprehensive from the start, for there was good reason to assume that the amateur or "displaced" soldiers who led the S.A. would not be content, once their Party was in power, to see military office remain a privileged preserve of the traditionally conservative Reichswehr.

But evidence that a considerable number of officers were favourably disposed towards Hitler's rise is not equivalent to evidence that they were instrumental in aiding his arrival in power—and still less that the Army in its corporate sense was instrumental. For that would only have been practicable if those who were then in control of the Army were favourably disposed. On this score the cardinal facts seem to point the other way. The political head of the Army at this crucial period was General von Schleicher, who had been made Reichswehr Minister in Papen's Cabinet; under him on that side came Colonel von Bredow, the Chief of the Ministerial Staff (the Ministeramt, which was later developed into the High Command of the Wehrmacht). The military head of the Army was General von Hammerstein (*Chef der Heeresleitung*).

Not long after Hitler came into power, Hammerstein was removed from the command of the Army. Then, in the bloody purge of June 30th, 1934, Schleicher and Bredow were murdered. Such treatment is presumptive evidence in support of what other soldiers say—that they had tried to prevent the Nazis' rise to power.

General Röhricht, who was one of Schleicher's assistants at the time, gave me an account of this critical phase, as well as subsequent phases of the conflict between the generals and Hitler. While it runs counter to outside impressions it deserves consideration as to testmony of one of the few surviving witnesses who were on the inside of events during the decisive weeks.

In his preliminary remarks Röhricht sketched the personalities of Schleicher and Hammerstein. This was the description of Schleicher—"He was not so much a soldier as an expert in home politics, though not tied to any party. He was very sympathetic towards, and popular with, the trade unions, while suspected by the Conservatives on account of his tendency to social reforms. He was anything but a 'Junker.' A very skilful and astute political tactician, but without the personality of a statesman that was needed at this period." Speaking of Hammerstein, Röhricht said—"He was gifted and extremely clever, politically level-headed, but a lazy soldier. He was strongly opposed to National Socialism, and followed Schleicher's political course."

Röhricht's narrative follows:

The Sequence of Events

In their struggle with the National-Socialist Party the Papen-Schleicher Government dissolved the Reichstag and resigned —in October, 1932. The elections, in spite of an obvious loss of votes for the National-Socialists, resulted in a Parliament without any clear basis of confidence and definite majority either for Papen or for the Opposition—which was split into Right and Left. At first the President intended to charge Papen anew with forming the Government. But there was high tension with all circles of revolutionary opposition. During the Berlin transport workers' strike in November, 1932, co-operation between Communists and National-Socialists was apparent. This had to be regarded as a critical symptom.

Based on this alarming situation, a conference and map exercise was held about the 20th November at the Ministeramt of the Reichswehr Ministry, in conjunction with the Ministry of the Interior, in order to examine the question whether the armed forces of the State would be sufficient to break a simultaneous revolutionary assault by the extremists of both the Right and the Left. This situation seemed likely to arise if a new Papen Government relied exclusively on the Conservative Right (Deutsch-Nationale), the Stahlhelm included.

The conclusion reached at this conference was that a general transport workers' strike would paralyze the entire structure and organization of the State and of the armed forces. For the Reichswehr was only motorized to a slight extent, and its emergency-units for technical work (Technische Nothilfe) were not in an efficient state. In Schleicher's opinion we ought to avoid a situation where the troops had to fire on their own countrymen. He did not want to "sit on bayonets."

At this moment, very much against his will, Schleicher was

driven to take over the office of Chancellor himself, with the idea that it would be for a limited time. Inasmuch as he was not—like Papen—regarded as a representative of conservative-reactionary circles, but as a neutral soldier, he was accepted as a lesser evil by the Centre Party and the Social-Democrats. The National-Socialists also acquiesced—regarding this stop-gap arrangement as a possible stepping stone to their own coming into power. Thus his appointment at the end of November had a calming effect and provided a breathing space.

Schleicher planned to break the onslaught of the National-Socialists by splitting up their faction in the Reichstag. The moment seemed favourable, as the Party was badly disappointed by their electoral setback and worried with financial difficulties. Negotiations started with Strasser and about eighty other M.P.s. The opening of the Reichstag was delayed.

The prospect looked better still when, at the beginning of December, a success was gained in the sphere of foreign affairs —the Disarmament Conference (presumably under the pressure of the stormy domestic development in Germany) conceding to Germany the right of military equality on principle.

But from the start Schleicher met with violent opposition from the Conservatives (Deutsch-Nationale) because his programme contained far-reaching social reforms. Thereupon Schleicher threatened to disclose nepotism in the use of the Eastern Relief funds (Osthilfe). The President—who, on account of his age, was no longer capable of clear judgement—fell under the influence of his contemporary conservative friends, who accused Schleicher of "Bolshevist" tendencies and spread the suspicion that he wanted to pervert the Army for his own political aims. At the same time Papen started an intrigue—negotiating with Hitler—by which he hoped to come back into power with the aid of the National-Socialists, but in the end was cheated himself.

The Hindenburg-Schleicher crisis reacted on Schleicher's attempt to split the National-Socialist Party—by wrecking the discussions, which had opened with good prospects.

Schleicher's situation, therefore, soon appeared hopeless—
no support by the President, no prospects of a majority in
Parliament. On January 26th or 27th General von Hammerstein, the Chief of the Army Command . . . attempted once
more for the last time to change the President's mind. He was
sharply rebuffed. Schleicher's resignation on the 29th January
was followed by Hitler's appointment as Chancellor on January 30th.

With General von Schleicher the only Chancellor who arose
from the Wehrmacht was overthrown. Schleicher was murdered at the first suitable moment (30th June, 1934) by agents
of the Nazi Party, together with Colonel von Bredow (apparently overrated as a politician) and Strasser.

By Hitler's appointment the Reichswehr lost their hitherto
existing monopoly as the final and decisive instrument of the
Government. Their 100,000 men were distributed in small units
all over the Reich, whereas the Party dominated the entire
apparatus of the State, all the means of transport, public communications and utilities, the opinion of the man in the street,
and a large part of the working class. The Army had lost its
importance.

In view of these events and facts I venture to suggest that it
is historically false to charge the Wehrmacht with having
assisted Hitler in his coming into power. The facts point to
the contrary.

In this connection I would like to examine the question,
whether there was the possibility for the Reichswehr to rise in
open rebellion.

The circles around Schleicher and Hammerstein, during the
critical days and after the Nazi Party came into power, considered the possibility of a *coup d'état* by the Reichswehr but rejected the idea as hopeless.

These were the reasons. Hitler had been appointed Chancellor by the President as leader of the strongest party according
to the constitution—therefore at first in a wholly legal manner.

A *coup d'état* by the Reichswehr ordered by Generals von Schleicher and von Hammerstein—who were but little known by the rank and file—would have appeared to be not only against the new Hitler-Papen-Hugenberg Cabinet but also against the greatly respected person of their universally venerated Commander-in-Chief, the President. A political alliance with the Communists was impossible; with the other republican parties it was not prepared. The troops, bound by their oath to Hindenburg, would have declined to follow such an attempt. Besides, the disproportion of power was now still more unfavourable than in November. Finally, the unhappy consequences of a failure could not be overlooked.

THE PERIOD UP TO HINDENBURG'S DEATH (JANUARY, 1933-AUGUST, 1934)

The Reichswehr stood aside from the political events which changed Germany's features with sweeping revolutionary measures. It was like an island—not commanded by Hitler, but by Hindenburg, who, however, was very old. Hammerstein was replaced by Fritsch on Hindenburg's order.

THE NEW MEN

Von Blomberg was appointed as War Minister ("Reichskriegsminister") in January, 1933. Until then he had been German Representative with the Disarmament Conference at Geneva —and had had no previous relations with Hitler. He was a gifted soldier, a man of the world, widely educated and with many interests, but not a strong character, and was easily influenced.

Von Reichenau was Chief of the Wehrmachtamt, until then the Ministeramt. He was a strong personality and full of initiative, a man of action and instinct rather than of intellect. Ambitious, clever, highly educated, even a poet, he was never-

theless of a sturdy nature and a sportsman. Well acquainted
with Hitler for some years, he felt himself bound to the person
of Hitler, not to the Party.

Freiherr von Fritsch (Chef der Heeresleitung, later Commander-in-Chief of the Army) was an excellent and distinguished soldier, but his ideas were limited to the military
sphere. He was a gentleman from top to toe, and also very
religious.

Blomberg and Reichenau had the task of assuring the position due to the Army within the new State—which they had
to accept as an established fact—and the task of helping to
recover normal public life by eliminating the revolutionary
elements of the Party.

The revolutionary S.A., dominating the masses and the
Party at that time, was opposed to the Army from the start.
The S.A. claimed to form the Army of the new State out of
its own ranks. The Army prepared to fight for its position
within the new State. Hitler, like every dictator, was forced
to rid himself of his S.A. rebels—his Prætorian Guard—who
had raised him to power. He sided with the Army and routed
the S.A. (Roehm) on 30th June, 1934, without calling in any
troops.

The Reichswehr regarded that day as a success—notwith-
standing serious excesses (the murder of Schleicher and
others). However, it proved a Pyrrhic victory. From that day,
with the founding of the Waffen-S.S., dated the rise of an
enemy much more dangerous to the Army.

THE PERIOD FROM HINDENBURG'S DEATH TO 1938

Following Hindenburg's death, Hitler declared himself Head
of the State—which made him at the same time the titular
Supreme Commander-in-Chief of the Wehrmacht.

Re-armament, at first only aiming at equality with Germany's neighbours, began to absorb the entire attention and
strength of the troops. Every new stage of re-armament weak-

ened the solid foundations of the hitherto unanimous professional army. The 4,000 professional officers had not only to
form the nucleus for the officers of the gradually expanding
army, but also for the Luftwaffe. To their numbers were
added the newly-reinstated officers, who came from the most
various professions and circles. These—especially the younger
ones—brought along their political ideas. The features of the
officer-corps were changing, and the Party began to gain
ground within the Army. Soon, one could not count any
longer on unity of mind.

With the reintroduction of conscription the whole army lost
its character as an instrument in domestic struggles. It was
further weakened by the formation of the Luftwaffe—which
was guided by National-Socialist principles from the outset.
For the Luftwaffe, not without purpose, embraced the Flak
(A.A.)—a decision which deprived the Army of every means
of anti-aircraft defence. The Army's scope of action for domestic struggle grew ever more hopeless.

For all that, the leaders of the Army once more considered
the question of a rebellion against Hitler, when, with the fall
of Blomberg, there arose a grave conflict over the person of
Colonel-General von Fritsch in January and February, 1938.
Hitler himself took over direct command of the Wehrmacht
in place of Blomberg, and retained Keitel (Reichenau's successor), whose importance never exceeded that of a pliant
head-clerk.

The incredible injustice with which the distinguished General von Fritsch was treated, exasperated the generals in positions of high command—no others were ever informed—to
great heat.[1] This boiling pot was stirred, already, by a secret
group of opposition (Goerdeler, Schacht) which was inclined
"to go all out." For decisive action, however, the generals
lacked unity in the sense of a solid acting corporation—which
had not been attained since the days of Seeckt. They lacked

[1] Civilian opponents of Hitler, however, complain that the fault of the
generals was that they simmered, but never came to the boil.

the instrument of power—troops ready to go into action for such a purpose. They lacked political leadership—that was ready for action and ready to take over political power. Rebellion remained untried. On the other hand, Hitler from the outset used his "insertion" within the leaders of the Wehrmacht in order to split up the body of military leaders and to break their back-bone. Each commander was reduced to his own counsel and guidance; it was no longer possible to reckon on uniform and united political action by the Army.

I X

THE RISE OF ARMOUR

WHILE THE RISE OF HITLER CHANGED THE MAP OF EUROPE more quickly than even Napoleon had done—though for a shorter period—it was the rise of armoured forces in the German Army that mainly enabled him to achieve his run of conquests. Without them his dreams would never have turned into realities. More even than the Luftwaffe, and much more than the Quislings, they were his decisive instrument. All his other means of softening opposition would not have sufficed for the quick success he sought without their unique capacity to penetrate and overrun a country. He had had the foresight to back this new development, though he ultimately paid forfeit for not backing it more fully.

I was fortunate in getting a long account of the rise of the "Panzers" from General von Thoma, the most famous of the original German tank leaders next to Guderian. A tough but likeable type, he is obviously a born enthusiast who lives in a world of tanks, loves fighting for the zest of it, but would fight without ill-feeling, respecting any worthy opponent. In the Middle Ages he would have been perfectly happy as a knight-errant, challenging all comers at any cross-road for the honour of crossing spears with them. The advent of the tank in warfare was a godsend to such a man, giving him a chance to re-live the part of the mail-clad knight.

He described the way it was developed in the German Army after this was released by Hitler from the restrictions of the Versailles Treaty. "It was wonderful to have real tanks for the first time in 1934, after being confined to tactical experiments with dummies for so many years. Until then our only practical experience was in an experimental camp that we had in Russia, by arrangement with the Soviet Government. This was near Kazan, and was particularly for studying technical problems. But in 1934 our first tank battalion was formed, at Ohrdruf, under the name 'Motor-Instruction Commando.' I was in charge of it. It was the grandmother of all the others.

"It was subsequently expanded into a regiment of two battalions, while two more were established at Zossen. They were equipped by degrees, rather slowly, according to the production of the factories—at first with the air-cooled Krupp tank, Mark I, with only two machine-guns; the next year with odd Maybach tanks, Mark II, that had water cooling; in 1937-38 came the first Mark III and Mark IV tanks, which were considerably better. Meantime our organization was growing. In 1936 two tank brigades were formed—one for each of the two armoured divisions that were then created. The German tank officers closely followed the British ideas on armoured warfare, particularly your own; also General Fuller's. They likewise followed with keen interest the pioneer activities of the original British tank brigade." (This was formed in 1931 for experiment, under Colonel (now General) Broad, and given permanent form in 1934 under Brigadier (now General) Hobart.)

I asked him whether the German tank methods had also been influenced by General de Gaulle's well-known book, as has been commonly reported. His answer was: "No, that did not receive much attention then, as we regarded it as rather 'fantastical.' It did not give much tactical guidance, and was rather up in the clouds. Besides, it came much later than the British exposition of the possibilities of tank warfare."

Thoma went on to say: "It may surprise you to hear that the development of armoured forces met with much resistance from the higher generals of the German Army, as it did in yours. The older ones were afraid of developing such forces fast—because they themselves did not understand the technique of armoured warfare, and were uncomfortable with such new instruments. At the best they were interested, but dubious and cautious. We could have gone ahead much faster but for their attitude."

Thoma himself was sent to Spain in 1936 when the Civil War broke out. "For it was seen that Spain would serve as 'the European Aldershot.' I actually started on the night that General Franco's revolt was due to begin, and went via Marseilles and Lisbon—meeting him at Merida, and arranging how we were to help him. I was in command of all the German ground troops in Spain during the war. Their numbers were greatly exaggerated in newspaper reports—they were never more than 600 at a time." (This excludes air and administrative personnel.) "They were used to train Franco's tank force —and to get battle experience themselves.

"Our main help to Franco was in machines, aircraft and tanks. At the start he had nothing beyond a few obsolete machines. The first batch of German tanks arrived in September, followed by a larger batch in October. They were the Krupp Mark I.

"Russian tanks began to arrive on the other side even quicker —at the end of July. They were of a heavier type than ours, which were armed only with machine-guns, and I offered a reward of 500 pesetas for every one that was captured, as I was only too glad to convert them to my own use. The Moors bagged quite a lot. It may interest you to hear that the present Marshal Koniev was my 'opposite number' on the other side.

"By a carefully organized dilution of the German personnel I was soon able to train a large number of Spanish tank-crews. I found the Spanish quick to learn—though also quick to forget. By 1938 I had four tank battalions under my command— each of three companies, with fifteen tanks in a company. Four of the companies were equipped with Russian tanks. I also had thirty anti-tank companies, with six 37 mm. guns apiece.

"General Franco wished to parcel out the tanks among the infantry—in the usual way of generals who belong to the old school. I had to fight this tendency constantly in the endeavour to use the tanks in a concentrated way. The Francoists' successes were largely due to this.

"I came back from Spain in June, 1939, after the end of the war, and wrote out my experiences and the lessons learned. I was then given command of a tank regiment in Austria. I had been offered a tank brigade, but said that I preferred to polish up my knowledge of recent German practice by handling a regiment first, as I had been out of touch so long with what was happening in Germany. General von Brauchitsch agreed. But in August I was given command of the tank brigade in the 2nd Panzer Division, for the Polish campaign.

"That division was in General von List's Army on the extreme southern wing, beyond the Carpathians. I was ordered to advance on the Jablunka Pass, but suggested instead that the motorized brigade should be sent there, while I carried out with my tank brigade a flanking move—through thick woods and over the ridge. On descending into the valley I arrived in a village to find the people all going to church. How astonished they were to see my tanks appearing! I had turned the enemy's defences without losing a single tank— after a night approach march of fifty miles.

"After the Polish campaign I was appointed to the General Staff, as Chief of the Mobile Forces. This directorate embraced the tank forces, the motorized forces, the horsed cavalry—of which there was still one division—and the cyclist units. In the Polish campaign we had six armoured divisions and four light divisions. The armoured divisions each had a tank brigade of two regiments with two battalions apiece—the combat strength of a regiment at the beginning was about 125 tanks. After an operation lasting several days, one must, in the light of experience, deduct one quarter from the number of tanks—to allow for those under repair—in reckoning the average combat strength."

As combat strength, Thoma explained, he included only

the fighting tanks in the companies (or squadrons). The total number in a regiment, including the light tanks used for reconnaissance, was 160.

"The light divisions were an experiment, and the strength of each of them varied. But the average was two motorized rifle regiments (of three battalions each) and one tank battalion. In addition they had an armoured reconnaissance battalion and a motor-cyclist battalion, as well as an artillery regiment—like the armoured divisions.

"We gave up this experiment after the Polish campaign, and converted them into armoured divisions. For the 1940 offensive in the West we had ten complete armoured divisions, and the S.S. tank regiment 'Leibstandarte'—the scale of which was considerably above a normal tank regiment. The proportion of medium tanks in a division was increased by that time. Even so, there were too many light tanks."

Thoma then made the surprising revelation that, for the invasion of France, the Germans had only 2,400 tanks altogether—not 6,000 as French reports at the time stated. He said that he did not count the light reconnaissance tanks, which he called "sardine tins." The French tanks were better than ours, and as numerous—but they were too slow. It was by speed, in exploiting the surprise, that we beat the French."

Discussing the different types of tank, and their respective qualities, Thoma remarked that if he had to choose between "a thick skin" or "a fast runner" he would always choose the latter. In other words, he preferred speed to heavy armour, having come to the conclusion, from much experience, that speed was a more desirable quality on balance. He went on to say that, in his view, the ideal tank regiment would be made up of two-thirds large tanks, fairly fast, and one-third very fast tanks, lightly armoured.

Talking of the 1940 offensive, Thoma said—"All the tank officers wanted to see Guderian in charge of the panzer army that carried out the thrust through the Ardennes. Kleist had not the same understanding of tanks—he had earlier been one of the chief opponents of them. To put a sceptic, even a converted sceptic, in supreme charge of the armoured forces was typical of the way things were done in the German Army—as in yours. But Guderian was regarded as a difficult subordinate. Hitler had the deciding voice in the issue, and he approved Kleist's appointment. Nevertheless, Guderian was called on to carry out the actual break-through, which he did on the same lines that he had practised in the 1937 Army Manœuvres. After that, he continued to lead the drive to the Channel. He concentrated all his thought on exploiting success, and took the attitude 'to hell with what is happening behind.' That thrustfulness was decisive, because it gave the French no time to rally.

"It was commonly said in the German Army that Guderian was always seeing red, and was too inclined to charge like a bull.[1] I don't agree with that opinion. I had personal experience of serving under him on the Stalingrad front in 1942, where opposition was very stiff, and I found him a very fine commander under those difficult circumstances."

I asked Thoma what he considered the principal elements in the success of the German armoured forces in achieving such a series of breaks-through as they did in the earlier part of the war. He gave five main reasons:

"1. The concentration of all forces on the point of penetration in co-operation with bombers.

"2. Exploiting the success of this movement on the roads during the *night*—as a result, we often gained success by surprise deep in, and behind, the enemy's front.

"3. Insufficient anti-tank defence on the enemy's part, and our own superiority in the air.

"4. The fact that the armoured division itself carried enough

[1] I have often noticed that when the senior German generals wanted to convey criticism of some exceptionally vigorous commander who did not conform to their own standards of methodical, and almost chess-like operation, they habitually spoke of him as "a bull." Such a term might be more suitably applied to those who butt at strongly defended positions than to those who loosen opposition by audacity and speed.

petrol for 150-200 kilometres—supplemented, if necessary, with supply of petrol to the armoured spearheads by air, dropped in containers by parachute.

"5. Carrying rations sufficient for three days in the tanks, for three more days in the regimental supply column, and three more days in the divisional supply column."

Thoma mentioned some of the examples of sustained speed in long-range drives by the armoured forces. In the Polish campaign, he said, the seven-day march from Upper Silesia to Warsaw averaged about thirty miles a day, fighting included. In the second stage of the French campaign the advance from the Marne to Lyon averaged the same. In the 1941 Russian campaign the advance from Rosslawl to beyond Kiev averaged fifteen miles a day over a period of twenty days, while the thrust from Glukov to Orel covered forty miles a day for three days. The record advance was up to sixty miles in the day.

Thoma stressed the importance of the commander of an armoured force being well forward—"in the midst of his tanks." He should give "saddle orders," like cavalry leaders of old. "The tactical task for a commander is up in front, and he must be on the spot. He should leave the administrative side to his chief staff officer."

Thoma then talked of the reorganization of the German armoured forces that was carried out before the Russian campaign, and made it clear that he considered it a grave mistake. "The armoured divisions each had one of their two tank regiments taken away from them, in order to form further armoured divisions—making twenty in all. I did not agree with this decision, and protested to Hitler—for he always took a personal interest in technical questions." Thoma argued that the net effect would be disadvantageous on balance, since it meant doubling the number of staffs and auxiliary troops without any effective increased in the armoured punch. "But I could not persuade Hitler—he was obsessed with the advantage of having an increased number of divisions. Numbers always inflamed his imagination.

"Hitler had not interfered in the Polish campaign, but the

immense public acclaim of 'his' strategy there, and still more after the French campaign, had given him a swelled head. He had a taste for strategy and tactics, but he did not understand the executive details. He often had good ideas, but he was stubborn as a rock—so that he spoilt the fulfilment of his own conceptions.

"Twenty armoured divisions sounded a great increase, but the actual number of tanks was no greater than before. Our combat strength was only 2,434 tanks—not 12,000, as the Russians stated. About two-thirds now were medium tanks, instead of two-thirds being light tanks as in our first campaign."

Discussing the Russian campaign, Thoma said that the German armoured forces developed a new method which they found very successful. "Armoured divisions would break through the Russian front at night, and then go into hiding in woods behind the front. The Russians meantime would close the gap. In the morning the German infantry would launch their attack on this partially cemented sector—which was naturally somewhat disorganized—while the armoured divisions would emerge from the place where they were lying up, and strike the defenders in the rear."

For the 1942 campaign four new armoured divisions were formed—this was achieved partly by breaking up the existing horsed cavalry division, which had not proved effective. Three more infantry divisions were also motorized—in addition to the ten which had been motorized for the 1941 campaign. "But only ten out of the twenty former armoured divisions were brought up to strength again—because, under Hitler's orders, an increase of tank production was neglected in favour of the U-boat programme."

Thoma strongly criticized the failure of the senior generals, and of Hitler, to appreciate the vital importance of the armoured forces, and to develop them in time to the scale that was required, as well as in the form required. "What we had was good enough to beat Poland and France, but not good enough to conquer Russia. The space there was so vast, and the going so difficult. We ought to have had twice as many tanks in our armoured divisions, and their motor-infantry regiments were not mobile enough.

"The original pattern of our armoured division was ideal —with two tank regiments and two motor-infantry regiments. But the latter should be carried in armoured tracked vehicles, even though it entails more petrol. In the earlier part of the Russian campaign it was possible to bring them up in their lorries close to the scene of action before they dismounted. They were often brought up as close as a quarter of a mile from the fighting line. But that ceased to be possible when the Russians had more aircraft. The lorry-columns were too vulnerable, and the infantry had to get out too far back. Only armoured infantry can come into action quickly enough for the needs of a mobile battle.

"Worse still, these clumsy lorries easily became bogged. France had been ideal country for armoured forces, but Russia was the worst—because of its immense tracts of country that were either swamp or sand. In parts the sand was two or three feet deep. When the rain came down the sand turned into swamp."

Thoma added: "Africa was paradise in comparison. Tank troops who had been in Russia found it easy to adapt themselves to the African conditions. It is a mistake to draw lessons from the African campaign and apply them to quite different conditions. For you in future it is only Russia that matters—not the desert any more." It was a characteristic ending.

Thoma emphasized that another great mistake of the Russian campaign was the lack of co-operation between armoured forces and airborne forces. "This forfeited many successes that we might have gained. The cause of it was that the parachute troops formed part of the Luftwaffe, and consequently there were conflicts of opinion in the highest places about their employment. Goering, in particular, was an obstacle. Another handicap was the defectiveness of our self-propelled artillery. This weapon is invaluable. But those we used were only makeshifts, and the chassis was overloaded."

As Thoma was captured at Alamein in the autumn of 1942 he could contribute no evidence based on experience in the last part of the war. But in that period Manteuffel was the outstanding exponent of armoured warfare and his conclusions bore out Thoma's earlier views, on the whole, while supplementing them in certain respects. Manteuffel gave me his views at too great length to set forth here, for non-technical readers, but some of his main points are worth citing—"Tanks *must* be fast. That, I would say, is the most important lesson of the war in regard to tank design. The Panther was on the right lines, as a prototype. We used to call the Tiger a 'furniture van'—though it was a good machine in the initial breakthrough. Its slowness was a worse handicap in Russia than in France, because the distances were greater."

He considered that the Russian "Stalin" tank was the finest in the world. It combined powerful armament, thick armour, low build, with a speed superior to the Tiger and not much less than that of the Panther. It had more general mobility than any German tank.

Manteuffel then spoke of two avoidable handicaps that the German armoured forces had suffered. "Every unit in the division should have its own Mobile Workshop, which should accompany the tactical echelon. Our army made a grave error in thinking that these Mobile Workshops should be kept in the rear. They ought to be well forward, under the command of a tactical leader who is in wireless touch with them. This is essential so that repairs can be done during the night, except in cases of serious damage. Such a system saves many of the accidental casualties that cause wastage. It would have counteracted the pernicious effect that our actual system had in leading the commanders to carry on with a dwindling tank strength because they could not afford to wait for tanks to be repaired. Too often they attempted tasks that were beyond their real strength—because the task was calculated on what a division should be able to achieve on its nominal strength.

"It is essential, too, for an armoured division to have its own air element—a reconnaissance squadron, a tactical bombing squadron, and a liaison squadron of slow-flying aircraft for the use of the commander and staff. The commander of an armoured division ought always to direct from the air. In the early part of the Russian campaign, the armoured divisions had their own air contingent. But the High Command took it away from them in November, 1941, in favour of centralized control. That proved a grave mistake. I would also emphasize that the air squadrons should be trained with the divisions in peace time.

"Air transport is also essential—to carry supplies of ammunition, fuel, food and men. For armoured divisions will have to operate at much longer distances in future. They must also be prepared to make advances of 200 kilometres a day. Having read so many of your translated writings in the years before the war, I know what attention you gave to the development of this air side of armoured warfare. This warfare is a different language from infantry warfare—and infantrymen don't understand it. That was one of our great troubles in the war."

Discussing tank design and tactics, Manteuffel spoke of the value of designing tanks that were low in height, and thus a less visible target. The difficulty was to combine low build with the necessity that the underside of the tank should be sufficiently clear of the ground to avoid becoming "bellied" in crossing obstructions such as bumps in the ground, rocks and tree stumps. "A slight handicap in ground clearance, however, can be overcome by a good eye for ground. That is the most vital quality in handling tanks."

Giving an example, Manteuffel narrated the story of a riposte he had delivered against the Russian break-through near Jassy, inside the Rumanian frontier, early in May, 1944. "A tank battle developed in which a total of some five hundred tanks were involved on the two sides. The Russians were repulsed, and only 60 of their tanks got away, most of them damaged. I lost only 11 of mine. It was here that I first met the Stalin tanks. It was a shock to find that, although my Tigers began to hit them at a range of 2,200 yards, our shells did not penetrate them until we had closed to half that distance. But I was able to counter their technical superiority by manœuvre and mobility, in making the best use of ground cover." Manteuffel concluded his account with the emphatic remark: "In a tank battle, if you stand still you are lost." Recalling the memory of that piece of tactics gave him obvious professional satisfaction, and he added: "It would have given you a lot of pleasure to see this fight."

He went on to speak of the importance of the careful selection of tank crews, in order to ensure tactical aptitude and gain the advantage which this offers in modern battle. "With that condition fulfilled, tank design must aim at a careful balance between armour, weapons and speed, taking into account particularly the special risks introduced by air attack, parachutists, and rocket weapons."

I asked him what he considered to be the ideal composition of an armoured division. His reply was: "In the first place, a tank regiment of three battalions, each of 60 tanks—so as to ensure that somewhere about 150 would be available for action, allowing for mechanical troubles. Secondly, two infantry regiments, each of two battalions carried in armoured half-track vehicles. In one regiment these should be well armoured—the 7 mm. of armour which they had in the war was not enough when it came to bringing them up close under fairly heavy fire. In the other regiment the carriers should be of a more lightly armoured type—so that they could move faster, and exploit opportunities of pushing forward where opposition was slight. Another essential element in the division is a strong reconnaissance unit, carried in full-track vehicles. In this war they had half-track vehicles, which were not good enough for a reconnaissance role, under the conditions met in Russia. There should also be a pioneer battalion—what you call engineers. This need not be larger than the present scale, because every unit in the division ought to have its own section of pioneers, capable of laying and lifting mines, and of building bridges. The other main element is the artillery. I should like four battalions of artillery, each of three batteries. Three of them should be mixed battalions, each of two light field howitzer batteries, and one heavy field howitzer battery. The fourth battalion should consist of three heavy batteries, with 150 mm. pieces. Two of the three mixed battalions at least should be self-propelled instead of tractor-drawn."

In another of our talks Manteuffel gave his views on the question of how armies should be organized in the future. "Modern conditions indicate that there should be two classes of army within the Army. The best policy would be to constitute an *élite*. A certain number of divisions should be picked out for this purpose, and they should be given the best possible equipment, ample money for training, and the pick of the personnel. A large country might be able to create an army of up to thirty divisions in this way. Of course, no country could equip an army of millions on this scale. But it is better to have an *élite* army for the main operational purposes than to have a much bigger army that is mediocrely equipped and trained throughout. That *élite* army would have an increased proportion of air support, airborne forces and rocket weapons. The present scale of artillery with armoured forces is a handicap on mobility. It is required by the need for plunging fire, such as only howitzers can provide under existing conditions, but the development of rocket weapons may provide an effective substitute."

Manteuffel went on to say that he agreed with the view I had often expressed in my writings that the basic military problem of the present time was to diminish the proportion of auxiliary troops and vehicles in comparison with the striking arms. "But for such progress to be attained the High Command must learn the new language of mechanized warfare.

"The new model army calls for the design of a new kind of strategy. For these ideas to win acceptance, it is important that all the new type of forces should be under a single chief of adequate status. At the same time in order to foster the *esprit de corps* of the troops composing this *élite* army they should not only have the best of equipment and training facilities but a distinctive uniform—the smartest possible."

PART III

THROUGH GERMAN EYES

X

HOW HITLER BEAT FRANCE— AND SAVED BRITAIN

THE REAL STORY OF ANY GREAT EVENT IS APT TO BE VERY DIF-ferent to what appears at the time. That is especially the case in war. The fate of millions of people turns on decisions that are taken by one man—who may be influenced by the most curious of motives in reaching a decision that changes the whole course of history. The way he makes up his mind is known only by a few men behind the scenes, who usually have good reason for keeping it quiet. The truth sometimes leaks out later; sometimes never.

When it emerges it often bears out the saying that "truth is stranger than fiction." A novelist has to appear plausible, and would hesitate to make use of such astounding contradictions as occur in history through some extraordinary accident or twist of psychology.

Nothing could be more extraordinary than the way that the decisive events of 1940 were shaped. France was over-come by an offensive in which few of the higher executants had any faith, and the invasion only succeeded through a be-lated change of plan on the German side that happened to fit the situation produced by rigidity of plan combined with over-confidence on the French side. Stranger still was the way that the British Army escaped, and Britain herself was preserved from invasion. The truth here runs quite contrary to the popular picture. It would have seemed incredible to the British people at that time, and equally incredible to most of Hitler's ardent followers in Germany. Little indication of it emerged in the revelations at Nuremberg. The bare facts were known to a small circle at the top of the German Army, but the essential clue was held by only a few, not the topmost, who were present one day at Rundstedt's headquarters when Hitler disclosed the way his thoughts were running.

The escape of the British Army from France has often been called "the miracle of Dunkirk." For the German armoured forces had reached the Channel coast behind the back of the British Army while this was still deep in the interior of Flanders. Cut off from its own bases, and from the bulk of the French Army, it seemed likely also to be cut off from the sea. Those who got away have often wondered how they managed to do so.

The answer is that Hitler's intervention saved them—when nothing else could have. A sudden order from him over the telephone stopped the armoured forces just as they were in sight of Dunkirk, and held them back until the retreating British had reached the port and slipped out of their clutches. Rundstedt and other generals concerned, as executive commanders or on the higher staffs, gave me accounts from their different angles of this staggering order and its effects.

But although the British Army thus escaped from the trap in France, it was in no state to defend England. It had left most of its weapons behind, and the stores at home were almost empty. In the following months Britain's small and scantily-armed forces faced the magnificently-equipped army that had conquered France—with only a strip of water between them. Yet the invasion never came.

At the time we believed that the repulse of the Luftwaffe in the "Battle *over* Britain" had saved her. That is only part of the explanation. The last part of it. The original cause, which goes deeper, is that Hitler did not want to conquer England. He took little interest in the invasion preparations, did nothing to spur them on, and cancelled them at the first plausible excuse.

Before relating in detail the inner story of these fateful decisions, there is a previous one to reveal. For the real character of earlier events is hardly less amazing than the climax—or anti-climax. While Hitler saved England, France was conquered in spite of his Generals.

When France lay prostrate under the German heel, the men of the victorious Army would have been astonished had they known that their highest military chiefs had not believed such a victory to be possible—and that the victory had been gained by a plan which had been forced on a doubting General Staff as the result of a backstairs approach. Most of them would have been horrified to hear that six months earlier they had nearly been ordered to march on Berlin instead of on Paris. Yet those were the facts hidden behind the triumphant façade.

SCHISM IN THE BRAIN

The conquest of the West, although it appeared so irresistible in retrospect, was conceived in an atmosphere of fear and doubt. The preceding period of "the phoney war" was so christened by American commentators in derision of the Allies' inactivity. In that sense it was hardly just, since the Allies lacked the equipment needed to take the offensive—as later events showed. But there *were* "phoney" factors on the German side.

After the conquest of Poland, and the division of the spoils with Russia, Hitler made a bid for peace with the Western Powers. When he was rebuffed he began to feel afraid of what he had started—and of his temporary partner. He expressed the view that a long-drawn-out war of attrition with Britain and France would gradually exhaust Germany's limited resources, and expose her to a fatal attack from behind by

Russia. "By no treaty or pact can Russia's lasting neutrality be ensured," he told his generals. His fear urged him to force peace on France by an offensive in the West. He hoped that if the French were defeated, the British would see reason and come to terms. He reckoned that *time* was working against him on every count.

Hitler did not dare to risk playing a waiting game, to see whether the French grew tired of war. He believed that for the moment he had the strength and equipment to beat France. "In certain arms, the decisive arms, Germany to-day possesses clear, indisputable superiority of weapons." Hitler felt that he must strike as soon as possible, before it was too late. His order was: "The attack is to be launched, if conditions are at all possible, this autumn."

Hitler's reckoning, and these instructions were set out in a long memorandum of October 9th, 1939. His analysis of the military factors in the situation was masterly, but he left out of account a vital political factor—the "bulldoggedness" of the British people when aroused.

His generals shared his long-term fears, but did not share his short-term confidence. They did not think that the German Army was strong enough to beat France.

All the top ones to whom I talked, including Rundstedt and his chief planner, Blumentritt, admitted that they were full of doubt about taking the offensive in the West. As Blumentritt remarked: "Hitler alone believed that a decisive victory was possible."

General Siewert, who had been Brauchitsch's personal assistant from 1939 to 1941, said that no plan for an offensive in the West had even been considered until after the Polish campaign, and that Brauchitsch was dismayed when, early in October, he received Hitler's directive to prepare such a plan. "Field-Marshal von Brauchitsch was dead against it. All the documents relating to this plan will be available in the archives wherever they are, and they will show that he advised the Führer against invading the West. He went to see the Führer personally, to demonstrate the unwisdom of such an attempt. When he found he could not convince the Führer, he began to think of resigning." I asked on what grounds the objection was made. Siewert replied: "Field-Marshal von Brauchitsch did not think that the German forces were strong enough to conquer France, and argued that if they invaded France they would draw Britain's full weight into the war. The Führer discounted this, but the Field-Marshal warned him: 'We know the British from the last war—and how tough they are.'"

Faced with such doubts on the part of the army chiefs, Hitler summoned a conference in Berlin, on November 23, with the aim of implanting his own conviction. I had an account of it from General Röhricht, who was head of the Training Department of the General Staff, and was subsequently responsible for compiling the lessons of the 1940 campaign. Röhricht said: "The Führer spent two hours in a lengthy review of the situation aimed to convince the Army Command that an offensive in the West was a necessity. But Field-Marshal von Brauchitsch argued against it, and drew upon himself a severe rebuke from the Führer. General Halder was equally dubious about taking the offensive. Both of them argued that the German Army was not strong enough—it was the only line of argument that could have any chance of deterring the Führer. But he insisted that his will must prevail. After this conference many new formations were raised, to increase the Army's strength. That was as far as the Führer would meet the opposing views."

In Hitler's address to the higher commanders he expressed his anxiety about ultimate danger from Russia, and the consequent necessity of being free in the West. But the Allies would not consider his peace offers, and lay behind their fortifications—out of reach, yet able to spring when they chose. How long could Germany endure such a situation? While she had the advantage at the moment, in six months it might no longer be so. "Time is working for our adversary." There was cause for anxiety even in the West. "We have an Achilles'

Heel—the Ruhr . . . If Britain and France push through Belgium and Holland into the Ruhr, we shall be in the greatest danger. That could lead to a paralysis of German resistance." The menace must be removed by striking first.

But even Hitler did not display much assurance of success at this time. He described the offensive as "a gamble," and a choice "between victory and destruction." Moreover, he ended his exhortation on the gloomy, and prophetic note—"I shall stand or fall in this struggle. I shall never survive the defeat of my people."

A copy of this address was found in the archives of the Supreme Command after Germany's collapse, and produced at Nuremberg. But there was no mention there of the opposition that Hitler had met in the discussion, nor of a sequel that might have cut short his career in the first autumn of the war.

For the generals were driven by their forebodings to consider desperate remedies. Röhricht told me: "It was mooted in O.K.H., by Brauchitsch and Halder that—if the Führer would not moderate his policy, and insisted on plans that would involve Germany in an all out struggle against Britain and France—they should order the German Army in the West to turn about, and march on Berlin to overthrow Hitler and the Nazi régime.

"But the one man who was really vital to the success of this counter-plan declined to co-operate. This was General Fromm, the Commander-in-Chief of the Home Forces, in Germany. He argued that if the troops were ordered to turn against the régime most of them would not obey—because they had too much trust in Hitler. Fromm was only too right on this score. His refusal to co-operate was not due to any love of Hitler. He disliked the régime just as much as the others did, and in the end became one of Hitler's victims—though not until March, 1945."

Röhricht went on to say: "Apart from Fromm's hesitation, I think that the plan would have failed. The Luftwaffe, which was enthusiastically pro-Nazi, could have broken any revolt which the Army attempted, since it had the *flak* under its control. The original step of making Goering and the Luftwaffe responsible for the anti-aircraft defence of the Army was a very shrewd move in weakening the power of the Army."

Fromm's calculation about the troops' reaction was probably correct. That is admitted by the generals who were upset at the time by his refusal to co-operate, and it tends to be confirmed by our knowledge of how hard it was to loosen the people's faith in Hitler even in the later days of devastation and disaster. But although this 1939 plot might not have succeeded in its immediate object of overthrowing Hitler, the attempt would have been worthwhile. For at the least it would have so shaken Germany as to nullify Hitler's plans for the conquest of France. In that case all the European peoples would have been spared the misery that befell them as a consequence of that illusory triumph. Even the German people would not have suffered anything like what they did after a long-drawn war, accompanied by ever-multiplying devastation from the air.

Although the generals' plot was still-born, Hitler did not succeed in delivering his offensive in 1939 as he wished. Rundstedt explained—"The weather intervened to frustrate him, more than anything else. The postponements continued throughout the winter."

Blumentritt revealed that on *eleven* occasions between November and April the armies received the order to "fall in" —to be ready to attack in forty-eight hours. "Each time it was cancelled before the time expired. These repeated cancellations led us to think that Hitler was merely bluffing, and was only using the threat of attack as a means of prompting the Allies to consider his peace offer." But when the twelfth order came, in the month of May, events took their fatal course.

THE VITAL CHANGE OF PLAN

The original plan, worked out by the General Staff under
Halder, was on broadly similar lines to that of 1914, though
its aim was less far-reaching. The main weight was to be concentrated on the right wing, for a drive through the plains of
Belgium, carried out by Army Group "B" under Bock. Army
Group "A" under Rundstedt, in the centre facing the Ardennes, was to play a secondary part. Army Group "C" under
Leeb, on the left, facing the frontier of France itself, was
simply to threaten and pin down the French armies that were
holding the Maginot Line. Bock had the 18th, 6th, and 4th
Armies—listing them from right to left; Rundstedt had the
12th and 16th Armies; Leeb had the 1st and 7th Armies. What
was more important, the bulk of the tank forces was to be
concentrated for Bock's blow. None were allotted to Rundstedt, whose task was merely to advance to the Meuse, and
there cover Bock's left flank.

In January, Rundstedt's strength was increased by providing
him with one panzer corps, and his part in the plan enlarged
to some extent—he was to push across the Meuse and establish a wide bridgehead beyond, linking up with Bock's flank
and covering it better. But that was only a modification, rather
than a radical change. The plan still placed the main weight
on the right wing.

It is clear now that if that plan had been carried out it
would have failed to be decisive. For the British Army and
the best equipped part of the French Army stood in the path.
The German attack would have met these forces head on.
Even if it had broken their front in Belgium it would merely
have pushed them back on their fortified line in Northern
France, and closer to their bases of supply.

The inner story of how the plan was changed is an extraordinary one. It was only by degrees that I got on the track of
it. From the outset the German generals were very forthcom-

ing in telling me about the military operations—such professional objectivity is a characteristic of theirs. Most of them, I found, were old students of my military writings, so that they were all the more ready to talk, and exchange views. They were equally frank in discussing most of the Nazi leaders, whose influence they heartily detested. In regard to Hitler they were more reserved at first. It was obvious that many of them had been so hypnotized by him or so fearful of him that they hesitated to mention his name. As they gradually became convinced that he was dead, this inhibition subsided, and they criticized his actions more freely—Rundstedt was always critical. But they still had a tendency, a very natural one, to cover up cleavages in their own ranks. So it was only after many discussions that I learnt the real truth about the brain-wave that beat France.

The new plan was inspired by General von Manstein, who was Rundstedt's chief of staff at the time. He thought that the existing plan was too obvious, and too much a repetition of the past—so that it was just the kind of move the Allied High Command would anticipate.

If the Allied forces advanced into Belgium, as was expected, there would be a frontal clash. That would not promise decisive results. Another drawback was that the decisive battle would be fought out with the British Army, which, Manstein argued, was likely to be a tougher opponent than the French. Moreover, the German tank forces, on whom the chances of victory depended, would have to make their drive through country which, though flat, was filled with rivers and canals. That was a serious handicap, since the whole issue turned on speed.

So Manstein conceived the bold idea of shifting the main stroke to the Ardennes. He argued that the enemy would never expect a mass of tanks to be used in such difficult country. Yet it should be practicable for the German tank forces, since opposition was likely to be slight during the crucial stage of the advance. Once they had emerged from the Ardennes, and crossed the Meuse, the rolling plains of Northern France would provide ideal country for tank manœuvre and for a rapid sweep to the sea.

This idea was too bold for his able but more conventional superiors to swallow easily. He found difficulty in persuading them until he took an opportunity of expounding his idea to Hitler, whose imagination was fired by it. That led to the adoption of Manstein's plan.

The man whose brain-wave produced the defeat of France had to pay forfeit for his audacity. He was not allowed any part in directing the execution of his own plan. The vigour with which he had pressed his ideas had been resented by his military superiors, and they suspected him of trying a back-stairs approach to Hitler. Their sore feelings were aggravated when it came to their ears that many of the younger members of the General Staff were saying that "Manstein ought to be made Commander-in-Chief." Three months before the offensive was launched he was appointed to command an army corps, and replaced by General von Sodenstern. That promotion was a convenient means of moving him out of the way, to the relief of his superiors yet with honour to both parties. Nevertheless, it was ironical that the man who had shown the most imagination in grasping the potentialities of highly mobile armoured warfare—though not himself a tank specialist—should have been sent to take charge of an infantry formation (which merely played a walking-on part in the offensive) just as the new type of mobility was to achieve its supreme fulfilment.

SHORT VIEWS

In discussing the campaign with the various generals concerned I found that almost every one of them admitted that he had not anticipated such a decisive victory as was actually gained. The general run of opinion was represented by Röhricht, who remarked—"We hoped to succeed far enough to reach the line of the Somme, separate the British from the main French armies, and occupy Belgium together with Northern France." Blumentritt was more explicit—"We were sure that the Allied left wing would advance into Belgium, to Brussels at least, and thus reckoned on cutting it off. Beyond that, we did not look. The completeness of our victory was a surprise."

Most of the generals said that they had feared a delay in crossing the Meuse. But they did not seem to have considered the problem of what might have happened if the breakthrough had failed, and they had been definitely checked. Underlying Brauchitsch's and Halder's objections to Hitler's plans there may have been such a thought; if so it was exceptional. Yet had the invasion failed to produce the collapse of France, but merely taken a bite of her soil, it would have made any settlement more difficult—by arousing and stiffening the spirit of France. Thus, for the Germans an indecisive offensive might have been worse than none, and much less wise than a policy of remaining quiet in the West, improving their defence, until the French became weary of a deadlock war. This point did not seem to have occurred to the German generals. Blumentritt said he had no recollection of it being discussed either in conference or in conversation among themselves. The reply that most of them made to me was that questions of this sort belonged to the political side of war, and were outside their ken.

The neglect to consider such obvious contingencies, and the vital questions involved, sheds a particularly revealing light on the limitations of their professional outlook. It shows how lacking they were in a sense of grand strategy, or in due regard for the objects of war, as distinct from its military objectives. Such pure strategists were bound to be ineffective in dealing with Hitler, who had a grasp of both aim and method, of politics and strategy—from the mating of which grand strategy proceeds. Since they could not argue on the same plane they were impotent to correct the mistakes of his grand strategy, or curb his increasingly excessive ambitions. Their professional skill on the lower planes—of strategy and tactics—only served to carry him, and them, deeper into a pit from which there was no way of extrication.

By an irony of history, however, the greatest contribution of all to the success which paved Hitler's path to the pit came from his opponents.

THE FRENCH PLAN

The shattering effect of the Ardennes stroke owed much to the design of the French plan—which fitted perfectly, from the Germans' point of view, into their own remodelled plan. What proved fatal to the French was not, as is commonly imagined, their defensive attitude or "Maginot Line complex," but the more offensive side of their plan. By pushing into Belgium with their left shoulder forward they played into the hands of their enemy, and wedged themselves in a trap —just as had happened with their near-fatal Plan XVII of 1914. It was the more perilous this time because the opponent was more mobile, manœuvring at motor-pace instead of at foot-pace. The penalty, too, was the greater because the left shoulder push—made by the 1st, 7th, and 9th French armies and the British Expeditionary Force—comprised the most modernly equipped and mobile part of the Allied forces, so that once these were deeply committed the French High Command lost most of its manœuvring power.

The supreme advantage of the new German plan was that every step forward that the Allies took made them more susceptible to Rundstedt's flanking drive through the Ardennes. That had been foreseen when the scheme was drafted. Rundstedt himself told me: "We expected that the Allies would try to advance through Belgium and Southern Holland against the Ruhr—and our offensive would thus have the effect of a counter-stroke, with the natural advantages this carries." Such an expectation went beyond the Allies' intentions, but that did not matter. For the opening of the German right wing assault on the frontiers of Belgium and Holland acted like a pistol in starting the Allies' dash forward into those countries, in fulfilment of Plan D—which they had framed in the autumn. Bock's direct thrust drew them out of their defences, and far forward into the open, leaving their flank and rear exposed to Rundstedt's indirect thrust.

While it was not difficult to foresee the Allies' reaction, the ultimate decision in favour of Manstein's scheme was guided by something more than intelligent anticipation. Blumentritt made a significant disclosure in giving me his account of events—"The opposition was finally overcome and the plan changed owing to definite news, emanating from Brussels, of the Allied plans."

THE MATADOR'S CLOAK

Hitler's invasion of the West opened with startling successes on the seaward flank. These focused attention to such an extent as to serve, like a matador's cloak, to distract attention from the thrust that was being delivered through the Ardennes— towards the heart of France.

The capital of Holland and the hub of its communications, at Rotterdam, were attacked in the early hours of May 10th, by airborne forces, simultaneously with the assault on its frontier defences a hundred miles to the east. The confusion and alarm created by this double blow, in front and rear, were increased by the widespread menace of the Luftwaffe. Exploiting the disorder, German armoured forces raced through a gap in the southern flank and joined up with the airborne forces at Rotterdam on the third day. They cut through to their objective under the nose of the 7th French Army which was just arriving to the aid of the Dutch. On the fifth day the Dutch capitulated.

The main gateway into Belgium was also forced by a dramatic opening coup. Airborne troops picked the lock—by seizing the bridges over the Albert Canal near Maastricht. By the second day, armoured forces pushed through into the open, outflanking the fortified bridgehead of Liége. That evening the Belgian Army was driven to abandon its fortified frontier line, and fall back westward as its Allies were rushing up to the line of the Dyle as planned.

At the time these direct assaults, on Holland and Belgium, carried the impression of tremendous strength. It is remarkable to find how light was the weight put into these strokes, especially in the case of Holland. The German 18th Army under General von Küchler, which dealt with the Dutch, was considerably smaller than the forces opposing it, and the path of its advance was intersected by a network of canals and rivers that should have been easy to defend. Its chances turned, primarily, on the effect of the airborne coup. But this new arm was astonishingly small.

General Student, its Commander-in-Chief, gave me the details. "Altogether, we had 4,500 trained parachute troops in the spring of 1940. To give the offensive against Holland a fair chance it was necessary to use the bulk of them there. So we allotted five battalions, some 4,000 men, to that task, supplemented by an air-transported division, the 22nd, which comprised 12,000 men.

"The limitations of our strength compelled us to concentrate on two objectives—the points which seemed the most essential to the success of the invasion. The main effort, under my own control, was directed against the bridges at Rotterdam, Dordrecht, and Moerdijk by which the main route from the south was carried across the mouths of the Rhine. Our task was to capture the bridges before the Dutch could blow them up, and keep them open until the arrival of our mobile ground forces. My force comprised four parachute battalions and one air-transported regiment (of three battalions). We achieved complete success, at a cost of only 180 casualties. We dared not fail, for if we did the whole invasion would have failed." Student himself was one of the casualties, being wounded in the head by a sniper's bullet, and he was out of action for eight months.

"The secondary attack was made against The Hague. Its aim was to get a hold upon the Dutch capital, and in particular to capture the Government offices and the Service headquarters. The force employed here was commanded by General Graf Sponeck; it consisted of one parachute battalion and two air-transported regiments. This attack did not succeed. Several hundred men were killed and wounded, while as many were taken prisoner."

❋   ❋   ❋

After meeting the paramount needs of the coup in Holland, only 500 airborne troops were left to help the invasion of Belgium, Student told me. They were used to capture the two bridges over the Albert Canal and the Fort of Eben Emael, Belgium's most modern fort, which flanked this waterline-frontier. That tiny detachment, however, made all the difference to the issue. For the approach to the Belgian frontier here lay across the southerly projection of Dutch territory known as the "Maastricht Appendix," and once the German Army crossed the Dutch frontier the Belgian frontier guards on the Albert Canal would have had ample warning to blow the bridges before any invading ground forces could cross that fifteen-mile strip. Airborne troops dropping silently out of the night sky offered a new way, and the only way, of securing the key-bridges intact.

The very limited scale of airborne forces used in Belgium gives a fantastic air to the reports at the time that German parachutists were dropping at scores of places, in numbers that cumulatively ran into thousands. Student provided the explanation. He said that to compensate the scantiness of the actual resources, and create as much confusion as possible, dummy parachutists were scattered widely over the country.

This ruse certainly proved most effective, helped by the natural tendency of heated imaginations to multiply all figures.

The course of the invasion was described to me by General von Bechtolsheim, then 1A (operations chief) to Reichenau's 6th Army, which carried out this frontal offensive. He was an old acquaintance, having been the German Military Attaché in London before the war.

"The axis of the 6th Army ran through Maastricht to Brussels, its right wing being directed from Roermond past Turnhout to Malines, and its left wing from Aachen past Liége to Namur. Maastricht was the vital point in the first phase—or, to be exact, the two bridges over the Albert Canal west of Maastricht. These were captured, before they could be blown up, by glider-landings on the west bank. Fort Eben Emael was captured in the same way, though not so quickly. The great disappointment of the first day was that the bridges over the Meuse in Maastricht were blown up by the Dutch, thus delaying the advance to support the glider-parties on the Albert Canal.

"However, Hoeppner's 16th Panzer Corps was pushed through as soon as the Meuse had been bridged, although it was strung out in excessive depth, as it had to use a single bridge, and thus had to be passed through a bottleneck. Once through, it drove towards Nivelles. Progress now became quick.

"Under the original plan there was no intention of attacking Liége. That fortified city was to be by-passed, while screened on the north by our left wing and on the south by the 4th Army's right wing. But our left wing, pushing down towards Liége, succeeded in driving into it from the rear without any serious opposition.

"Our main forces pushed on westward, and made contact with the British Army on the Dyle line. We paused to close up our divisions for the attack, while staging a turning movement from the south, but before it developed the British had fallen back to the Scheldt, so we halted for a short time on the Dyle to enable our divisions to close up.

"Throughout our advance to Brussels we were continually expecting an Allied counter-attack from Antwerp against our right flank.

"Meanwhile, the 16th Panzer Corps had driven ahead, on our southern flank, and fought battles near Hannut and Gembloux with the French mechanized Cavalry Corps. At first our tanks were outnumbered, but the French tanks fought in a static way that forfeited their advantage, and their lack of enterprise allowed time for the rest of Hoeppner's corps to arrive on the scene. That decided the Gembloux battle in our favour on the 14th. But we were deprived of the chance to exploit our success, for Hoeppner's corps was now taken away to back up the break-through which had been achieved south of the Meuse, in the Ardennes. This decision of the Supreme Command left the 6th Army without any armoured forces."

This order caused much heartburning, and a heated protest from Reichenau. But he was overruled in the higher interests of the general offensive plan. The 6th Army had well performed its rôle of attracting the attention of the French High Command, and distracting their attention from the greater threat that was developing in the Ardennes. It had also pinned down the mobile forces of the Allied left wing during the crucial days. For on the 13th Rundstedt's armoured spearheads crossed the Meuse around Sedan and burst into the rolling plains of northeastern France. When Gamelin, the French Commander-in-Chief, thought of switching his mechanized cavalry from the left wing to stem the flood at Sedan he was told that they were too fully engaged at Gembloux.

Once that object had been fulfilled there was good reason for reducing Reichenau's punching power, since it was not desirable to hustle the Allied left wing into too rapid a retreat before Rundstedt's net had been stretched across its rear.

Reichenau's air support had been reduced even before his armour was switched away, Bechtolsheim said. "In the first phase of the offensive the 6th Army was given very powerful support by the Luftwaffe, for the crossings of the Meuse and the Albert Canal near Maastricht, but the corps of dive-bombers were then concentrated southward against the cross-ings of the Meuse near Sedan." I asked Bechtolsheim whether the freedom from bombing which the B.E.F. had enjoyed dur-ing its advance to the Dyle was deliberately intended to entice it forward. He replied: "Not so far as we were concerned at 6th Army H.Q., but it may have been planned on a higher level."

✵   ✵   ✵

Before passing to the story of Rundstedt's break-through from the Ardennes to the Channel coast, which trapped the whole Allied left wing, it is worth giving some of the main points from Bechtolsheim's account of the 6th Army's later advance in following up the belated Allied retreat from the Dyle line.

"The axis of our advance was now directed on Lille, with our right flank moving on Ghent, and our left on Mons and Condé. The first serious contact with the British was on the Scheldt. General von Reichenau wanted to envelop Lille by a turning movement round the north, but O.K.H. ordered the main effort to be made on the other flank—in order to assist General von Kluge's 4th Army (on the right wing of General von Rundstedt's Army Group), which was heavily engaged in the area Roubaix-Cambrai. In this advance our 4th Corps had a tough fight at Tournai, where it did not succeed in penetrating the British defence.

"Better reports then came from the Cambrai area, and Gen-eral von Reichenau persuaded O.K.H. to approve his plan of swinging round north of Lille towards Ypres. A powerful attack by the 11th Corps broke through the Belgian front here on the Lys near Courtrai. Following this success, we concen-trated all possible strength towards Roulers and Ypres. The final overthrow of the Belgian Army was now achieved by the 6th Army.

"On the evening of May 27th word came from the 11th Corps that a Belgian general had arrived at its H.Q. and asked for the conditions of an armistice. This request was referred back to O.K.W., which sent back orders that unconditional surrender must be demanded." This was accepted, and the Belgians laid down their arms early next morning. "I called on King Leopold at Bruges the day after. He did not like the idea of going to the castle of Laeken for internment, and asked if he might go to his country house. I passed on his request, but it was not granted."

I asked Bechtolsheim whether he considered that the Belgian Army could have held out longer. He replied: "I think it could, for its losses were not severe. But when I drove through the lines of Belgian troops most of them seemed to be very relieved that the struggle had ended."

Another question I put was whether he had any news at this time of preparations to evacuate the B.E.F. He said: "We had reports that a large concentration of shipping had been seen at Dunkirk. This led us to suspect that an evacuation was contemplated. Previously, we had expected the British to withdraw southward."

Summing up the brief campaign, he remarked: "The only real difficulty we met was the crossing of rivers and canals, not from opposition. When the 16th Panzer Corps had been taken away, most of our bridging units went with it, and this became a handicap on our subsequent progress."

He also enumerated what he regarded as the four main lessons of the campaign:

"First. The outstanding lesson was the necessity of air-ground liaison in actual battle. This was good in the main efforts, at Maastricht and Sedan, but not in general. At Maastricht the 6th Army had excellent support from and co-operation with Richthofen's Stukas, but these were then subsequently sent to support Kleist's thrust through Sedan. The Air Force should always know when to switch from attacking communications to close co-operation in the battle. There is need for great flexibility.

"Second. Even after the Panzer Group had been taken away, events proved that infantry attack was still possible without tank support—thanks to the way that the infantry had been trained; to well-controlled supporting fire; and to infiltration tactics. Widely dispersed threats create openings for concentrated thrusts.

"Third. When armoured forces are fairly equal, a kind of standing battle develops—where space is lacking for manoeuvre.

"Fourth. The need of flexibility in switching forces when they are checked in battle along any particular line of advance."

THE MATADOR'S THRUST

Before dawn of May 10th the greatest concentration of tanks yet seen in war was massed opposite the frontier of Luxembourg. It was poised for a dash through that state and then through Belgian Luxembourg to the French frontier near Sedan, seventy miles distant. Made up of three Panzer corps, these were arrayed in three blocks, or layers, with armoured divisions in the first two, and motorized infantry divisions in the third. The van was led by General Guderian, Germany's chief tank expert, and the whole was commanded by General von Kleist.

"Like a great phalanx, the three blocks stood densely closed up one behind the other"—that was Blumentritt's description. Even so, this armoured array was more than a hundred miles deep from head to tail—which lay nearly fifty miles *east* of the Rhine. A vivid impression of its scale was conveyed in a remark which Kleist made to me: "If this Panzer Group had advanced on a single road its tail would have stretched right back to Koenigsberg in East Prussia, when its head was at Trier."

To the right of Kleist's group lay a separate panzer corps under Hoth, which was to dash through the northern part of the Ardennes, to the Meuse between Givet and Dinant.

These armoured phalanxes, however, formed only a fraction of the armed mass that was drawn up along the German frontier ready to plunge into the Ardennes. According to Blumentritt: "Army Group A had altogether 86 divisions of all kinds closely packed on a narrow but very deep front." He went on: "This advance through the Ardennes was not really an operation, in the tactical sense, but an approach march. In making the plan we had reckoned it unlikely that we should meet any serious resistance before reaching the Meuse. That calculation proved correct. We met no resistance in Luxembourg, and only slight resistance in Belgian Luxembourg—from the *Chasseurs Ardennais* and some French cavalry. It was weak opposition, and easily brushed aside.

"The main problem was not tactical but administrative—the complicated movement and supply arrangements. It was essential to utilize all roads and tracks that were to any degree practicable. The greatest possible precision was required in plotting the route on the map; in the regulation of traffic; and in the arrangements for protecting the movement against both ground and air interference. The many infantry divisions had to march on field paths and across country, interspersed among the armoured divisions that were using the roads. The most intricate staff work was demanded in laying down start-lines for the successive panzer blocks, while the beginning and end of each division's passage was precisely regulated by the clock. The terrain was difficult—mountainous and wooded—and the roads, though they had a good surface, were often steep and full of bends. The worst problem of all came later, in the passage of these densely-crowded columns of tanks and infantry over the deep-cut valley of the Meuse—a very awkward obstacle."

The chances of success largely depended on the quickness with which Kleist's forces could push through the Ardennes and cross the Meuse near Sedan. Only when they were across that river-barrier would their tanks have room for manœuvre. They must get across before the French realized what was happening, and collected reserves to stop them. But the German air photographs showed what appeared to be a large fortified bridgehead covering the approach to the river at Sedan. Its presence reinforced the doubts of all who questioned the practicability of the Hitler-Manstein plan. They felt that the tanks could not rush such a fortified position, and that the advance would be hung up for days in the effort to capture it.

A few days before the attack was launched, however, an Austrian officer with a flair for interpreting air photographs was given the opportunity to re-examine them. He spotted what no one else had discovered—that the French fortifications here were not completed, but merely in process of construction. His report was sent off in haste to Kleist. It dispelled the final hesitations. Kleist realized that he could speed up the advance by pushing his armoured and infantry divisions forward simultaneously, without waiting until the latter had cleared the way. The advance to the Meuse became a race rather than a normal military operation. The infantry corps of List's 12th Army, "marching like the devil," reached the Meuse only one day after the armoured divisions, but the latter were already over the river by the time they arrived.

In the desire to keep his finger on the pulse of the battle, Rundstedt himself came forward to see the armoured divisions in the Forest of Sedan, before they made their pounce on the Meuse, and subsequently followed them down to the river to watch the engineers bridging it.

Giving me a detailed account of the operation, Kleist said: "My leading troops, after traversing the Ardennes, crossed the French frontier on May 12th. General Schmundt, the Führer's adjutant, came forward to see me that morning, and asked whether I would prefer to continue the advance at once, and tackle the Meuse, or wait until the infantry corps came up. I decided to make the attempt without loss of time. General Schmundt then said that the Führer would place at my disposal next day, the 13th, the maximum support from the Luftwaffe—including the whole of Richthofen's air corps, of dive-bombers. Detailed arrangements were settled at a conference on the evening of the 12th with General Sperrle, who flew up to see me for the purpose—my headquarters were then near Bertrix.

"During the day my leading troops had pushed through the wooded belt north of the Meuse, and reached its southern edge, overlooking the river. That night the reserves closed up, ready for an advance in strength. On the morning of the 13th the infantry regiments of the armoured divisions pushed down to the river bank. The Luftwaffe—about a thousand aircraft— appeared on the scene at midday. Crossings were achieved early in the afternoon—at two places near Sedan, by General Guderian's corps, and near Monthermé, by General Reinhardt's corps. All three attempts were successful, but the one near Monthermé proved rather more difficult than the others, mainly because of the difficult terrain and steeply winding route of approach.

"The opposition was not serious. That was fortunate, for my artillery had only fifty rounds per battery—as the ammunition columns had been delayed by the congestion on the roads through the Ardennes. By the evening of the 13th my armoured divisions had established strong bridgeheads over the Meuse. The leading infantry corps only began to arrive on the 14th."

I asked Kleist about the state of the French defences. He replied: "Along the Meuse there was a moderate amount of fortification, in the way of pillboxes, but these were not properly armed. If the French troops here had been adequately equipped with anti-tank guns we should certainly have noticed it, as the majority of our tanks were of the early Mark I type, and thus very vulnerable! The French divisions in the sector were poorly armed, and of low quality. Their troops, as we repeatedly found, gave up the fight very soon after being subjected to air bombing or gunfire."

On the French side, four 2nd Reserve divisions, of oldish men, were holding a front of over forty miles. Besides being thinly stretched, they were not even provided with the meagre normal scale of anti-tank guns, while lacking anti-aircraft guns. Assailed by swarms of dive-bombers while the Germans were bridging the river and then by masses of tanks, it is not surprising these low-grade French infantry quickly collapsed.

A FIRST PAUSE

The German commanders, however, could hardly believe their luck. They were still more surprised that no counter-offensive developed. Rundstedt had feared the delivery of a heavy stroke against his left flank while he was pushing through the Ardennes. "I knew Gamelin before the war, and, trying to read his mind, had anticipated that he would make a flank move from the Verdun direction with his reserves. We estimated that he had thirty to forty divisions which could be used for the purpose. But nothing of the sort developed."

Hitler shared these apprehensions. In consequence he put a curb on the advance—it was the first of two interventions on his part, the second of which had greater consequences. Telling of this first case, Siewert said: "After we had crossed the Meuse, the Commander-in-Chief wanted to make a quick dash for Abbeville and Boulogne. But the Führer was nervous about the risk that the main French armies might strike westward, and wanted to wait until a large number of infantry divisions had been brought up to provide flank cover along the Aisne." Röhricht, then acting as chief liaison officer between O.K.H. and 12th Army H.Q., was more explicit: "The 12th Army, which was following Kleist's panzer group, was ordered to wheel south to the Aisne, when he wheeled west after crossing the Meuse and headed for the Channel coast. Weichs's 2nd

Army was brought up from the rear to provide the infantry backing for this seaward drive. In my opinion this decision was a bad mistake. I reckon it cost us two days. It would have been better if the 2nd Army had carried out the wheel south to the Aisne, while the 12th Army marched straight on to support the armoured forces."

Kleist himself, however, qualified these opinions. "My forces were actually halted only for one day. The order came when my leading elements had reached the Oise, between Guise and La Fère. I was told that it was a direct order from the Führer. But I don't think it was the direct consequence of the decision to replace the 12th Army by the 2nd as our backer-up. It was due to the Führer's anxiety about the danger of a counter-stroke against our left flank; he did not care to let us push too deeply until the situation there was clearer."

THE DRIVE TO THE SEA

Such uneasiness is understandable, especially on the part of Hitler, who was far in rear. For the quickness of the French collapse on the Meuse, and the absence of any strong counter-offensive reaction, naturally seemed too good to be true. But events in the battle-zone soon dispelled these apprehensions. The shock of the mechanized *blitzkrieg* had paralyzed the French Army, which was mentally and materially unfitted to cope with it. In that state of paralysis it was incapable of profiting by the brief relaxation of pressure which Hitler's first intervention provided.

After crossing the Meuse and turning westward, Kleist's drive met little resistance. His tanks rolled along what was virtually an open corridor, behind the back of the Allied left wing in Belgium. There was no "Battle of the Bulge" such as the official commentators described so graphically at the time. It was a smooth run. The few counter-attacks against its flank were spasmodic and unco-ordinated. The first had been at Stonne, just south of Sedan, where the French 3rd Armoured

Division caused a momentary jolt before it was itself taken in flank and swept back. The next was near Laon, by the newly-formed 4th Armoured Division, under General de Gaulle. In regard to this Kleist remarked: "It did not put us in any such danger as later accounts have suggested. Guderian dealt with it himself without troubling me, and I only heard of it the day after." Of the two other armoured divisions which the French possessed, the 1st ran out of petrol and was encircled while helpless, while the 2nd was frittered away in packets by the higher command to guard bridges.

The German armoured forces, apart from their brief pauses at the Oise, raced westward so fast that their opponents were utterly confused. As an example, Kleist related—"I was half-way to the sea when one of my staff brought me an extract from the French radio which said that the commander of their 6th Army on the Meuse had been sacked, and General Giraud appointed to take charge of the situation. Just as I was reading it, the door opened and a handsome French general was ushered in. He introduced himself with the words, 'I am General Giraud.' He told me how he had set out in an armoured car to look for his Army, and had found himself in the midst of my forces far ahead of where he had expected them to be. My first encounter with the British was when my tanks came upon, and overran, an infantry battalion whose men were equipped with dummy cartridges, for field exercises. This was a sidelight on the apparent unexpectedness of our arrival." The Germans poured like a flood across the back areas of the B.E.F. while the bulk of it was still deep in Belgium.

Kleist continued: "In sum, our advance met no serious opposition after the break-through. Reinhardt's Panzer Corps had some fighting near Le Cateau, but that was the only noteworthy incident. Guderian's Panzer Corps, sweeping farther south, reached Abbeville on the 20th, thus splitting the Allied armies. Wietersheim, with the motorized divisions, was close on its heels, and promptly took over the defence of the sector along the Somme from Peronne to Abbeville, while Guderian

turned north next day." He had already cut the B.E.F.'s communications with its bases; he was now aiming to cut it off
from retreat to the sea.

The German higher command had a bad shock that day,
however, although it did not affect Kleist—who was unaware
of it at the time, as he had gone forward to Abbeville on the
20th immediately after the place was occupied. As he had
driven deeper into France his flank guards had been relieved
in turn by a system of relays—as part of the process of maintaining the momentum of the advance. The infantry corps
were backing up his panzer corps, and they came under his
orders for a day or two at each stage while they took up defensive positions on the flanks. But, in the later stages, the pace
of the panzers became so fast as to leave a dangerous interval
behind them. A small British counter-attack force suddenly
inserted a wedge into the gap.

Rundstedt told me: "A critical moment in the drive came
just as my forces had reached the Channel. It was caused by
a British counter-stroke southward from Arras towards Cambrai, on May 21. For a short time it was feared that our armoured divisions would be cut off before the infantry divisions
could come up to support them. None of the French counter-
attacks carried any serious threat as this one did." (It is remarkable to learn what a jar this gave the Germans and how
it nearly upset their drive, for it was delivered by a very small
force, part of General Martel's 50th Northumbrian Division
with the 4th and 7th Battalions Royal Tank Regiment. It is
clear that if there had been two British armoured divisions,
instead of battalions, the whole German plan might have been
paralyzed.)

That proved to be the last effort to cut the net which the
Germans had cast across the rear of the Allied armies in Bel-
guim—a net which was soon drawn tighter. Hitler was justified by the issue, against all the judgment of his generals. Yet
they were justified in their doubts on any basis of probability.
No reasonable estimate of the prospect could have reckoned

that the French Commander-in-Chief, General Gamelin, would have made such an elementary blunder as to leave the hinge of his advance almost uncovered when he rushed the whole of his left wing armies into the central plains of Belgium to meet the threat there. But for that extraordinary oversight, it is almost certain that Hitler's attack would have had only a limited success. If it had penetrated only a short distance over the French frontier, and stuck there, the whole course of the war, and of the world in our time, would have been very different.

Blumentritt said (and others endorsed this): "The fact that Hitler's 'judgment' had been justified in face of his generals intoxicated him, and made it much more difficult for them ever to argue with, or restrain him, again." Thus, in the end, the 13th May proved even more unlucky for them—and for Germany—than it did for France.

The turn of fortune began barely a week later. Ironically, it started from a strange instance of restraint on Hitler's part, not from his generals' caution.

HITLER'S "HALT" ORDER

On wheeling north, Guderian's Panzer Corps headed for Calais while Reinhardt's swept west of Arras towards St. Omer and Dunkirk. On the 22nd, Boulogne was isolated by Guderian's advance, and next day Calais. That same day Reinhardt reached the Aire-St. Omer Canal, less than twenty miles from Dunkirk—the only escape port left to the B.E.F. The German armoured forces were much nearer to it than the bulk of the B.E.F.

"At that moment," Rundstedt told me, "a sudden telephone call came from Colonel von Grieffenberg at O.K.H., saying that Kleist's forces were to halt on the line of the canal. It was the Führer's direct order—and contrary to General Halder's view. I questioned it in a message of protest, but received a curt telegram in reply, saying: 'The armoured divisions are to remain at medium artillery range from Dunkirk' (a distance of eight or nine miles). 'Permission is only granted for reconnaissance and protective movements.'"

Kleist said that when he got the order it seemed to make no sense to him. "I decided to ignore it, and to push on across the Canal. My armoured cars actually entered Hazebrouck, and cut across the British lines of retreat. I heard later that the British Commander-in-Chief, Lord Gort, had been in Hazebrouck at the time. But then came a more emphatic order that I was to withdraw behind the canal. My tanks were kept halted there for three days."

Thoma, who was chief of the tank side of the General Staff, told me that he was right up forward with the leading tanks, near Bergues, where he could look into the town of Dunkirk itself. He sent back wireless messages direct to O.K.H., begging for permission to let the tanks push on. But his appeal had no effect. Referring to Hitler's attitude, he bitingly remarked: "You can never talk to a fool. Hitler spoilt the chance of victory."

Meanwhile the British forces streamed back towards Dunkirk, and cemented a defensive position to cover their re-embarkation. The German tank commanders had to sit and watch the British slipping away under their very nose.

"After three days the ban was lifted," Kleist said, "and the advance was resumed—against stiffening opposition. It had just begun to make headway when it was interrupted by a fresh order from Hitler—that my forces were to be withdrawn, and sent southward for the attack on the line that the remainder of the French Army had improvised along the Somme. It was left to the infantry forces which had come down from Belgium to complete the occupation of Dunkirk —after the British had gone."

A few days later Kleist met Hitler on the airfield at Cambrai, and ventured to remark that a great opportunity had been lost of reaching Dunkirk before the British escaped. Hitler replied: "That may be so. But I did not want to send the tanks into the Flanders marshes—and the British won't come back in this war."

To others Hitler gave a somewhat different excuse—that so many of the tanks had fallen out from mechanical break-downs that he wanted to build up his strength and reconnoitre the position before pushing on. He also explained that he wanted to be sure of having sufficient tanks in hand for the subsequent offensive against the rest of the French Army.

I found that most of the generals, including Kleist, had accepted these explanations with little question, though they were sore about the decision that had deprived them of complete victory. They felt that Hitler's anxiety about the marshy ground was exaggerated, and were convinced that they could have easily avoided it. They knew that lots of fresh tanks had been arriving daily to replace wastage. Nevertheless, Hitler's decision was assumed to be purely an error of judgment or excess of caution.

But certain members of Rundstedt's staff regarded the excuses as thin, and believed that Hitler had a deeper motive for his halt order. They connected it with the surprising way he had talked when visiting their headquarters at Charleville on May 24th, the day after the armoured forces had been halted in their stride.

Hitler was accompanied by only one of his staff, and talked in private to Rundstedt and the two key men of his staff—Sodenstern and Blumentritt. Here is what the latter told me—"Hitler was in very good humour, he admitted that the course of the campaign had been 'a decided miracle,' and gave us his opinion that the war would be finished in six weeks.

After that he wished to conclude a reasonable peace with France. and then the way would be free for an agreement with Britain.

"He then astonished us by speaking with admiration of the British Empire, of the necessity for its existence, and of the civilization that Britain had brought into the world. He remarked, with a shrug of the shoulders, that the creation of its Empire had been achieved by means that were often harsh, but 'where there is planing, there are shavings flying.' He compared the British Empire with the Catholic Church—saying they were both essential elements of stability in the world. He said that all he wanted from Britain was that she should acknowledge Germany's position on the Continent. The return of Germany's lost colonies would be desirable but not essential, and he would even offer to support Britain with troops if she should be involved in any difficulties anywhere. He remarked that the colonies were primarily a matter of prestige, since they could not be held in war, and few Germans could settle in the tropics.

"He concluded by saying that his aim was to make peace with Britain on a basis that she would regard as compatible with her honour to accept.

"Field-Marshal von Rundstedt, who was always for agreement with France and Britain, expressed his satisfaction, and later, after Hitler's departure, remarked with a sigh of relief—'Well if he wants nothing else, then we shall have peace at last.'"

When Hitler continued to keep on the brake, Blumentritt's thoughts ran back to this conversation. He felt that the "halt" had been called for more than military reasons, and that it was part of a political scheme to make peace easier to reach. If the British Army had been captured at Dunkirk, the British people might have felt that their honour had suffered a stain which they must wipe out. By letting it escape Hitler hoped to conciliate them.

This conviction of Hitler's deeper motive was confirmed

by his strangely dilatory attitude over the subsequent plans for the invasion of England. "He showed little interest in the plans," Blumentritt said, "and made no effort to speed up the preparations. That was utterly different to his usual behaviour." Before the invasion of Poland, of France, and later of Russia, he repeatedly spurred them on. But on this occasion he sat back.

Since the account of his conversation at Charleville and subsequent holding back comes from a section of the generals who had long distrusted Hitler's policy and became more hostile to him as the war continued, that makes their testimony on this point more notable. They have criticized Hitler on almost every score. It would be natural to expect, that, in the present circumstances, they would portray him as intent on the capture of the British Army, and themselves as holding him back. Their evidence has the opposite effect. They very honestly admit that, as soldiers, they wanted to finish off their victory, and were upset at the way they were checked from doing so. Significantly, their account of Hitler's thoughts about England at the decisive hour before Dunkirk fits in with much that he himself wrote earlier in *Mein Kampf*—and it is remarkable how closely he followed his own bible in other respects.

Was this attitude of his towards England prompted only by the political idea, which he had long entertained, of securing an alliance with her? Or was it inspired by a deeper feeling which reasserted itself at this crucial moment? There were some complex elements in his make-up which suggest that he had a mixed love-hate feeling towards England similar to the Kaiser's.

Whatever be the true explanation, we can at least be content with the result. For his hesitations came to Britain's rescue at the most critical moment of her history.

XI

THE END IN FRANCE AND THE FIRST FRUSTRATION

THE SECOND AND FINAL PHASE OF THE CAMPAIGN IN FRANCE opened on June 5th, when the new German offensive was launched southward over the Somme. That was barely a week after the bulk evacuation of the B.E.F. from Dunkirk had begun, and the day after the last ship had sailed from there.

In their severed left wing the French had lost 30 divisions, nearly a third of their total forces, including the best part of their scanty number of mechanized divisions. They had also lost the help of 12 British divisions, for all that remained in France were two that had not been with the main body of the B.E.F. when the blow fell. Weygand, who had now replaced Gamelin, was left with 66 divisions, mostly depleted or of inferior quality, to hold a stretch that was longer than the original front. The Germans, on the other hand, had now had time to bring up the mass of their marching divisions, which had taken little part in the first offensive.

The most striking feature of the new offensive was in its prelude—the fact that the German armoured divisions, all of which had been engaged in the westward drive to the Channel, could be switched southwards or eastwards in so short a time ready for the next stroke. Such rapidity of reconcentration in a fresh direction was proof that mechanized mobility had transformed strategy.

In the new offensive Rundstedt's Army Group once again played the decisive rôle. It was not definitely cast for that in the plan. While Rundstedt had the larger front and forces, six of the ten German armoured divisions were allotted to Bock's Army Group at the outset. But the planning was flexible and the pattern developed from the course of the battle. The change of pattern was another proof of the power conferred by mechanized mobility.

Nothing could have been more concise than the way Rundstedt summed up the battle in our first talk—"There was tough going for a few days but the issue was hardly in doubt. The offensive was opened by Bock's Army Group, on the right wing. I waited until his attack had made headway, across the Somme, before joining in the offensive. My armies met with strong resistance in crossing the Aisne, but after that it was easy. The vital thrust was that made over the Plateau de Langres towards Besançon and the Swiss frontier, behind the back of the French right wing in the Maginot Line."

The opening of the offensive, by the German right wing, had not fulfilled expectations where success was most desired, though it had surpassed expectations on a secondary sector where the obstacles had appeared greater.

On the extreme right, between Amiens and the sea, the attack was delivered by Kluge's 4th Army, as the 18th Army, originally the right of the line, had been left behind to clear up the position at Dunkirk. Kluge was given one panzer corps, and owing to a speedy cut-through by Rommel's 7th Armoured Division, his advance soon reached the Seine at and around Rouen. The French troops here were thrown into confusion and made little attempt to defend the crossings, so that the Germans got over the river on the heels of the French.

But it was not here that the decisive stroke had been contemplated—for no reasonable plan could have reckoned on

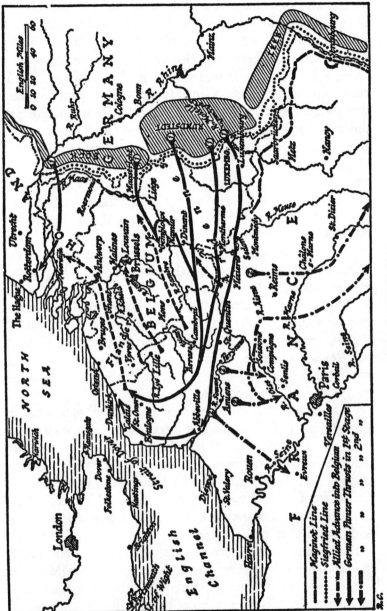

WESTERN FRONT 1940

such a smooth passage of a broad river-line that was easy to defend. The main weight of the attack by Bock's Army Group had been placed with Reichenau's 6th Army, on the sector east of Amiens, where more decisive results were anticipated.

What happened here was related by Bechtolsheim, Reichenau's operations chief. "General von Kleist's Panzer Group was placed under the 6th Army for this attack. Its composition differed from that in the first offensive, for Guderian had been transferred to Army Group "A" in Champagne, and his corps had been replaced by Hoeppner's 16th Panzer Corps. We made a two-pronged thrust. Wietersheim's 14th Panzer Corps attacked from the bridgehead over the Somme that we had gained at Amiens, and Hoeppner's from the bridgehead at Peronne. The idea was that they should converge to join hands on the Oise beyond St. Just-en-Chaussée. After that, the decision was to be taken whether the advance should be pursued east or west of Paris.

"In planning the attack there were some arguments about this method. Personally, I should have preferred to concentrate the two panzer corps in a single punch, but in the end General von Reichenau decided in favour of the pincer stroke from the two bridgeheads. The drive might have gone quicker if the weight had been concentrated.

"When the attack was launched it met stiff opposition in the 'Weygand Line' for the first three or four days. As a result, contrary to anticipation, the decisive break-through was not made on our sector, but on the Aisne east of Soissons. Thereupon O.K.H. decided to withdraw General von Kleist's Panzer Group from us, and move it east to exploit this breach. Naturally we were disappointed, for it was a repetition of what had happened to us in Belgium."

Kleist continued the story. "Wietersheim's Corps had actually gained a bridgehead over the Oise at Pont Sainte Maxence, but Hoeppner's advance was delayed by heavy fighting west of Noyon. By this time a break-through had been achieved in Champagne. Although the attack there did not start until the 9th, the passage of the Aisne was quickly forced and Guderian's Panzer Group pushed through the gap made by the 12th Army east of Reims. The 9th and 2nd Armies had also broken through west of Reims, and I now received orders to pull out of the battle I was fighting, and bring my forces back and round to exploit this opening. We made a long circuit behind the front, north of Compiègne, then crossed the Aisne at Soissons, and next the Marne at Château Thierry, after which we headed for Troyes. By this time the French were collapsing in confusion, so we drove on past Dijon down the Rhône valley to Lyons without check. Another big switch took place before this drive finished, for Wietersheim's Corps was brought back and round for a southwesterly drive to Bordeaux, and then to the Spanish frontier beyond Biarritz."

What had happened in the course of the break-through on the Aisne was told by Blumentritt. "There was only one big strategic decision taken during this offensive. When Guderian's Panzer Group was right through the French front and reached the area between St. Dizier and Chaumont, on the upper Marne, the question arose which of three courses it should take. Should it turn east, over the Plateau de Langres, towards the Swiss frontier, in order to cut off the French armies in Alsace? Should it advance south-east over the plateau to Dijon and Lyon, in order to reach the Mediterranean and to help the Italians over the Alps? Should it turn south-west towards Bordeaux, in order to cut off the French armies retreating from the Paris area to the Loire and beyond? Three short wireless cues were prepared beforehand for this purpose."

In the event, Guderian was directed to follow the first course, while Kleist's Panzer Group, racing up on its right after passing through the gap on the Aisne, carried out both the second and third. For by that time the French armies were breaking up into incoherent fragments, and the Germans could safely take the risk of splitting their own forces.

Guderian was already sweeping across the rear of the Maginot Line when, on June 14th, Leeb's Army Group "C" joined in the battle by striking at that famous barrier. Significantly, the Germans had not ventured to attack it direct until it was undercut; and even then their efforts were in the nature of probing. The main one was a narrow-fronted assault by Heinrici's 12th Corps (of the 1st Army) near Puttlingen, south of Saarbrucken, while a secondary effort was made a hundred miles to the south, on the 7th Army front, where the Rhine was crossed near Colmar.

Heinrici told me that he broke through the Line in twelve hours. But in further discussion he admitted that this breakthrough took place only after the defence had been weakened and the French were in process of withdrawing. "On the 14th my troops penetrated at two points, after stiff fighting. I had ordered a continuance of the attack for the 15th when at midnight an intercepted French order was brought to me, showing that the defenders of the Maginot Line had been ordered to withdraw. So our operation next day became a pursuit rather than an assault."

What had been happening meanwhile on the other flank, where the German offensive had started, was described by Bechtolsheim—resuming his account from the point where one of Kleist's panzer corps had gained a bridgehead over the Oise at Pont Sainte Maxence, before being pulled out and switched to the Aisne. "When our infantry relieved the tanks and pushed on beyond the Oise, an awkward problem was presented by the outer line of fortifications covering the approach to Paris that the French had built near Senlis. General von Reichenau was doubtful about the best way of tackling this obstacle, but then decided to turn it by moving round the eastern flank. However, the French retreat saved us trouble. When they abandoned Paris, our right corps was transferred to the 18th Army, which had now arrived from the north, for the move into the capital, while we continued our advance southward. After crossing the Seine at Corbeil and Montereau, we pushed on to the Loire. We found the bridges at Sully and Gien had been blown up, but we captured those at Orleans intact by a *coup de main*. The advance was essentially a pursuit all the way from the Marne to the Cher, where it ended. There was not much fighting."

Summing up the general course of the offensive, Blumentritt said: "Only the crossing of the Aisne, which was strongly defended by the French, involved a serious engagement. Here, the armoured divisions were not launched until the infantry had forced the passage; even so, they had some stiff opposition beyond the river before they broke through. After that, the fighting became less and less strenuous. The armoured divisions pushed on without stopping, or without bothering about their exposed flanks, and flooded the south of France. The German infantry followed them up in forced marches of forty to sixty kilometres a day, liquidating such fractions of the French Army as were still holding out after the tanks had driven on. On many of the main roads our armoured forces advanced without opposition past French columns that were marching back in the same direction.

"During this stage the Luftwaffe worked in close cooperation with the armoured divisions, in a new form of 'street tactics.' When a place was defended, the bombers were called up to attack it, and then the advanced detachment of the division took it; meanwhile the bulk of the division, without leaving the road, usually waited in a long column (nearly a hundred miles in length) until the road ahead was clear. This was possible only because we had air superiority, because the enemy's anti-tank defence was inadequate, and mines were as yet little used.

"In the 1940 campaign the French fought bravely, but they were no longer the French of 1914-18—of Verdun and the Somme. The British fought much more stubbornly, as they did in 1914-18. The Belgians in part fought gallantly; the Dutch, only a few days. *We* had superiority in the air combined with more up-to-date tanks than the French. Above all, the German tank troops were more mobile, quicker and better at in-fighting, and able while in movement to turn wherever

required by their leader. This, the French at that time were
unable to do. They still fought and fought more in the tradition
of the First World War. They were not up to date either in
leadership or in wireless control. When they wanted to change
direction on the move, they had to halt first, give fresh orders,
and only then were they able to start again. Their tank tactics
were out of date—but they *were* brave!"

This authoritative German verdict should correct the hasty
judgments that the world passed on the defenders of France.
While the final collapse was accelerated by a rapidly spreading
breakdown of morale, it is clear that the issue of the second
offensive was a foregone conclusion. Defeat was inevitable from
its outset, though it might have been delayed a little longer.

On an elementary calculation of forces in relation to space
—the space that had to be covered between the Somme and
the Swiss frontier—Weygand had an insoluble problem to
meet. A calculation in terms of quantity multiplied by technical quality only makes the situation look more hopeless. It
is more surprising that the British Government, and even part
of the French, continued to cherish illusions after Dunkirk,
than that soldiers like Weygand and Petain abandoned hope
as soon as the Somme-Aisne line began to crack. But the
strangest feature of the whole period is that the German
generals should have counted on cutting off the Allied left
wing in Belgium, yet not expected a general collapse of French
resistance—its almost mathematically calculable consequence.
When that collapse came, it was soon clear that they had failed
to reckon with such a probability, and were unprepared to
follow it up.

RECUMBENT "SEA-LION"

After the collapse of France the German Army relaxed with
a happy feeling that the war was over and that the fruits of
victory could be enjoyed at leisure. Blumentritt's account of
the sequel conveys a vivid impression of the prevailing atti-

tude. "Immediately following the armistice with France, orders came from O.K.H. to form the staff for the victory parade in Paris, and to despatch the troops that were assigned to take part in the parade. We spent a fortnight working on the organization of this parade. Spirits were high, as everyone counted on a general peace. Preparations for demobilization had already begun, and we had received a list of the divisions that were to be sent home for disbanding."

After a few weeks, however, the victory mood began to subside, and a feeling of uneasiness grew in the absence of any sign that Britain was disposed to make peace. Hopeful rumours filled the void. "There was talk of negotiations with Britain being conducted through Sweden; then, through the Duke of Alba." But nothing definite came in the way of confirmation.

The first indication that Hitler was considering an invasion of England came on July 2nd, when he directed the heads of the three Services to study the problem, and called for intelligence appreciations from them. But he ended by emphasizing that "the plan is in its infancy," and added: "So far it is only a question of preparing for a possible event." Two weeks passed before the next development.

On July 16th, nearly a month after the collapse of France, Hitler issued a directive saying: "Since England, in spite of her militarily hopeless situation, shows no sign of coming to terms, I have decided to prepare a landing operation against England and, if necessary, to carry it out. . . . The preparations for the entire operation must be completed by mid-August." The order, however, sounded very "iffy."

Hitler's disinclination to invade England had been manifest at a conference with the Commander-in-Chief of the Navy, Admiral Raeder, on July 11th. The record of this conference was in the archives captured after the war. Proceedings began with a long discussion, not of the problem of invading England, but of the development of Norway—a matter in which Hitler showed more interest. He expressed his intention of

building "a beautiful German city" in the fiord near Trond-
heim, and ordered plans to be submitted. Later, the question
of invading England was discussed. Raeder considered that
"an invasion should be used only as a last resort to force
Britain to sue for peace." He dwelt on the many difficulties of
the venture, and the lengthy transport preparations required,
as well as the need for air superiority. When he had finished
Hitler expressed his views, which are thus summarized in the
record: "The Führer also views invasion as a last resort, and
also considers air superiority a prerequisite."

Although the operational directive was issued on the 16th,
its tentativeness was emphasized by Hitler's step three days
later in making a peace appeal to Britain in his speech to the
Reichstag on the victory in France. He struck a remarkably
moderate note, deploring the possibility of a war to the bitter
end, and dwelling on the sacrifices it would entail for both
sides. Even the cynical Italian Foreign Minister, Count Ciano,
was impressed and noted in his diary: "I believe that his desire
for peace is sincere. In fact, late in the evening, when the first
cold British reactions to the speech arrive, a sense of ill-
concealed disappointment spreads among the Germans . . .
they are hoping and praying that this appeal will not be
rejected."

Next morning he called on Hitler, and noted in his diary:
"He confirms my impressions of yesterday. He would like
an understanding with Great Britain. He knows that war with
the British will be hard and bloody, and knows also that people
everywhere to-day are averse to bloodshed." On returning to
Rome, however, Ciano found that Mussolini was upset by
the speech, fearing that the English would respond to Hitler's
appeal and consider a negotiated peace. "That would be sad
for Mussolini, because now more than ever he wants war."

On the 21st Hitler held a conference of his higher commanders. His opening remarks showed that he was puzzled
as to the grounds for Britain's persistence in carrying on the
war. He could only imagine that she was hoping that America

or Russia would enter the war, but it did not seem likely that either would, though Russia's entry "would be unpleasant for Germany especially on account of the threat from the air." Then he came to the question of invading England, and began by pointing out that it would be "an exceptionally hazardous undertaking, because even if the way is short, this is not just a river crossing, but the crossing of a sea which is dominated by the enemy. Operational surprise cannot be expected; a defensively prepared and utterly determined enemy faces us." He went on to emphasize the difficulties of reinforcement and supply after a landing. He insisted that "complete mastery of the air" was essential before starting, and that as the venture depended on sustained air support, which in turn depended on the weather—which was usually bad during the second half of September—the main operation must be completed by the 15th. The survey ended with the declaration: "If it is not certain that preparations can be completed by the beginning of September, other plans must be considered." The whole address breathed doubt, and the final note implied that his mind was turning elsewhere.

It is interesting to look up one's notes of the situation in England at that time. The Navy's dispositions did not promise a very prompt intervention in the Channel, for the British admirals were almost as anxious about the menace of the German Air Force as the German admirals were about the interference of the British Navy. But on the same day that Hitler's directive was issued, I heard authoritatively that Britain's fighter strength, gravely depleted in covering the evacuation from Dunkirk, had been built up again to its former level—its fifty-seven squadrons now comprised over a thousand machines, with reserves.

During the six weeks since Dunkirk the land forces available to meet an invasion had been so scanty that even a few enemy divisions might have brushed them aside. But although the reorganization and re-equipment of the land forces evacuated from France was still a slow process, one felt that with the restoration of our fighter strength in the air the primary assurance against invasion had been achieved, and that the danger of this succeeding was on the wane. Nevertheless, a glimpse of "the other side of the hill," as an unseen onlooker at Hitler's conferences, would have been still more cheering. So would a glimpse into the reports of the German Intelligence service. For they grossly over-estimated even the strength of our land forces. It is not surprising that Hitler and his generals had growing doubts as they studied the problem.

Only the air marshals, headed by Goering, showed confidence in fulfilling their part—the double rôle of dominating the Royal Air Force and checking the Royal Navy's intervention. It may have been only their assurance which kept the plan alive.

The German generals and admirals had a common mistrust of Goering's promises, but they did not agree among themselves. A landing force of 40 divisions was originally proposed, but had to be scaled down to 13 divisions because the Naval High Command declared that it was impossible to transport more. The remainder were to be sent over at intervals, in three more waves, if conditions allowed. The panzer menace would not have been as great as the British expected, for only small elements were included in the landing force, and the bulk were held back until a later stage. The Army High Command insisted that the landings should be made on the widest possible front—from Ramsgate to Lyme Bay at least—in order to distract and stretch the British reserves. But the Naval High Command insisted that they could only protect a passage and landing on a narrow front, no farther west than Eastbourne. The argument raged for two or three weeks. Halder declared that the Navy's proposal spelt "complete suicide" for the Army—"I might just as well put the troops that have been landed straight through a mincing machine." The Naval Chief of Staff retorted that it would be equally suicidal to cross the Channel on a wider front.

Eventually the controversy ended in a compromise, ordained by Hitler, that satisfied neither service. By that time it was the middle of August, and the completion of the preparations had been deferred until the middle of September. As Goering had begun his preliminary air offensive on the 13th, both the generals and the admirals felt the more inclined to wait and see whether the Luftwaffe mastered the R.A.F., or whether by failing it conclusively settled the issue against attempting invasion.

Discussing the invasion plans with Rundstedt, I asked him about the timing and the reasons for cancelling the invasion. He replied: "As the first steps to prepare for an invasion were taken only after the French capitulation, no definite date could be fixed when the plan was drafted. It depended on the time required to provide the shipping, to alter ships so they could carry tanks, and to train the troops in embarking and disembarking. The invasion was to be made in August if possible, and September at the latest. The military reasons for its cancellation were various. The German Navy would have had to control the North Sea as well as the Channel, and was not strong enough to do so. The German Air Force was not sufficient to protect the sea crossing on its own. While the leading part of the forces might have landed, there was the danger that they might be cut off from supplies and reinforcements." I asked Rundstedt whether it might not have been possible to keep the invasion forces supplied by air for a time—as was done on a very large scale in Russia during the winter of 1941. He said the system of air supply was not sufficiently developed in 1940 for this possibility to be considered.

Rundstedt then outlined the military side of the plan. "The responsibility of commanding the invasion fell to me, as the task was assigned to my Army Group. The 16th Army under General von Busch was on the right, and the 9th Army under General Strauss was on the left. They were to sail from ports stretching from Holland to Le Havre. The 16th Army was to use ports from Antwerp to Boulogne, while the 9th Army was to use the ports between the Somme and the Seine. No

landing was to be made north of the Thames." Rundstedt
indicated on the map the sector over which the landings were
to be made, stretching from Dover to near Portsmouth. "We
were then to push forward and establish a much larger bridgehead along an arc south of London. It ran up the south shore
of the Thames to the outskirts of London, and then south-
westwards to Southampton Water." In answer to a further
question, he said the original idea was that part of Reichenau's
6th Army—from Bock's Army Group—was to land on the
coast west of the Isle of Wight, on both sides of Weymouth, to
cut off the Devon-Cornwall peninsula, and drive north to
Bristol. But that was dropped, except as a possible later development.

In further discussion he conveyed that he never had much
confidence in the prospects of successful invasion, and that he
was often thinking of how Napoleon had been baffled. In that
sense the German generals seem to have been hampered by
being historically minded—as they were once again in Russia
the following autumn.

Brauchitsch seems to have been rather more hopeful than
Rundstedt. That is the impression I gathered from General
Siewert, who was with him at the time. When I asked him
about Brauchitsch's views as to the practicability of the plan,
he replied: "If the weather was favourable, and given time to
prepare, and considering Britain's great losses at Dunkirk,
Field-Marshal von Brauchitsch thought it a possibility." But I
gathered that the thought was prompted by the wish, because
he could see no other way of gaining peace in face of Mr.
Churchill's refusal to consider any proposals for peace. "Our
idea was to finish the war as soon as possible, and we *had* to
get across the water to do that." "Then why wasn't it carried
out?" I asked. "There were many preparations in progress, but
the weather outlook was not too good. The attempt was supposed to be carried out in September but Hitler cancelled all
the preparations because he thought it impracticable. The
Navy's heart was not in it, and it was not strong enough to

protect the flanks. Neither was the German Air Force strong enough to stop the British Navy."

What the soldiers told me about the Navy's attitude was amply borne out by the views gathered from a number of admirals, among them Voss, Brinkmann, Breuning, and Engel. One very significant comment seemed to express the common view: "The German Navy was utterly unprepared to hold off the British Navy, even for a short time. Moreover, the accumulation of barges brought from the Rhine, the Elbe and the Dutch canals were quite unsuitable." In discussion some said that they did not believe these barges were massed with the idea of using them, and doubted whether an invasion of England was really intended. There was a sense of play-acting—as if most of the higher people concerned were pretending to be more serious about the project than they were. "From what we learnt later about Britain's situation, it would seem that the war might have been won in July, 1940, if the German Intelligence service had been better; but most senior naval officers considered it lost on September 3rd, 1939." In other words, from the day Britain entered the war.

General Student gave me details of the part that the airborne forces were to have played in the invasion plan, as well as some more interesting comments on the way he would have wished them to be used. As Student himself was then in hospital, recovering from the head wound he had suffered at Rotterdam, the airborne forces were commanded by General Putzier: "Two divisions [1] were to be employed, as well as 300 gliders—each of these carried a pilot and nine other men, three thousand in all. The intention was to use the airborne force for securing a bridge-head near Folkstone, about twenty miles wide and twelve miles deep. The intended dropping zone was kept closely under air observation. It was seen that obstacles were being quickly prepared—that the suitable landing fields were being filled with upright stakes—and it was assumed that

[1] The Parachute Division and the 22nd Air-Landing Division, forming the XI Air Corps.

minefields were also being laid there. For these reasons Putzier reported, at the end of August, that an airborne invasion was now out of the question.

"If I had been still on the scene I should have urged the use of the parachute forces against England while your evacuation from Dunkirk was still in progress, to seize the ports where your troops were landing. It was known that most of them had left Dunkirk without any of their heavier weapons.

"Even if this project had been vetoed, my plans for the airborne part of the invasion would have been different to what was actually decided. I should have used my force to capture airfields considerably deeper inland than the intended bridgehead. Having captured these, I should have transported infantry divisions over by air, without tanks or heavy artillery—some to turn outwards and attack the coast defences from the rear, and some to move on London. I reckoned that one infantry division could be brought over by air in a day and a half to two days, and that this rate of reinforcement could be kept up." It seemed to me that Student's plan was optimistic, taking account of the small force that could be carried in this way, and the time it would take to increase.

"But the best time," Student again emphasized, "was immediately after Dunkirk—before your defensive measures were developed. We heard later that the people in Britain had a parachute psychology. That amused us, but there is no doubt it was the best defensive precaution, properly directed."

The attitude shown in the decision that the airborne operation should be abandoned was symptomatic. Although the preparations continued, the nearer they came to completion the further the will to invade receded. The progress of the air offensive was not very encouraging, and all the doubters in the other services were prompt to stress that Goering's expectations were not being fulfilled as quickly as promised. The strain that this "battle over Britain" was imposing on the defenders was unduly discounted. At the same time, the Intelligence reports emphasized, and exaggerated, the growth of the

British defences on land—there is reason to suspect that this was, in part, deliberate. Hitler himself tended to emphasize not only the difficulties, but the ill-effects of failing in an invasion attempt. The "wait and see" note became louder as the provisional date approached. Hitler kept on putting off the crucial decision about fixing a definite date, and on September 17th decided "to postpone 'Sea-Lion' indefinitely."

Throughout the whole period the minutes of his conferences reek, not only of doubt, but of a deeper disinclination. They tend to bear out the account that Blumentritt gave me. "Although 'Operation Sea-Lion' was ordered, and preparations made, the affair was not pushed forward. Hitler scarcely seemed to bother about it at all—contrary to his usual way—and the staffs went on with their planning without any inclination. It was all regarded as a 'war game.' Field-Marshal von Rundstedt did not take the affair seriously, and busied himself little with the work. His Chief of Staff, General von Sodenstern, frequently went on leave. After about the middle of August no one believed in its execution any longer, and from mid-September the means of transport—which were quite insufficient—were already being silently dispersed. By the end of September it was quite clear that the plan was not intended seriously, and it was dropped completely. Among ourselves we talked of it as bluff, and looked forward to news that an understanding with Britain had been reached."

It seems evident that the generals had no heart in the attempted invasion, and that the admirals were even more disinclined to make the venture. They took the gloomiest view of what the British Navy might do. Goering and the heads of the air force were the only people who were keen on the plan. They were allowed to test the British strength in the air, but when they failed to drive the R.A.F. out of the sky the generals and the admirals were quick to renew their objections to the venture—and Hitler was surprisingly ready to accept their excuses for a postponement. It was a permanent postponement. For his mind was already turning eastward.

XII

MISFIRES IN THE MEDITERRANEAN

DISCUSSION WITH THE GERMAN GENERALS BROUGHT FRESH LIGHT on many facets of the campaign in North Africa and the war in the Mediterranean as a whole. Here are some of the chief points that came out.

Egypt and the Suez Canal were saved, at the time the British forces were weakest, by the Italians' jealousy of the Germans coupled with Hitler's indifference to the opportunity of capturing these keys to the Middle East.

Cyprus was saved by the price the British made the Germans pay for the capture of Crete.

Gibraltar was saved by Franco's reluctance to let the Germans into Spain.

Malta was saved by Hitler's distrust of the Italian Navy.

All that happened during 1941, when Britain's fortunes were at their lowest. In 1942 the tide began to turn, with Russia's sustained resistance to Hitler's invasion, with the entry of America into the war following Japan's assault, and with the growth of Britain's own strength. But there was a long road to travel. It might have been longer but for Hitler's help.

It was Hitler who ensured the British the chance to win such a victory at El Alamein as to decide the war in North Africa. For he forbade his generals to forestall Montgomery's attack by a timely step back that would have preserved them from crushing defeat.

I gathered these revelations from various generals, but most of all from General von Thoma, the famous tank commander who was finally captured at Alamein, and from General Student, the Commander-in-Chief of Germany's airborne forces.

Thoma related the origins of Germany's entry into the Mediterranean field. "I was sent to North Africa in October, 1940, to report on the question whether German forces should be sent there, to help the Italians turn the British out of Egypt. After seeing Marshal Graziani, and studying the situation, I made my report. It emphasized that the supply problem was the decisive factor—not only because of the difficulties of the desert, but because of the British Navy's command of the Mediterranean. I said it would not be possible to maintain a large German Army there as well as the Italian Army.

"My conclusion was that, if a force was sent by us, it should be an armoured force. Nothing less than four armoured divisions would suffice to ensure success—and this, I calculated, was also the maximum that could be effectively maintained with supplies in an advance across the desert to the Nile valley. At the same time, I said it could only be done by replacing the Italian troops with German. Large numbers could not be supplied, and the vital thing was that every man in the invading force should be of the best possible quality.

"But Badoglio and Graziani opposed the substitution of Germans for Italians. Indeed, at that time they were against having any German troops sent there. They wanted to keep the glory of conquering Egypt for themselves. Mussolini backed their objections. While, unlike them, he wanted some German help, he did not want a predominantly German force."

The importance of this revelation can be better realized if we remember that Thoma's mission to Africa was made two months before O'Connor's brilliant riposte, under Wavell's direction, broke up Graziani's attempted invasion of Egypt.

The small and scantily-equipped British forces were capable of smashing the larger but worse equipped Italian Army. But the prospects would have been very dim if a German armoured force had been on the scene.

It is all too likely that a picked force of four armoured divisions, such as Thoma suggested, would have swept into Egypt—any time that winter. For O'Connor's force then consisted of only one armoured and one infantry division, both incompletely equipped.

Now comes another remarkable disclosure. Mussolini got his own way—to defeat—partly because Hitler was not fired by the idea of throwing the British out of Egypt. That was very different to what the British imagined at the time. Yet it may be compared with his equally surprising attitude to the invasion of England. Thoma was struck by Hitler's indifference, though he is not the sort of man to speculate about the underlying motives.

"When I rendered my report, Hitler said he could not spare more than one armoured division. At that, I told him that it would be better to give up the idea of sending any force at all. My remark made him angry. His idea in offering to send a German force to Africa was political. He feared Mussolini might change sides unless he had a German stiffening. But he wanted to send as small a force as possible." (It is to be noted, here, that Hitler had already suspended the plans for the invasion of England, and was considering plans for the invasion of Russia.)

Thoma went on to say: "Hitler thought that the Italians were capable of holding their own in Africa, with a little German help. He expected too much of them. I had seen them in Spain, 'fighting' on the same side as we were. Hitler seemed to form his idea of their value from the way their commanders talked when he met them at the dinner-table. When he asked me what I thought of them, I retorted: 'I've seen them on the battlefield, not merely in the Officers' Mess.'" (If Thoma spoke to Hitler like that, it is not surprising that he was out of

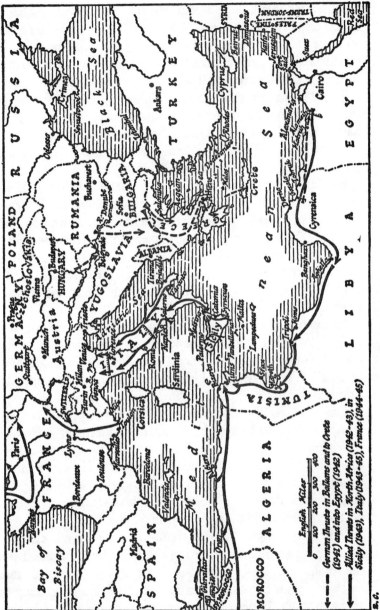

THE MEDITERRANEAN

favour after this talk.) "I told Hitler: 'One British soldier is better than twelve Italians.' I added: 'The Italians are good workers, but they are not fighters. They don't like noise.'"

The German General Staff was also against sending German forces to Africa, either on a big scale or a small scale. According to Thoma, Brauchitsch and Halder did not want to get involved in the Mediterranean at all. "Halder told me that he had tried to impress on Hitler the dangers of extending too far, and had pointedly remarked—'Our danger is that we win all the battles except the last one.'"

But Hitler would not refrain from interfering in the Mediterranean, though he hesitated to go all out there. After Graziani's defeat, he sent a picked detachment there, under Rommel, to restore the situation. It was strong enough to frustrate British plans for the conquest of Libya—and to go on frustrating them for more than two years—but not strong enough to be decisive. The battle swayed to and fro, from the spring of 1941 to the autumn of 1942.

Meanwhile, Britain's position in the Mediterranean was subject to serious threats elsewhere, though they never matured. That has tended to conceal how deadly they might have been. I gathered details of them from General Student, the Commander-in-Chief of Germany's airborne forces.

The most serious was the projected attack on Gibraltar—which could have barred the Western Mediterranean. He told me that in January, 1941, he was instructed to draft a plan for capturing Gibraltar by a parachute descent. He came to the conclusion that it was too big a job to be done by the parachute forces alone. His summing up was—"Gibraltar cannot be taken if the neutrality of Spain is observed by us.

"After my report," Student went on, "the plan was changed into the bigger one of capturing Gibraltar by an attack from the mainland. Eight divisions from France were to race through Spain. But this depended on the Spanish agreeing to let us through. Hitler did not want to take the risk of having to fight a way through Spain. He tried to persuade Franco, but Franco would not agree. The discussions went on for some time, but they proved fruitless. So the Gibraltar plan had to be dropped."

Student then made the surprising disclosure that Hitler was not at all keen about the stroke that captured Crete—and gave the British such a shock in the Eastern Mediterranean. "He wanted to break off the Balkan campaign after reaching the south of Greece. When I heard this, I flew to see Goering and proposed the plan of capturing Crete by airborne forces alone. Goering—who was always easy to enthuse—was quick to see the possibilities of the idea, and sent me on to Hitler. I saw him on April 21st. When I first explained the project Hitler said: 'It sounds all right, but I don't think it's practicable.' But I managed to convince him in the end.

"In the operation we used our one Parachute Division, our one Glider Regiment and the 5th Mountain Division, which had no previous experience of being transported by air. The 22nd Air-landing Division, which had the experience of the Dutch campaign, had been flown to Ploesti in March, to protect the Rumanian oilfields, as the Führer was afraid of sabotage there. He was so concerned with this danger that he refused to release the division for the Crete operation."

The air support was provided by the dive-bombers and fighters of Richthofen's 8th Air Corps, which had played such a vital part in forcing the entry into Belgium and France in turn. Student said: "I asked that this should be placed under my command, as well as the airborne forces, but my request was refused. Then the higher direction of the whole operation was entrusted to General Lohr, who had been in command of all the air forces taking part in the Balkan campaign. However, I worked out all the plans for the operation—and was allowed a free hand in this respect. The 8th Air Corps was excellent, but its action would have been more effective if it had been placed under my direct control.

"No troops came by sea. Such a reinforcement had been intended originally, but the only sea transport available was a number of Greek caiques. It was then arranged that a convoy of these small vessels was to carry the heavier arms for the expedition—anti-aircraft and anti-tank guns, the artillery and some tanks—together with two battalions of the 5th Mountain Division. Escorted by Italian torpedo-boats, they were to sail to Melos, and wait there until we had discovered the where-abouts of the British fleet. When they reached Melos, they were told that the British fleet was still at Alexandria—whereas it was actually on the way to Crete. The convoy sailed for Crete, ran into the fleet, and was scattered. The Luftwaffe avenged this setback by 'pulling a lot of hairs' out of the British Navy's scalp. But our operations on land, in Crete, were much handicapped by the absence of the heavier weapons on which we had reckoned.

"Although we succeeded in capturing the island, our casualties were heavy. We lost 4,000 killed and missing, apart from wounded, out of 22,000 men we dropped on the island—14,000 of these were parachute troops and the rest belonged to the Mountain division. Much of the loss was due to bad landings—there were very few suitable spots in Crete, and the prevailing wind blew from the interior towards the sea. For fear of dropping the troops in the sea, the pilots tended to drop them too far inland—some of them actually in the British lines. The weapon-containers often fell wide of the troops, which was another handicap that contributed to our excessive casualties. The few British tanks that were there shook us badly at the start—it was lucky there were not more than two dozen. The infantry, mostly New Zealanders, put up a stiff fight, though taken by surprise.

"The Führer was very upset by the heavy losses suffered by the parachute units, and came to the conclusion that their surprise value had passed. After that, he often said to me: 'The day of parachute troops is over.'

"He would not believe reports that the British and Americans were developing airborne forces. The fact that none were used in the St. Nazaire and Dieppe raids confirmed his opinion. He said to me: 'There, you see! They are not raising such forces. I was right.' He only changed his mind after the Allied conquest of Sicily in 1943. Impressed by the way the Allies had used them there, he ordered an expansion of our own airborne forces. But that change of mind came too late—because by then you had command of the air, and airborne troops could not be effectively used in face of a superior air force."

Returning to the events of 1941, Student said: "When I got Hitler to accept the Crete plan, I also proposed that we should follow it up by capturing Cyprus from the air, and then a further jump from Cyprus to capture the Suez Canal. Hitler did not seem averse to the idea, but would not commit himself definitely to the project—his mind was so occupied with the coming invasion of Russia. After the shock of the heavy losses in Crete, he refused to attempt another big airborne effort. I pressed the idea on him repeatedly, but without avail.

"A year later, however, he was persuaded to adopt a plan for capturing Malta. This was in April, 1942. The attack was to be carried out in conjunction with the Italians. My airborne forces, together with the Italian ones, were to be dropped on the island and capture a bridgehead, which would then be reinforced by a large Italian seaborne force—of six to eight divisions. My force comprised our one existing Parachute division, three additional regiments that had not yet been organized as a division, and an Italian parachute division.

"I hoped to carry out the plan not later than August—it depended on suitable weather—and spent some months in Rome preparing it. In June I was summoned to Hitler's headquarters for the final conference on the operation. Unfortunately, the day before I got there, Hitler had seen General Crüwell, who was just back from North Africa, and had been given a very unfavourable account of the state of the Italian forces and their morale.

"Hitler at once took alarm. He felt that if the British Fleet appeared on the scene, all the Italian ships would bolt for their home ports—and leave the German airborne forces stranded. He decided to abandon the plan of attacking Malta."

That decision was the more significant because Rommel had just won a striking victory over the British in North Africa, turning the Eighth Army out of the Gazala position and capturing Tobruk. Exploiting its confusion Rommel pursued it helter-skelter through the Western Desert. He came within reach of the Nile valley before he was checked on the Alamein line, at the beginning of July.

That was the worst crisis which the British passed through in the Middle East. The situation was made all the more grave by the simultaneous collapse of Russia's southern armies in face of Hitler's new drive to the Caucasus. At Alamein, Rommel was hammering on the front door to the Middle East; in the Caucasus, Kleist was threatening the back door.

Thoma declared, however, that the threat was accidental rather than intended. "The great pincer movement against the Middle East, which your people imagined to be in progress, was never a serious plan. It was vaguely discussed in Hitler's entourage, but our General Staff never agreed with it, nor regarded it as practicable."

Even the threat to Egypt only developed haphazardly—out of the unexpected collapse of the Eighth Army in the Gazala-Tobruk battle. Rommel's forces were nothing like strong enough to attempt the conquest of Egypt. But he could not resist the temptation to push on in the flush of victory. That was his undoing.

I asked Thoma whether it was true that Rommel was so confident of reaching the Suez Canal as appeared in some of the remarks he made to his officers. Thoma replied: "I'm sure he was not! He only expressed such confidence to encourage his troops, especially the Italians. He soon cooled down when he was checked by the British on the Alamein position. He knew that he needed surprise in order to throw the British off their balance, and he didn't see how he could possibly achieve a fresh surprise in face of the Alamein defences. Moreover, he knew that British reinforcements were continously arriving.

"Rommel realized that he had gone too far—with his limited forces and difficult supply line—but his success had caused such a sensation that he could not draw back. Hitler would not let him. The result was that he had to stay there until the British had gathered overwhelming forces to smash him."

Thoma said that he had learnt most of this from Rommel and Rommel's chief subordinates. He himself had only gone to Africa, from Russia, in September. "When I received orders to relieve Rommel, who was sick with jaundice, I telephoned back that I did not want to take the job, saying: 'See what I wrote two years ago.' But back came a message that the Führer insisted on my going, as a personal order, so nothing more could be done. I arrived in Africa about September 20th, and spent a few days discussing the situation with Rommel— who then went for treatment to Wiener Neustadt, near Vienna. A fortnight later General Stumme arrived on the scene, having been appointed to take charge of the African theatre as a whole. This meant that I only had command of our troops at the front, facing the El Alamein position, which limited my capacity to improve the administrative organization. Soon afterwards Stumme had a stroke, and died. All this complicated our preparations to meet the coming British offensive.

"I did what I could to improve our dispositions, under difficult conditions, as any idea of withdrawing before the British offensive opened was vetoed. But we would have had to retreat in spite of Hitler's order but for the fact that we were able to feed our troops with the supplies which we had captured from your stores at Tobruk. They kept us going."

On hearing this, I remarked that it looked as if our own loss of Tobruk—disastrous as it seemed at the time—had really helped to win us the war in North Africa. For if the German forces had retreated from Alamein before Montgomery struck, it was unlikely that they would have been so decisively smashed as they were. This point did not seem to have occurred to Thoma.

Thoma then gave me his impressions of the battle, which opened on October 23, 1942. He said that the Eighth Army's immense superiority of strength in all the decisive weapons made its victory almost a certainty before the battle opened. "I reckoned that you had 1,200 aircraft available at a time when I was reduced to barely a dozen. Rommel arrived back from Vienna a week after the offensive had begun. It was too late for him to change any of the dispositions. He was in a nervy state, being still ill, and was very apt to change his mind. After he arrived I had command of only part of the front, but then he suddenly wanted me to take charge of the whole once more, under his general direction. The British pressure grew heavier, straining us to the limit.

"When it was clear that we could not hope to check the British break-through, we decided to carry out a withdrawal, in two stages, to a line near Daba, 50 miles to the west. That might have saved us. The first stage of the withdrawal was to be made on the night of November 3. It had already begun when a wireless order came from Hitler forbidding any such withdrawal, and insisting that we must hold our old positions at all costs. This meant that our troops had actually to go forward again—to fight a hopeless battle that could only prove fatal."

Thoma then related to me how he himself came to be captured. He had been racing in a tank from one critical point to another during the battle, being hit several times, and in the end was trapped when his tank caught fire and he was pitched out. "I felt it was a fitting finish." He showed me his cap, which had several holes in it—symbols of lucky escapes. With a note of regret he said he had only been able to take part in 24 tank fights during the war—in Poland, France, Russia and Africa. "I managed to fight in 192 tank actions during the Spanish Civil War."

After Thoma's capture he was taken to see Montgomery,

and with him discussed the battle over the dinner-table. "Instead of asking me for information, he said he would tell me the state of our forces, their supplies and their dispositions. I was staggered at the exactness of his knowledge, particularly of our deficiencies and shipping losses. He seemed to know as much about our position as I did myself."

Then, speaking of the victor's handling of the battle, he said: "I thought he was very cautious, considering his immensely superior strength, but"—Thoma paused, then added with emphasis—"he is the only Field-Marshal in this war who won all his battles.

"In modern mobile warfare," he concluded, "the tactics are not the main thing. The decisive factor is the organization of one's resources—to maintain the momentum."

XIII

FRUSTRATION AT MOSCOW

HITLER'S GAMBLE IN RUSSIA FAILED BECAUSE HE WAS NOT BOLD enough. He wobbled for weeks at the critical phase, losing time he could never regain. After that he ruined himself, and Germany, because he could not bring himself to cut his losses. There, in a nutshell, is the sum of the evidence I gathered from his generals.

It is the story of Napoleon over again—but with important differences. While Hitler missed the chance of capturing Moscow, he came nearer decisive victory, conquered far more of Russia, and maintained his army there much longer, only to reach an even more catastrophic end.

Hitler had counted on destroying the bulk of the Red Army before reaching the Dnieper. When he missed his mark—by a hair's breadth—he could not make up his mind what to do. When at last he decided to drive for Moscow it was too late to win before the winter.

But that was not the only cause of failure revealed in what the German generals told me. Sometimes they themselves did not perceive the conclusions, having been too deep "in the trees to see the wood." But they did provide the facts from which conclusions could be drawn.

Here is the most startling of all. What saved Russia above all was, not her modern progress, but her backwardness. If the

Soviet regime had given her a road system comparable to that of western countries, she would probably have been overrun in quick time. The German mechanized forces were baulked by the badness of her roads.

But this conclusion has a converse. The Germans lost the chance of victory because they had based their mobility on wheels instead of on tracks. On these mud-roads the wheeled transport was bogged when the tanks could move on.

Panzer forces with *tracked* transport might have overrun Russia's vital centres long before the autumn, despite the bad roads. World War I had shown this need to anyone who used his eyes and his imagination. Britain was the birthplace of the tank, and those of us here who preached the idea of mobile mechanized warfare after 1914-1918 had urged that the new model forces should have cross-country vehicles throughout. The German Army went further than our own army, or any other, in adopting the idea. But it fell short in the vital respect of neglecting to develop such cross-country transport. In brief, the German Army was more modern than any other in 1940-41, but missed its goal because it had not yet caught up with ideas that were twenty years old.

The German generals had studied their profession with the greatest thoroughness, devoting themselves from youth on to the mastery of its technique, with little regard to politics and still less to the world outside. Men of that type are apt to be extremely competent, but not imaginative. It was only late in the war that the bolder minds of the tank school of thought were allowed free rein, and then it was too late—fortunately for other countries.

Now for the main points of their evidence on the war in Russia.

THE EFFECT OF THE BALKAN CAMPAIGN

Preliminary to the issues of the Russian campaign itself is the question whether the Greek campaign caused a vital delay in its launching. British Government spokesmen have claimed that the despatch of General Wilson's force to Greece, though it ended in a hurried evacuation, was justified because it produced six weeks' postponement of the invasion of Russia. This claim has been challenged, and the venture condemned as a political gamble, by a number of soldiers who were well acquainted with the Mediterranean situation—notably General de Guingand, later Montgomery's Chief of Staff, who was on the Joint Planning Staff in Cairo.

They argued at the time, and argue still more strongly now, that a golden opportunity of exploiting the defeat of the Italians in Cyrenaica, and capturing Tripoli before German help arrived, was sacrificed in order to switch inadequate forces to Greece that had no real chance of saving her from a German invasion. They emphasize that the Greek leaders were very dubious about accepting the British Government's offer to intervene, and were jockeyed into acceptance by Mr. Eden's persuasiveness, supported by an inflated impression of the extent of help that Britain could provide.

The historian must recognize that this military view was confirmed by events. In three weeks, Greece was overrun and the British thrown out of the Balkans, while the reduced British force in Cyrenaica was also driven out by the German Africa Corps under Rommel, which had been enabled to land at Tripoli. These defeats spelt a damaging loss of prestige and prospect for Britain, while bringing misery on the Greek people. Even if the check campaign was found to have retarded the invasion of Russia that fact would not justify the British Government's decision, for such an object was not in their minds at the time.

It is of historical interest, however, to discover whether the campaign actually had such an indirect and unforeseen effect. The most definite piece of evidence in support of this lies in the fact that Hitler had originally ordered preparations for the attack on Russia to be completed by May 15th, whereas at the end of March the tentative date was deferred about a month, and then fixed for June 22nd. Field-Marshal von Rundstedt told me how the preparations of his Army Group had been hampered by the late arrival of the armoured divisions that had been employed in the Balkan campaign, and that this was the key-factor in the delay, in combination with the weather.

Field-Marshal von Kleist, who commanded the armoured forces under Rundstedt, was still more explicit. "It is true," he said, "that the forces employed in the Balkans were not large compared with our total strength, but the proportion of tanks employed there was high. The bulk of the tanks that came under me for the offensive against the Russian front in Southern Poland had taken part in the Balkan offensive, and needed overhaul, while their crews needed a rest. A large number of them had driven as far south as the Peloponnese, and had to be brought back all that way."

The views of Field-Marshals von Rundstedt and von Kleist were naturally conditioned by the extent to which the offensive on their front was dependent on the return of these armoured divisions. I found that other generals attached less importance to the effect of the Balkan campaign. They emphasized that the main rôle in the offensive against Russia was allotted to Field-Marshal von Bock's Central Army Group, in Northern Poland, and that the chances of victory principally turned on its progress. A diminution of Rundstedt's forces, for the secondary rôle of his Army Group, might not have affected the decisive issue, as the Russian forces could not be easily switched. It might even have checked Hitler's inclination to switch his effort southward in the second stage of the invasion —an inclination that, as we shall see, had a fatally retarding effect on the prospects of reaching Moscow before the winter. The invasion, at a pinch, could have been launched without awaiting the reinforcement of Rundstedt's Army Group by the arrival of the divisions from the Balkans. But, in the event, that argument for delay was reinforced by doubts whether the ground was dry enough to attempt an earlier start. General

Halder said that the weather conditions were not suitable before the time when the invasion was actually launched.

The retrospective views of generals are not, however, a sure guide as to what might have been decided if the situation had been devoid of Balkan complications. Once the tentative date had been postponed on that account the scales were weighted against any idea of striking before the extra divisions had returned from that quarter.

But it was not the Greek campaign that caused the postponement. Hitler had already reckoned with that commitment when the invasion of Greece was inserted in the 1941 programme, as a preliminary to the invasion of Russia. The decisive factor in the change of timing was the unexpected *coup d'état* in Yugo-Slavia that took place on March 27th, when General Simovich and his confederates overthrew the Government that had just previously committed Yugo-Slavia to a pact with the Axis. Hitler was so incensed by the upsetting news as to decide, that same day, to stage an overwhelming offensive against Yugo-Slavia. The additional forces, land and air, required for such a stroke involved a greater commitment than the Greek campaign alone would have done, and thus impelled Hitler to take his fuller and more fateful decision to put off the intended start of the attack on Russia.

It was the fear, not the fact, of a British landing that had prompted Hitler to move into Greece, and the outcome set his mind at rest. The landing did not even check the existing Government of Yugo-Slavia from making terms with Hitler. On the other hand, it may have encouraged Simovich in making his successful bid to overthrow the government and defy Hitler—less successfully.

THE IMPULSE TO INVADE RUSSIA

As a next stage in my enquiry I sought such light as the generals could shed on the question why Hitler invaded Russia. It was a dim light. Although the project had been incubating in his mind since July, 1940, and had taken definite form before the end of that year, it was remarkable how hazy most of his generals were about the reasons for a step that had decided their fate. Most of them had been apprehensive when they were told of the decision, but they were told very little, and told very late. Hitler was clever in the way he kept his commanders in separate "water-tight compartments"—each was told only what Hitler considered necessary for him to know in carrying out his own localized task. They were almost like prisoners on piecework in a row of cells.

As I heard from all of them that Rundstedt had been the strongest opponent of the invasion—and the first to urge its abandonment—I was anxious to get his views on the question. He told me: "Hitler insisted we must strike before Russia became too strong, and that she was much nearer striking than we imagined. He provided us with information that she was planning to launch an offensive herself that same summer, of 1941. For my part, I was very doubtful about this—and I found little sign of it when we crossed the frontier. Many of us who had feared such a stroke had been reassured by the way the Russians had remained quiet during our battles in the West, in 1940, when we had our hands full. I felt that our best way of guarding against the danger was simply to strengthen our frontier defence, leaving the Russians to take the offensive if they chose. That would be the best test of their intentions, and less risk than launching into Russia."

I asked him further about the reasons that had led him to discredit Hitler's belief in an imminent Russian offensive. He replied: "In the first place, the Russians appeared to be taken by surprise when we crossed the frontier. On my front we found no signs of offensive preparations in the forward zone, though there were some farther back. They had twenty-five divisions in the Carpathian sector, facing the Hungarian frontier, and I had expected that they would swing round and strike at my right flank as it advanced. Instead, they retreated. I deduced from this that they were not in a state of readiness for offensive operations, and hence that the Russian Command had not been intending to launch an offensive at an early date."

I next questioned General Blumentritt, who at the time was Chief of Staff to Kluge's 4th Army on the main line of attack, and who at the end of the year became Deputy Chief of the General Staff at O.K.H.—where he was in close touch with the records, and the "post-mortems" into the course of the invasion.

Blumentritt told me that the Commander-in-Chief, Brauchitsch, and the Chief of the General Staff, Halder, as well as Rundstedt, were opposed to the attempt to invade Russia. "All three realized the difficulties presented by the nature of the country from their experiences in the 1914-18 war—above all, the difficulties of movement, reinforcement, and supply. Field-Marshal von Rundstedt asked Hitler bluntly: 'Have you weighed up what you are undertaking in an attack on Russia?'"

Hitler was not moved from his decision. But he was brought to declare that the Russian campaign must be decided west of the Dnieper. He admitted beforehand the difficulties of bringing up, and maintaining, sufficient reinforcements if the advance extended beyond that line. When he found that the Russian Armies had not been decisively beaten in the battles west of the Dnieper, he was led, like Napoleon, to order a continuance of the offensive beyond this river line. That was the most fateful decision of the whole campaign. It was made fatal by Hitler's own indecision as to the best direction to take then.

Further sidelights came in discussion with Field-Marshal von Kleist, who remarked that he was only told of Hitler's intention to invade Russia a short time before the attack was launched. "It was the same with the other high commanders. We were told the Russian armies were about to take the offensive, and it was essential for Germany to remove the menace. It was explained to us that the Führer could not

THE EASTERN FRONT

proceed with other plans while this threat loomed close, as too large a part of the German forces would be pinned down in the east keeping guard. It was argued that attack was the only way for us to remove the risks of a Russian attack.

"I believe that Jodl was opposed to Hitler's conclusion, as well as Brauchitsch and Halder. Keitel, too, was doubtful about it, but he was more hesitant to make his doubts clear to Hitler."

Kleist went on: "We did not underrate the Red Army, as is commonly imagined. The last German military attaché in Moscow, General Köstring—a very able man—had kept us well informed about the state of the Russian Army. But Hitler refused to credit his information.

"Hopes of victory were largely built on the prospect that the invasion would produce a political upheaval in Russia. Most of us generals realized beforehand that, if the Russians chose to fall back there was very little chance of achieving a final victory without the help of such an upheaval. Too high hopes were built on the belief that Stalin would be overthrown by his own people if he suffered heavy defeats. The belief was fostered by the Führer's political advisers, and we, as soldiers, didn't know enough about the political side to dispute it.

"There were no preparations for a prolonged struggle. Everything was based on the idea of a decisive result before the autumn." The Germans paid a terrific price for that short view, when winter came.

An even more astonishing fact is that Hitler embarked on the invasion of Russia in face of the knowledge that his forces would be fewer than those opposing him at the outset, and were bound to be increasingly outnumbered if the campaign were prolonged. That alone made the invasion an offensive gamble without precedent in modern history. When Hitler's plan had been unfolded to the generals in February, they had been perturbed by Keitel's estimate of the comparative strengths on either side. For, even on his figures, the Red Army had the equivalent of 155 divisions available in Western

Russia, whereas the invading forces could muster only 121. (Actually Keitel's estimate was a little under the mark.) The assurance that the German forces were "far superior in quality" did not suffice to allay their qualms.

The advantage of the initiative enabled the Germans to produce a moderate superiority of strength on the sector, north of the Pripet Marshes, where Field-Marshal von Bock's Central Army Group advanced astride the Minsk-Moscow highway. But Leeb's Northern Army Group near the Baltic had bare equality to the opposition and Rundstedt's Southern Army Group had to perform its part with the handicap of a marked inferiority of strength, especially in armour—the most essential element. Kleist told me that his Panzer Army, which formed Rundstedt's spearhead, comprised only 600 tanks. "That will probably seem incredible to you, but it was all we could assemble after the return of the divisions from Greece. Budenny's Army Group, facing us in the South, had some 2,400 tanks. Apart from surprise, we depended for success simply on the superior training and skill of the troops. These were decisive assets until the Russians gained experience."

In the light of events it becomes clear that Hitler's belief in the power of technical quality to discount superior numbers had more justification than appeared in the final issue of the war. The test of battlefield results for long bore out his assurance of the decisive advantage of quality over quantity. It brought his gamble dangerously near fulfilment.

THE MISCARRIAGE OF THE INVASION

The next question I explored was how the plan went wrong. Kleist's answer was: "The main cause of our failure was that winter came early that year, coupled with the way the Russians repeatedly gave ground rather than let themselves be drawn into a decisive battle such as we were seeking."

Rundstedt agreed that this was "the most decisive" cause. "But long before winter came the chances had been diminished

owing to the repeated delays in the advance that were caused
by bad roads, and mud. The 'black earth' of the Ukraine
could be turned into mud by ten minutes' rain—stopping all
movement until it dried. That was a heavy handicap in a race
with time. It was increased by the lack of railways in Russia—
for bringing up supplies to our advancing troops. Another
adverse factor was the way the Russians received continual
reinforcements from their back areas, as they fell back. It
seemed to us that as soon as one force was wiped out, the path
was blocked by the arrival of a fresh force."

Blumentritt endorsed these verdicts except for the point
about the Russians yielding ground. On the Moscow route, the
principal line of advance, they repeatedly held on long enough
to be encircled. But the invaders repeatedly failed to reap the
opportunity through becoming immobilized themselves. "The
badness of the roads was the worst handicap, but next to that
was the inadequacy of the railways, even when repaired. Our
Intelligence was faulty on both scores, and had underestimated
their effect. Moreover the restoration of railway traffic was
delayed by the change of gauge beyond the Russian frontier.
The supply problem in the Russian campaign was a very serious one, complicated by local conditions." Nevertheless, Blumentritt considered that Moscow could have been captured if
Guderian's unorthodox plan had been adopted, or if Hitler
had not wasted vital time through his own indecision. Blumentritt's evidence on these issues will be given later.

Another factor, emphasized by Kleist, was that the Germans
had no such definite advantage in the air as they had enjoyed
in their 1940 invasion of the West. Although they took such a
heavy toll of the Russian Air Force as to turn the numerical
balance in their favour, the diminished opposition in the air
was offset by the stretching of their own air cover as they
pushed deeper. The faster they advanced on the ground, the
longer the stretch became. Talking of this, Kleist said: "At
several stages in the advance my panzer forces were handicapped through lack of cover overhead, due to the fighter air-

fields being too far back. Moreover, such air superiority as we enjoyed during the opening months was local rather than general. We owed it to the superior skill of our airmen, not to a superiority in numbers." That advantage disappeared as the Russians gained experience, while being able to renew their strength.

Besides these basic factors there was, in Rundstedt's opinion, a fault in the original German dispositions that had a delayed ill-effect on the course of operations subsequent to the initial break-through. Under the plan of the Supreme Command a wide gap was left between his left flank and Bock's right flank, opposite the western end of the Pripet Marshes—the idea being this area could be safely neglected because of its nature, and the maximum effort put into the two rapid drives, north and south of the marsh-belt. Rundstedt doubted the wisdom of this assumption when the plan was under discussion. "From my own experience on the Eastern Front in 1914-18 I anticipated that the Russian cavalry would be able to operate in the Pripet Marshes, and thus felt anxious about the gap in our advancing front, since it left the Russians free to develop flank threats from that area."

In the first stage of the invasion no such risk materialized. After Reichenau's 6th Army had forced the crossings of the Bug, south of the Marshes, Kleist's armoured forces passed through and swept rapidly forward, capturing Luck and Rovno. But after crossing the old Russian frontier, and heading for Kiev, the invaders were heavily counter-attacked in flank by Russian cavalry corps that suddenly emerged from the Pripet Marshes. This produced a dangerous situation, and although the threat was eventually curbed after tough fighting, it delayed the advance, and spoilt the chance of an early arrived on the Dnieper.

While it is not difficult to see how this interruption weighed on Rundstedt's mind, it is not so clear that the general prospects of the invasion suffered in consequence. For no similar interference played any considerable part in checking Bock's advance north of the Pripet Marshes, where the centre of gravity of the whole offensive lay.

It was here, along the direct route to Moscow, that Hitler had concentrated his strongest forces, and had planned to bring off the decisive battle. While the course of events on that front brought out with even greater emphasis the difficulties that Rundstedt and Kleist had encountered on the southern front, it also turned on more personal factors—of human misjudgment.

A clear picture of the offensive design was given me by General Heinrici, who traced the moves on the map. He is a small, precise man with a parsonical manner—he talks as if he were saying grace. Although he hardly looks like a soldier, proof of his military ability is provided by the fact that, starting as a corps commander, he finished as Army Group Commander conducting the final battle of the Oder in defence of Berlin. His outline of the pattern of the operation was filled in with fuller details and background disclosures by General Blumentritt, who was Chief of Staff to Kluge's Army throughout the advance from Brest-Litovsk to Moscow.

The plan, in brief, was to trap the bulk of the Russian forces by a vast encircling manœuvre—with the infantry corps moving on an inner circle, and two great groups of tanks on an outer circle. The pincers nearly closed round the Russians near Slonim, but most of them managed to slip out. Then the pincers opened out again, and a still bigger encirclement was attempted around Minsk—it was hoped to make this the decisive battle. But it fell short of full success, though masses of Russians were captured. The pincers failed to close in time— "owing to sudden heavy rain." These moves had been executed at great speed, and Minsk was captured on the ninth day. But the Germans were now two hundred miles deep in Russia— and had missed their real aim.

Beyond Minsk the country became worse, and the weather no better. Blumentritt vividly described the conditions. "It was appallingly difficult country for tank movement—great virgin forests, widespread swamps, terrible roads, and bridges not strong enough to bear the weight of tanks. The resistance also became stiffer, and the Russians began to cover their front with minefields. It was easier for them to block the way because there were so few roads.

"The great motor highway leading from the frontier to Moscow was unfinished—the one road a Westerner would call a 'road.' We were not prepared for what we found because our maps in no way corresponded to reality. On those maps all supposed main roads were marked in red, and there seemed to be many, but they often proved to be merely sandy tracks. The German intelligence service was fairly accurate about conditions in Russian-occupied Poland, but badly at fault about those beyond the original Russian frontier.

"Such country was bad enough for the tanks, but worse still for the transport accompanying them—carrying their fuel, their supplies, and all the auxiliary troops they needed. Nearly all this transport consisted of wheeled vehicles, which could not move off the roads, nor move on it if the sand turned into mud. An hour or two's rain reduced the panzer forces to stagnation. It was an extraordinary sight, with groups of tanks and transport strung out over a hundred-mile stretch, all stuck—until the sun came out and the ground dried."

Despite such repeated delays the German forces pushed on to the Dnieper. Near the end of July, a month from the start, a third encirclement was attempted around Smolensk, on a larger scale than ever. "Half a million Russians seemed to be trapped. The trap was almost closed—within about six miles —but the Russians once again succeeded in extricating a large part of their forces. That narrow failure brought Hitler right up against the question whether to stop or not. We were now over four hundred miles deep into Russia. Moscow lay two hundred miles farther ahead."

Blumentritt revealed that, from the start, there was a vital conflict of ideas about the method of operations. "Hitler always wanted to carry out encirclements—according to the principles of orthodox strategy—and Bock agreed with him. So did most of the senior generals on this issue. But Guderian and the new school of tank experts had a different idea—to drive deep, as fast as possible, and leave the encircling of the enemy to be completed by the infantry forces that were following up. Guderian urged the importance of keeping the Russians on the run, and allowing them no time to rally. He wanted to drive straight on to Moscow, and was convinced he could get there if no time was wasted. Russia's resistance might be paralyzed by that thrust at the heart of Stalin's power. But Hitler insisted on having the plan carried out in his own way, and kept a curb on the advance of the armoured forces.

"Guderian's plan was a very bold one—and meant big risks in maintaining reinforcements and supplies. But it might have been the lesser of two risks. By making the armoured forces turn in each time, and forge a ring round the enemy forces they had by-passed, a lot of time was lost.

"After we had reached Smolensk there was a stand-still for several weeks on the Desna. This was due partly to the need of bringing up supplies and reinforcements, but even more to a fresh conflict of views within the German command —about the future course of the campaign. There were endless arguments."

Bock wanted to push on to Moscow. Hitler, after three failures to trap the Russian armies on that front, was inclined to turn south. There, Rundstedt had broken through south of Kiev, on a slant to the Black Sea. It suggested to Hitler the idea of a bigger encirclement on a fresh line. Eventually he decided on this course. From Rundstedt's front, Kleist's tank army was to swing upward; from Bock's front, Guderian's tank army was to swing downward; and between them trap the massed Russian forces around Kiev. Hitler halted the march on Moscow in favour of this southerly pincer-manœuvre.

A significant point about this crucial decision was mentioned by Blumentritt: "Although Field-Marshal von Bock desired to continue the advance on Moscow, von Kluge did not share his view and was strongly in favour of the alternative plan of encircling the Russian forces around Kiev. It was his idea, and desire, that his own 4th Army should swing south to carry out this pincer-movement along with Guderian's panzer forces. When setting forth the arguments for this plan, he said to me, with emphasis: 'It would also mean that *we* should be under Field-Marshal von Rundstedt, instead of Field-Marshal von Bock.' Von Bock was a very difficult man to serve, and von Kluge would have been glad to get out of his sphere. This was an interesting example of the influence of the personal factor in strategy."

The Kiev encirclement succeeded, and over 600,000 prisoners were bagged. But it was late in September before the battle was completed. Winter was drawing near.

Now Hitler had to face the question whether to be content with what he had gained, or to make another bid for final victory in 1941. Rundstedt was quite definite; telling me of his view, he said: "We ought to have stopped on the Dnieper after taking Kiev. I argued this strongly, and Field-Marshal von Brauchitsch agreed with me. But Hitler, elated by the victory at Kiev, now wanted to push on, and felt sure he could capture Moscow. Field-Marshal von Bock naturally tended to concur, for his nose was pointing towards Moscow."

So Hitler gave the order for the advance, which began on October 2. "But," as Blumentritt remarked, "its chances were shortened because Hitler had given the Russians two months' grace on the Moscow front. We had been halted during August and September—the best two months of the year. That proved fatal."

But this decision was accompanied by another, which involved him in further complications and in a loss of concentration. For Hitler could not resist the temptation to exploit the success in the South at the same time as he pursued the aim of capturing Moscow.

FRUSTRATION AT THE "GATE TO THE CAUCASUS"

When Hitler made up his mind to push on, he assigned Rundstedt the extremely ambitious fresh task of clearing the Black

Sea coast and reaching the Caucasus. The objectives, as Rundstedt traced them for me on the map, were to gain the line
of the Don from Voronezh eastward to its mouth near Rostov,
and drive far enough beyond it to secure the Maikop oilfields
with his right wing and Stalingrad on the Volga with his left
wing. When Rundstedt pointed out the difficulties and risks
of advancing a further 400 miles beyond the Dnieper, with his
left exposed over such a long stretch, Hitler confidently asserted that the Russians were incapable of offering serious
opposition and that the frozen roads would enable a quick
advance to the objective.

Describing what happened, Rundstedt said: "The plan was
handicapped from the start by the diversion of forces to the
Moscow front. A number of my mobile divisions were drawn
off for a north-easterly advance past Orel towards the southern flank of Moscow. That achieved little, and lost an opportunity. I had wanted von Bock's right wing to turn south-
eastward, and strike across the rear of the Russian armies that
were opposing me near Kursk, thus cutting them off. It
seemed to me a great mistake to swing the offensive centre
of gravity northeastward, as the Russians were much better
placed, with the help of the railways radiating from Moscow,
to counter a move in that direction.

"As it was, my 6th Army on the left wing was blocked
beyond Kursk, and fell short of its objective, Voronezh, on the
Don. This check reacted on the progress of its neighbour, the
17th Army, and constricted the width of the advance towards
the Caucasus. The 17th Army met stiff resistance along the
Donetz. It could not push far enough forward to protect the
flank of von Kleist's 1st Panzer Army. In consequence, von
Kleist's flank was endangered by the strong counter-attacks
which the Russians developed in a southerly direction, towards
the Black Sea.

"On the other flank, von Manstein's 11th Army pierced the
defences of the Perekop Isthmus and broke into the Crimea,
quickly overrunning most of that peninsula except for the
fortress of Sevastopol and the eastern tip at Kerch. But this

divergent move, ordered by Hitler, reduced the strength I had available on the mainland."

The story of what happened to the Caucasus drive is best given in Kleist's own words. "Before we reached the Lower Don it became clear that there was no longer time or opportunity to reach the Caucasus. Although we had trapped most of the enemy forces west of the Dnieper, and thus gained an apparently open path, the Russians were bringing up many fresh divisions by rail and road from the east. Bad weather intervened and our advance was bogged down at a crucial time, while my leading troops ran short of petrol.

"My idea now was merely to enter Rostov and destroy the Don bridges there, not to hold that advanced line. I had reconnoitred a good defensive position on the Mius River, and taken steps to organize it as a winter line. But Goebbels's propaganda made so much of our arrival at Rostov—it was hailed as having 'opened the gateway to the Caucasus'—that we were prevented from carrying out this plan. My troops were forced to hang on at Rostov longer than I had intended, and as a result suffered a bad knock from the Russian counteroffensive that was launched in the last week of November. However, they succeeded in checking the Russian pursuit as soon as they had fallen back to the Mius River line, and although the enemy pushed on far beyond their inland flank they managed to maintain their position here, only 50 miles west of Rostov, throughout the winter. It was the most advanced sector of the whole German front in the East."

Kleist added: "The German armies were in grave danger during that first winter. They were virtually frozen in, and unable to move. That was a great handicap in meeting and checking the Russian encircling movements."

Rundstedt's account confirmed Kleist's, and also brought out the story of his own first removal from command. "When I wanted to break off the battle and withdraw to the Mius River, Field-Marshal von Brauchitsch agreed, but then an overriding order came from the Führer, which forbade any such withdrawal. I wired back that it was nonsense to hold on where we

were, and added: 'If you do not accept my view you must find
someone else to command.' That same night a reply came from
the Führer that my resignation was accepted—I left the Eastern
Front on December 1st, and never returned there. Almost
immediately afterwards the Führer flew down to that sector;
after seeing the situation, he changed his mind and sanctioned
the step-back. Significantly, the Mius River line was the only
sector of the front that was not shaken during the winter of
1941-42."

Nevertheless, Rundstedt made it clear to me that he considered the deep advance of his Army Group had been a fundamental mistake in strategy. In contrast to most generals, of
any nationality, he did not blame the miscarriage of the plan
on the failure to provide his particular effort with sufficient
resources, but rather suggested that the error lay in developing
it at all. For in further discussion he said: "The 1941 operations in Russia should, in my opinion, have had their main
effort directed, not at first towards Moscow, but towards Leningrad. That would have linked up with the Finns. Then, in the
next stage, should have come an attack on Moscow from the
north, in co-operation with the advance of Field-Marshal von
Bock's Army Group from the west."

FRUSTRATION AT MOSCOW

The offensive aimed at Moscow, starting on October 2nd, was
carried out by three armies—the 2nd on the right, the 4th in
the centre, and the 9th on the left—with the two panzer
groups of Hoth and Hoeppner. The latter had replaced Guderian's, which had been sent southward for the Kiev encircling
manœuvre.

The course of the offensive was vividly described by Blumentritt: "The first phase was the battle of encirclement around
Vyasma. This time, the encirclement was perfectly completed,
and 600,000 Russians were captured. It was a modern Cannae
—on a greater scale. The panzer groups played a big part in

this victory. The Russians were caught napping, as they did not expect a big drive for Moscow to be launched at such a late date. But it was too late in the year for us to harvest its fruits—for the operation was not completed until the end of October.

"After the Russian forces had been rounded up, we pushed on towards Moscow. There was little opposition for the moment, but the advance was slow—for the mud was awful, and the troops were tired. Moreover, they met a well-prepared defensive position on the Nara River, where they were held up by the arrival of fresh Russian forces.

"All the commanders were now asking: 'When are we going to stop?' They remembered what had happened to Napoleon's army. Many of them began to re-read Caulaincourt's grim account of 1812. That book had a weighty influence at this critical time in 1941. I can still see von Kluge trudging through the mud from his sleeping quarters to his office, and there standing before the map with Caulaincourt's book in his hand. That went on day after day."

This point was of particular interest to me as in August, 1941—when the German tide of invasion seemed to be flowing irresistibly—I had written an article for the October *Strand* on the relation of Napoleon's campaign to Hitler's, basing it on extensive quotations from Caulaincourt, to bring out my implied conclusion. I remarked that we had evidently been thinking on the same lines, though the German generals had begun to remember Caulaincourt a bit late! Blumentritt agreed, with a wry grin.

Resuming his account, he said: "The troops themselves were less depressed than their generals. They could see the flashes of the A.A. guns over Moscow at night, and it fired their imagination—the city seemed so near. They also felt that they would find shelter there from the bitter weather. But the commanders felt that they were not strong enough to push those last forty miles.

"The generals expressed their doubts in conference, but

Hitler overruled them, and Bock tended to agree with him. Hitler said he had good reason to believe that Russian resistance was on the verge of collapse. He gave the order for a final attempt to take Moscow. The order said that the Kremlin was to be blown up, to signalize the overthrow of Bolshevism."

The dispositions were reshuffled before the offensive was launched. On the southern wing it was to be carried out by Kluge's 4th Army, with the 1st Panzer Corps; and on the northern wing by Hoeppner's Panzer Group, with some infantry divisions of the 9th Army. The whole attack was placed under Kluge's direction. This was ironical in view of his disbelief in the possibility of achieving what he must undertake.

Blumentritt continued: "The offensive was opened by Hoeppner's Panzer Group on the left. Its progress was slow, in face of mud and strong Russian counter-attacks. Our losses were heavy. The weather then turned adverse, with snow falling on the swampy ground. The Russians made repeated counter-attacks from the flank across the frozen Moskwa, and Hoeppner had to divert more and more of his strength to check these thrusts. The 2nd Panzer Division succeeded in penetrating far enough to get a sight of the Kremlin, but that was the nearest it came.

"These unpromising conditions raised the question whether the 4th Army should join in the offensive or not. Night after night Hoeppner came through on the telephone, to urge this course; night after night von Kluge and I sat up late discussing whether it would be wise or not to agree to his insistence. Von Kluge decided that he would gain the opinion of the front-line troops themselves—he was a very energetic and active commander who liked to be up among the fighting troops—so he visited the forward posts, and consulted the junior officers and N.C.O.s. The troop leaders believed they could reach Moscow and were eager to try. So after five or six days of discussion and investigation, von Kluge decided to make a final effort with the 4th Army. The snow was thick on the ground, and the earth was frozen to a depth of several inches. The hardness of the ground was more favourable for artillery movement than if it had been otherwise.

"The attack was launched on December 2nd, but by afternoon reports were coming back that it was held up by strong Russian defences in the forests around Moscow. The Russians were artists in forest fighting, and their defence was helped by the fact that darkness came as early as 3 o'clock in the afternoon.

"A few parties of our troops, from the 258th Infantry Division, actually got into the suburbs of Moscow. But the Russian workers poured out of the factories and fought with their hammers and other tools in defence of their city.

"During the night the Russians strongly counter-attacked the isolated elements that had penetrated their defences. Next day our corps commanders reported that they thought it was no longer possible to break through. Von Kluge and I had a long discussion that evening, and at the end he decided to withdraw these advanced troops. Fortunately the Russians did not discover that they were moving back, so that we succeeded in extricating them and bringing them back to their original position in fairly good order. But there had been very heavy casualties in those two days' fighting.

"The decision was just in time to avert the worst consequences of the general counter-offensive that the Russians now unleashed, into which Marshal Zhukov threw a hundred divisions. Under their converging pressure our position became daily more dangerous. Hitler was at last brought to realize that we could not check them, and gave reluctant permission for a short withdrawal to a line in rear. We had been badly misled about the quantity of reinforcements that the Russians could produce. They had hidden their resources all too well."

That was the end of Hitler's bid for Moscow—and it proved his last bid on that capital front. Never again would any German soldiers catch sight of the Kremlin, except as prisoners.

XIV

FRUSTRATION IN THE CAUCASUS
AND AT STALINGRAD

WHEN MOSCOW REMAINED OUT OF REACH, AND WINTER SET IN at its worst, fear spread among the German troops. With it grew the danger of a collapse as terrible as befell Napoleon's *Grande Armée*.

It was Hitler's decision for "no withdrawal" that averted a panic in that black hour. It appeared a display of iron nerve—though it may only have been due to sheer mulish obstinacy. For it was against his generals' advice.

But his success in surviving that crisis was his undoing in the end. First, it led him to plunge deeper into Russia the next summer, 1942. He started well but soon went astray. He missed taking Stalingrad because his eyes were fixed on the Caucasus, and then forfeited the Caucasus in belated efforts to capture Stalingrad.

When winter came he was led to gamble again on his "Moscow" inspiration. This time it produced a disaster from which he never recovered. Even then, he might have spun out the war until Russia was exhausted, by practising elastic defence in the vast buffer-space he had gained. But he stuck rigidly to his rule of "no withdrawal," and so hastened Germany's fall.

THE WINTER CRISIS

It is clear from all the generals told me that the German armies were placed in the gravest danger after being repulsed before Moscow in December, 1941. The generals urged Hitler to make a long step back to a secure winter line. They pointed out that the troops were not equipped for the rigours of a winter campaign. But Hitler refused to listen. He gave the order: "The Army is not to retire a single step. Every man must fight where he stands."

His decision seemed to invite disaster. Yet the event justified him—once again. The basic region was brought out by General von Tippelskirch, lean and professorial, a corps and later an army commander there. "Frontal defence was much stronger in this war even than in 1914-18. The Russians always failed to break our front, and although they pushed far round our flanks, they had not yet the skill nor sufficient supplies to drive home their advantage. We concentrated on holding the towns that were rail and road centres, rolling up round them like 'hedgehogs'—that was Hitler's idea—and succeeded in holding them firmly. The situation was saved."

Many of the generals think now that Hitler's decision was the best in the circumstances, though they did not agree with it at the time. "It was his one great achievement," said Tippelskirch. "At that critical moment the troops were remembering what they had heard about Napoleon's retreat from Moscow, and living under the shadow of it. If they had once begun a retreat, it might have turned into a panic flight."

Other generals endorsed this. Rundstedt, however, caustically remarked: "It was Hitler's decision for rigid resistance that caused the danger in the first place. It would not have arisen if he had permitted a timely withdrawal."

Indirect support for that view was provided by the account Blumentritt gave me of what happened on the Moscow front during December. It brought out the needless perils that resulted from Hitler's excessive insistence on rigid defence combined with his unstable way of revoking any concessions he had granted.

"Following the final check before Moscow, General von Kluge advised the Supreme Command that it would be wise to make a general withdrawal to the Ugra, between Kaluga and Vyasma, a line which had already been partially prepared. There was prolonged deliberation at the Führer's Headquarters over this proposal before reluctant permission was granted. Meanwhile the Russian counter-offensive developed in a menacing way, especially on the flanks. The withdrawal was just beginning when a fresh order came from the Führer, saying: 'The 4th Army is not to retire a single step.'

"Our position became all the worse because Guderian's Panzer Group was lying out beyond our right wing, near Tula, and this much-depleted force had to be extricated before the main part of the 4th Army could withdraw. The delay quickly produced a fresh complication, for the Russians attacked Guderian's thin line and rolled it back precipitately over the Oka River. At the same time Hoeppner's Panzer Group on our left was being very hard pressed by the Russians, who threatened to outflank it.

"In consequence the 4th Army became isolated in its forward position, and in imminent danger of encirclement. The rivers were all frozen, so that they provided an inadequate barrier against the Russian thrusts. Soon the danger became acute, for a Russian cavalry corps pressed round our right flank well to the rear of it. This corps was composed of horsed cavalry and sledge-borne infantry, while roping in all the men from the recaptured villages who were capable of carrying a rifle.

"Such was the grim situation of the 4th Army on December 24th—and it had arisen from Hitler's refusal to permit a timely step back. My chief, von Kluge, had gone on the 15th to replace von Bock, who was sick, and I was left in charge of the army. I and my staff spent Christmas Day in a small hut—our headquarters in Malo Yaroslavits—with tommy guns on the table and sounds of shooting all round us. Just as it seemed that nothing could save us from being cut off, we found that the Russians were moving on westward, instead of turning up north astride our rear. They certainly missed their opportunity.

"The situation remained very precarious, for Hitler still delayed a decision, and it was not until January 4th that he at iast sanctioned the general withdrawal to the Ugra. I had left just before—to become Deputy Chief of the General Staff—and General Kuebler had arrived to take command. But he soon found that he could not stand the strain and was replaced by General Heinrici, who managed to maintain the new position until spring came, and longer, though it was deeply enveloped on both flanks."

Talking of the conditions under which the forces had to be extricated, Blumentritt said: "The roads were so deep in snow that the horses were up to their bellies. When the divisions withdrew, part of the troops had to shovel a path by day along the route their transport was to move by night. You may understand what their trials were when I mention that the temperature was twenty-eight degrees below freezing, Fahrenheit."

Even though Hitler's decision may have saved a collapse on the Moscow front, a terrible price was paid for it. "Our losses had not been heavy until the final attack for Moscow," Blumentritt told me, "but they became very serious during the winter—both in men and material. Vast numbers perished from the cold." More specific details came out in discussion with Tippelskirch, who spent the winter as a divisional commander in the Second Corps among the Valdai Hills, between Leningrad and Moscow, and told me that his strength was reduced to one third of its establishment. "Divisions were down to 5,000 men before the end of the winter, and companies to barely 50 men."

He also threw light on a more far-reaching effect of Hitler's "no withdrawal" policy. "That winter ruined the Luftwaffe—

because it had to be used for flying supplies to the garrisons of the 'hedgehogs,' the forward positions that were isolated by the Russian flanking advances. The Second Corps required 200 tons of supplies a day, which called for a daily average of 100 transport aircraft. But as bad weather often intervened, the actual number had had to be considerably larger, so as to make full use of an interval of passable weather—on one day as many as 350 aircraft were used to reprovision this single corps. Many aircraft crashed as flying conditions were bad. The overall strain of keeping up supplies by air to all the isolated positions on such a vast front was fatal to the future development of the Luftwaffe."

I questioned the generals about the course and effect of the Russian winter offensive of 1941-42. All testified to the nerve strain caused by the deep flanking threats of the Russian forces, which lapped round their positions and communications, but the general verdict was epitomized in Blumentritt's comment that the indirect results were greater than the direct danger. "The principal effect of that winter offensive was in upsetting the German plans for 1942. The weather was a more damaging and dangerous factor than the Russian offensive operations. Besides lowering morale, the weather accounted for the greater part of the German casualties—which were at least as heavy as the Russians' during that winter."

He went on to say that the strain was increased by the way that the German forces were stretched. "The average extent of a divisional frontage was 20 to 25 miles, and even on crucial sectors, such as those near Moscow, they were 10 to 15 miles. That thinness of the front was made more precarious because of the difficulty of bringing up and distributing supplies, which in turn was aggravated by the difficulty of building roads and railways."

I asked him how he accounted for the fact that such thin fronts had, in general, been able to withstand attack, since they were far more widely stretched than what had been regarded in World War I as the limit that a division could hold in defence. He replied: "In that war, the fronts were narrowed by the great depth in which divisions were distributed. New weapons and the improvement of automatic small arms partly accounted for the possibility of holding wider fronts than we could then. The greater mobility of defensive means was the other main reason. If the attackers broke through the front, small detachments of tanks and motorized troops often checked them by mobile counter-moves before they could expand the penetration into a wide breach."

But the way that the disaster was repeatedly averted by this underlying increase of defensive advantage had the ironical effect of encouraging Hitler to gamble more heavily on the offensive. The fact that the crisis was survived exalted Hitler's faith in himself; he felt that his judgment had been justified, against that of his generals. From now on he was less inclined than ever to tolerate their advice.

After the final repulse at Moscow he had got rid of Brauchitsch, and himself taken over the Supreme Command of the Army ("O.K.H.") in addition to his existing position as Supreme Commander of the Wehrmacht, the forces as a whole ("O.K.W."). The announcement that Brauchitsch had been removed naturally suggested to the credulous public that the faults of the military chiefs had been the cause of the failure. By that adroit step Hitler shifted the blame on to their shoulders while adding to his own power. An apt comment was provided by Blumentritt: "Only the admirals had a happy time in this war—as Hitler knew nothing about the sea, whereas he felt he knew all about land warfare."

Even the admirals, however, had their troubles. Like Napoleon's admirals, they had to deal with a leader who was too continental-minded to take full account of the obstacles created by British seapower, and its indirect effect on his continental designs. They had not succeeded in making Hitler realize the primary importance of cutting away the bases of that seapower—where these were within reach of landpower—before tackling further objectives.

The generals, on the other hand, were the less able to put a brake on Hitler because their outlook was too exclusively military, besides being continental. That narrowing vision tended to offset the effect of their greater caution. In this connection, Kleist contributed some significant reflections in the course of one of our talks: "Clausewitz's teachings had fallen into neglect in this generation—even at the time when I was at the War Academy and on the General Staff. His phrases were quoted, but his books were not closely studied. He was regarded as a military philosopher, rather than as a practical teacher. The writings of Schlieffen received much greater attention. They seemed more practical because they were directed to the problem of how an army inferior in strength—which was always Germany's position in relation to the whole—could overcome enemies on both sides who, in combination, were superior in strength. But Clausewitz's reflections were fundamentally sound—especially his dictum that war was a continuation of policy by other means. It implied that the political factors were more important than the military ones. The German mistake was to think that a military success would solve political problems. Indeed, under the Nazis we tended to reverse Clausewitz's dictum, and to regard peace as a continuation of war. Clausewitz, also, was prophetically right about the difficulties of conquering Russia."

PLANS FOR 1942

The question of what should be done in the spring had been debated throughout the winter. The discussion had begun even before the final assault on Moscow. Relating what happened, Blumentritt told me: "A number of the generals declared that a resumption of the offensive in 1942 was impossible, and that it was wiser to make sure of holding what had been gained. Halder was very dubious about the continuance of the offensive. Von Rundstedt was still more emphatic and even urged that the German Army should withdraw to their original front in Poland. Von Leeb agreed with him. While other generals did not go so far as this, most of them were very worried as to where the campaign would lead. With the departure of von Rundstedt as well as von Brauchitsch, the resistance to Hitler's pressure was weakening and that pressure was all for resuming the offensive."

As Blumentritt had become Deputy Chief of the General Staff early in January, under Halder, no one was better placed to know the motives and ideas behind Hitler's decision. He summed them up as follows:

First, Hitler's hope of obtaining in 1942 what he had failed to obtain in 1941. He did not believe that the Russians could increase their strength, and would not listen to evidence on this score. There was a "battle of opinion" between Halder and him. The Intelligence had information that 600 to 700 tanks a month were coming out of the Russian factories, in the Ural Mountains and elsewhere. When Halder told him of this, Hitler slammed the table and said it was impossible. He would not believe what he did not want to believe.

Secondly, he did not know what else to do—as he would not listen to any idea of a withdrawal. He felt that he must do something and that something could only be offensive.

Thirdly, there was much pressure from economic authorities in Germany. They urged that it was essential to continue the advance, telling Hitler that they could not continue the war without oil from the Caucasus and wheat from the Ukraine.

I asked Blumentritt whether the General Staff had examined the grounds for these assertions, and also whether it was true, as reported at the time, that the manganese ore round Nikopol in the Dnieper Bend was vital to the German steel industry. Replying to the latter question first, he said he did not know about this, as he was not acquainted with the economic side of the war. It seemed to me a significant revelation of the way that the German strategists had been divorced from the study of factors that were vital to their planning. He went on to say that it was more difficult to question such assertions by the economic experts as the General Staff was not represented at conferences on these issues—evidence of Hitler's desire to keep them in the dark.

While taking the fateful decision to plunge deeper still into the depths of Russia, Hitler found he no longer had enough strength left for an offensive on the whole front, such as he had carried out the year before. Forced to choose, and hesitating to make another attack towards Moscow, he decided to strike south for the Caucasus oilfields, though it meant extending his flank, like a telescope, past the main body of the Red Army. When his forces reached the Caucasus, they would be exposed to a counter-stroke at any point for nearly a thousand miles back.

The only other sector on which offensive operations were to be undertaken was on the Baltic flank. The 1942 plan originally included an attempt to taken Leningrad in the course of the summer, in order to secure safe communications with Finland and bring relief to her semi-isolated situation. With this exception, the Northern and Central Army Groups were to remain on the defensive, merely improving their positions.

A special Army Group "A" was created for the advance to the Caucasus and placed under Field-Marshal von List, while the reduced Army Group South operated on its left flank. Reichenau had replaced Rundstedt in command of the latter, but he died suddenly from a heart attack in January, and Bock was brought back to command it, only to be shelved finally before the offensive was launched. Kluge remained in command of the Central Army Group and Busch replaced Leeb in command of the Northern Army Group. Explaining this, Blumentritt said: "Field-Marshal von Leeb was so dissatisfied with the decision to resume the offensive that he asked to be allowed to give up his command. His heart was not in it. Apart from regarding it as a hopeless venture on military grounds, he was also opposed to the Nazi régime, and thus glad of a pretext on which he could ask to resign. Resignation would not have been possible without a reason that satisfied Hitler."

In further discussion of the way that the plans for 1942 came to be formulated, Blumentritt made some general observations that are worth inclusion as a sidelight. "My experience on the higher staffs showed me that the vital issues of war tended to be decided by political rather than by strategical factors, and by mental tussles in the rear rather than by the fighting on the battlefield. Moreover, those tussles are not reflected in the operation orders. Documents are no safe guide for history—the men who sign orders often think quite differently from what they put on paper. It would be foolish to take documents that historians find in the archives as a reliable indication of what particular officers really thought.

"I began to perceive that truth long ago when I was working on the history of the 1914-18 war, under General von Haeften, a very conscientious historian who taught me both the technique and the difficulties of historical research. But I came to see it much clearer from my own close observation of high headquarters in this war—under the Nazi system.

"That system had some strange by-products. While the German, with his liking for organization and order, has a tendency to put more down in writing than others do, a lot more 'paper' than ever before was produced in this war. The old army were trained to write brief orders, that allowed freedom to the executants. In this last war the practice was changed because mental freedom was more and more chained. Every step, and all conceivable cases had to be regulated in order to protect ourselves from penalization. Hence the abundance and length of the orders—the very contrary to our training. Their often bombastic language and use of superlatives was against all the rules of the old style—with its pregnant shortness and concise phrasing. But our orders now had to be 'stimulating,' in the style of propaganda. Many of the orders of the Führer and O.K.W. were reproduced word for word in subordinate orders, so as to ensure that, if things went wrong, the latter could not be charged with having failed to convey the Führer's intention.

"The conditions of compulsion in Germany under the Nazi system were almost as bad as in Russia. I often had evidence of what they were like there. For example, quite early in the campaign, I was present at the interrogation of two high Russian officers who were captured at Smolensk. They made it clear that they were entirely in disagreement with the plans they had executed, but said they had either to carry them out to the letter or lose their heads. It was only in such circumstances that men were able to talk freely—while in the grip of the régime they were forced to echo it and suppress their own thoughts.

"The systems of National Socialism and Bolshevism were similar in many ways. Talking in his own circle one day, when General Halder was present, the Führer said how much he envied Stalin, who could deal in a more radical way with the obstinate generals than he could himself. He went on to speak about the pre-war purge of the Red Army Command and how he envied the Bolshevists who had an army and generals completely impregnated with their own ideology and thus acting unconditionally as one man—whereas the German generals and the General Staff had no similar fanatical belief in the National Socialist idea. 'They have scruples, make objections, and are not sufficiently with me.'

"As the war went on Hitler indulged more and more in tirades of this kind. He still needed the class that he personally despised, as he could not carry out his operational functions without them, but he controlled their functions more and more closely. Many of the orders and reports thus bear two faces. Often what was signed did not represent the mind of the man concerned, but he had to sign it unless the two familiar consequences were to follow. Future psychologists, as well as historians, should pay attention to these phenomena."

THE DRIVE FOR THE CAUCASUS

The 1942 offensive had a curious shape, even in its original design. It was to be launched from the backward-slanting line Taganrog-Kursk—the right flank of which, on the sea of Azov, was already close to the Don at Rostov, while the left flank at Kursk lay more than 100 miles behind, to the west. The offensive was to start with a powerful thrust from this rearward flank. The objectives were dual, the Caucasus and Stalingrad, but the latter had only a protective purpose—to safeguard the flank of the advance to the Caucasus. At Stalingrad it was intended only to go far enough beyond the city to ensure the tactical security of that strategical point.

The fact that Stalingrad was not a main objective will surprise most people. For in that crucial summer of the war the fight for Stalingrad filled the minds of the Allied public. They felt that their own fate was bound up with it, as much as Russia's.

Further light on this point was provided by Kleist, who explained: "The capture of Stalingrad was subsidiary to the main aim. It was only of importance as a convenient place, in the bottleneck between the Don and the Volga, where we could block an attack on our flank by Russian forces coming from the East. At the start Stalingrad was no more than a name on the map to us." Blumentritt, however, told me that: "Hitler originally had the idea of wheeling north from Stalingrad with the aim of getting astride the rear of the Russian armies at Moscow, but he was persuaded, after considerable argument, that this was an impossibly ambitious plan. Some of his entourage had even been talking about an advance to the Urals, but that was still more a fantasy."

Even as it was, the plan was a hazardous one, and became more hazardous from the way it worked out in practice.

Kleist, who commanded the armoured drive to the Caucasus, was sent for by Hitler on April 1—an ominous date. "Hitler

said we must capture the oilfields by the autumn because
Germany could not continue the war without them. When I
pointed out the risks of leaving such a long flank exposed, he
said he was going to draw on Rumania, Hungary, and Italy
for troops to cover it. I warned him, and so did others, that it
was rash to rely on such troops, but he would not listen. He
told me that these Allied troops would only be used to hold
the flank along the Don from Voronezh to its southerly bend,
and beyond Stalingrad to the Caspian, which, he said, were
the easiest sectors to hold."

The warnings, and forebodings, of Hitler's military executants were justified by the ultimate course of events. Nevertheless, it has to be recognized that his second-year gamble did
not fall far short of success. The summer of 1942 saw Russia's
tide at its lowest ebb. It was fortunate for her that so much of
Germany's initial strength had evaporated. A little greater
impetus might have spread the many local collapses into a
general collapse.

The summer offensive opened with brilliant success. For
the Russians were suffering from their huge losses of men
and equipment in 1941, and their newly-raised armies had
not yet appeared on the scene. The German left wing made
a rapid advance from Kursk to Voronezh. Its progress was
helped because the Russian reserves were scanty—they mostly
lay farther north in the Moscow sector. Another helpful factor
was the Russian offensive towards Kharkov that had been
carried out, with great persistence, during the month of May.
Referring to this, Blumentritt said: "It used up much of the
strength that might otherwise have been available to meet our
offensive." He went on: "The 4th Panzer Army was the
spearhead of this advance from Kursk to the Don and Voronezh. The 2nd Hungarian Army then took over that sector,
while our armoured forces swerved south-eastward along the
right bank of the Don."

Remembering the stirring reports at the time about the
Russians' stubborn defence at Voronezh and the way it had

blocked the German efforts to continue their drive in that sector, I questioned him further on this score. He replied: "There was never any intention of pushing beyond Voronezh and continuing this direct easterly drive. The orders were to halt on the Don near Voronezh and assume the defensive there, as flank cover to the south-eastward advance—which was carried out by the 4th Panzer Army, backed up by the 6th Army under Paulus."

This slanting drive down the corridor between the Don and the Donetz helped in turn to screen, and ease the way for, the thrust of Kleist's 1st Panzer Army, which was entrusted with the principal rôle. Starting near Kharkov, it made a rapid advance past Chertkovo and Millerovo towards Rostov. The 17th Army, south of the Donetz, only joined in the offensive when Kleist approached Rostov. Relating the story of that lightning stroke, Kleist told me that his army crossed the Lower Don above Rostov and then pushed eastward along the valley of the Manych River. The Russians blew up the dam there and the consequent floods threatened to upset the German plans. But his armoured forces succeeded in getting across the river after two days' delay and then swung southward, in three columns. Kleist himself accompanied the right column, which reached Maikop as early as the 9th of August. At the same time his centre and left columns were approaching the foothills of the Caucasus mountains, 150 miles farther to the south-east. This fan-shaped armoured drive was backed up by the 17th Army, which was pushing forward on foot.

Thus in six weeks from the outset the Germans had reached and captured the more westerly oilfields, but they never succeeded in reaching the main sources—which lay beyond the mountains. "The primary cause of our failure," Kleist said, "was shortage of petrol. The bulk of our supplies had to come by rail from the Rostov bottleneck, as the Black Sea route was considered unsafe. A certain amount of oil was delivered by air, but the total which came through was insufficient to maintain the momentum of the advance, which came to a halt just when our chances looked best.

"But that was not the ultimate cause of the failure. We could still have reached our goal if my forces had not been drawn away bit by bit to help the attack at Stalingrad. Besides part of my motorized troops, I had to give up the whole of my flak corps and all my air force except the reconnaissance squadrons.

"That subtraction contributed to what, in my opinion, was a further cause of the failure. The Russians suddenly concentrated a force of 800 bombers on my front, operating from airfields near Grozny. Although only about a third of these bombers were serviceable, they sufficed to put a brake on my resumed advance, and it was all the more effective because of my lack of fighters and of flak."

Paying tribute to the stubbornness of the Russian defence here, Kleist made an interesting psychological point. "In the earlier stages of my advance I met little organized resistance. As soon as the Russian forces were by-passed, most of the troops seemed more intent to find the way back to their homes than to continue fighting. That was quite different to what had happened in 1941. But when we advanced into the Caucausus, the forces we met there were local troops, who fought more stubbornly because they were fighting to defend their homes. Their obstinate resistance was all the more effective because the country was so difficult for the advance."

Dealing in more detail with the course of operations in the later bound—after the capture of Maikop—he went on to say that the first objective assigned to him was to secure the whole length of the great highway from Rostov across the Caucasus mountains to Tiflis. Baku was to be a second objective. The advance met its first serious check on the Terek. He then tried to cross this river by a manœuvre farther to the east and succeeded. But after this he was held up again in the very difficult country beyond the Terek, which was not only precipitous, but densely wooded. The brake imposed by this frontal resistance was increased by the exposure of his left flank, in the Steppes between Stalingrad and the Caspian.

"The Russians brought reserves round from the southern Caucasus and also from Siberia. These developed a menace to my flank here, which was so widely stretched that the Russian cavalry could always penetrate my outposts whenever they chose. This flank concentration of theirs was helped by the railway that the Russians built across the Steppes, from Astrakhan southward. It was roughly laid, straight over the level plain without any foundation. Efforts to deal with the menace by wrecking the railway proved useless, for as soon as any section of the railway was destroyed a fresh set of rails was quickly laid down, and joined up. My patrols reached the shores of the Caspian, but that advance carried us nowhere, for my forces in this quarter were striking against an intangible foe. As time passed and the Russian strength grew in that area the flanking menace became increasingly serious."

Kleist went on trying to reach his objective until November —by repeated surprise attacks at different points. After failing to get through from Mozdok he made a turning movement from Nalchik on his western flank and succeeded in reaching Ordzhonikidze, in combination with a converging stroke from Prokhladnaya. He traced this multiple manœuvre for me on the map, describing it, with professional satisfaction, as "a very elegant battle." For it, he had at last been given a measure of air support. But then bad weather held him up, and after a short interval the Russians counter-attacked. "In this counter-attack a Rumanian division, which I reckoned as a good one, suffered a sudden collapse and threw my plan out of joint. After that, a stalemate set in."

The other generals confirmed Kleist's evidence on the causes of the failure, especially the shortage of petrol—the armoured divisions were sometimes at a standstill for weeks on end, waiting for fresh supplies. Owing to this shortage the petrol lorries themselves were immobilized and petrol was brought forward on camels—an ironical revival of the traditional "ship of the desert." Blumentritt furnished a supplementary point in saying that the chance of overcoming the resistance in the mountains was diminished because most of the Germans' expert mountain troops, instead of being used to support Kleist, had been employed to help the 17th Army's advance along the Black Sea coast towards Batum. "That coastal advance was less important than von Kleist's thrust, and it was a mistake to put so much effort into it. When it was checked at Tuapse, and reinforcements were demanded, some of us demurred. The argument went on raging. We used to say, to those who pressed the need of the coastal advance— 'Yes, children, but the oil is over there'—pointing to Baku. But the clamour for the reinforcement of the Tuapse operations prevailed, with the consequent splitting of our efforts in the Caucasus, until it was too late."

The divergence of effort that took place in the Caucasus area was repeated, on a greater scale, in the splitting of the forces between the Caucasus and Stalingrad. But on this question, too, Blumentritt differed from the prevailing view. "It was absurd to attempt to capture the Caucasus and Stalingrad simultaneously in face of strong resistance. My own preference, which I expressed at the time, was to concentrate first on taking Stalingrad. I felt that capturing the oil was less important than destroying the Russian forces. Although it was not possible to contradict economic experts who asserted that it was essential to obtain the oil, if we were to continue the war, events disproved their contention. For we managed to carry on the war until 1945 without ever securing the Caucasus oil."

DEFEAT AT STALINGRAD

The supreme irony of the 1942 campaign was that Stalingrad could have been taken quite early if it had been considered of prime importance. Kleist's account revealed this—"The 4th Panzer Army was advancing on that line, on my left. It could have taken Stalingrad without a fight, at the end of July, but was diverted south to help me in crossing the Don. I did not need its aid, and it merely congested the roads I was using. When it turned north again, a fortnight later, the Russians had gathered just sufficient forces at Stalingrad to check it."

Never again did the prospect look so bright for the Germans as in the second half of July. The rapid sweep of the two panzer armies had not only hustled the Russians out of successive positions but created a state of confusion favourable to further exploitation. That accounted for the ease with which the German armoured forces were able to gain crossings over the Lower Don. There was hardly anything to stop them at that moment from driving where they wished—south-eastward to the Caucasus or north-eastward to the Volga. Most of the Russian forces were still to the west of the Lower Don, outstripped in their retreat by the pace of the panzers.

When the 4th Panzer Army missed the chance of taking Stalingrad with a rush, through its temporary diversion south-eastward, the situation began to change. The Russians had time to rally and collect forces for the defence of Stalingrad. The Germans, after their first check, had to wait until the bulk of Paulus's 6th Army had fought its way forward to the Don, mopped up the Russian forces that were cornered in the bend of the river, and were ready to join in a converging attack on Stalingrad. But its arrival on the scene was retarded not only because it was a foot-marching force but because its pushing power dwindled, as division after division was dropped to guard the continually extending flank along the Middle Don.

By the time that the more deliberate bid for Stalingrad began, in the second half of August, the Russians had collected more reserves there. Check followed check. It was easier for the Russians to reinforce Stalingrad than the Caucasus, because it was nearer their main front. Hitler became exasperated at these repeated checks. The name of the place—"the City of Stalin"—was a challenge. He drew off forces from his main line, and everywhere else, in the effort to overcome it—and exhausted his army in the effort.

The three months' struggle became a battle of battering-ram tactics on the Germans' side. The more closely they converged on the city, the narrower became their scope for tactical manœuvre, as a lever in loosening resistance. At the same time, the narrowing of the front made it easier for the defender to switch his local reserves to any threatened point on the defensive arc. The more deeply the Germans penetrated into the densely built-up area of the city, the slower their progress became. In the last stages of the siege the front line was barely half a mile from the west bank of the Volga, but by then the strength of their efforts was fading, as a result of very heavy losses. Each step forward cost more and gained less.

The inherent difficulties of street fighting, in face of stubborn opponents, tended to outweigh the handicaps which the defence suffered in this case. The most serious of these was the fact that reinforcements and supplies had to come across the Volga by ferries and barges, under shell-fire. This limited the scale of the forces that the Russians could use, and maintain, on the west bank for the defence of the city. In consequence the defenders were often hard-pressed. The strain on them was the more severe because the higher command, with cool strategic calculation, reinforced the direct defence as sparingly as possible—preferring to concentrate most of its gathering reserves on the flanks, with a view to a counter-offensive. In the later stages, only on two occasions did it divert to Stalingrad itself a division from the armies that it was assembling for the counter-offensive. The margin by which the gallant defenders of Stalingrad held on was narrow, but it sufficed.

The story of the prolonged battle for Stalingrad has been graphically related from the Russian side. On the German side, detail is lacking because most of the executive commanders, as well as their troops, fell into the Russians' hands. So far as it is known, it appears to have been a rather dull process of battering at blocks of the city, with diminishing resources. The hopes of the attackers faded long before the initiative was wrested from them—but they were forced to continue trying under Hitler's unrelaxing demands for renewed efforts.

More historical interest lies in the evidence as to the way that the push for Stalingrad turned into a trap for the armies engaged. The collapse of the flanks was foreshadowed long before it actually occurred. Emphasizing this fact Blumentritt said: "The danger to the long-stretched flank of our advance developed gradually, but it became clear early enough for anyone to perceive it who was not wilfully blind. During August the Russians by degrees increased their strength on the other side of the Don, from Voronezh south-eastward. A number of short and sharp attacks on their part explored the weaknesses of the German defence along the Don. These exploratory attacks showed them that the Second Hungarian Army was holding the sector south of Voronezh, and the Eighth Italian Army was holding the sector beyond that. The risk became worse after September, when the Rumanians took over the more south-easterly sector as far as the Don bend, west of Stalingrad. There was only a slight German stiffening in this long 'Allied' front.

"Halder had sent me on a flying visit to the Italian sector, as an alarming report had come that the Russians had penetrated it and made a large breach. On investigating it, however, I found the attack had been made by only one Russian battalion, but an entire Italian division had bolted. I took immediate steps to close the gap, filling it with an Alpine division and part of the 6th German division.

"I spent ten days in that sector and after returning made a written report to the effect that it would not be safe to hold such a long defensive flank during the winter. The railheads were as much as 200 kilometres behind the front, and the bare nature of the country meant that there was little timber available for constructing defences. Such German divisions as were available were holding frontages of 50 to 60 kilometres. There were no proper trenches or fixed positions.

"General Halder endorsed this report and urged that our offensive should be halted, in view of the increasing resistance that it was meeting, and the increasing signs of danger to the long-stretched flank. But Hitler would not listen. During September the tension between the Führer and Halder increased, and their arguments became sharper. To see the Führer discussing plans with Halder was an illuminating experience. The Führer used to move his hands in big sweeps over the map—'Push here; push there.' It was all vague and regardless of practical difficulties. There was no doubt he would have liked to remove the whole German Staff, if he could, by a similar sweep. He felt that they were half-hearted about his ideas.

"Finally, General Halder made it clear that he refused to take the responsibility of continuing the advance with winter approaching. He was dismissed, at the end of September, and replaced by General Zeitzler—who was then Chief of Staff to Field-Marshal von Rundstedt in the West. I was sent to the West to take Zeitzler's place.

"Arriving fresh on the scene, and being newly appointed to such a high position, Zeitzler did not at first worry the Führer by constant objections in the way that General Halder had done. Thus Hitler pursued his aims unchecked, except by the Russians, and our armies were committed more deeply. Before long, Zeitzler became gloomy about the prospect and argued with the Führer that his intention of maintaining our armies forward near Stalingrad throughout the winter was impossible. When the outcome proved the truth of his warnings, the Führer became increasingly hostile to Zeitzler. He did not dismiss him, but he kept him at arm's length."

Summing up the situation Blumentritt said: "There would have been no risk of panic in withdrawing this time, for the German troops were now properly equipped for winter fighting, and had got over the fear of the unknown that had frightened them the year before. But they were not strong enough to hold on where they were, and the Russian strength was growing week by week.

"Hitler, however, would not budge. His 'instinct' had proved right the year before, and he was sure that it would be justified again. So he insisted on 'no withdrawal.' The result was that when the Russians launched their winter counter-offensive his army at Stalingrad was cut off, and forced to surrender. We were already too weakened to bear such a loss. The scales of the war had turned against Germany."

XV

AFTER STALINGRAD

A QUESTION THAT I PUT TO MANY GENERALS WAS: "DO YOU think that Germany could have avoided defeat after Stalingrad?" Rundstedt's reply was: "I think so, if the commanders in the field had been allowed a free hand in withdrawing when and where they thought fit, instead of being compelled to hold on too long, as repeatedly happened everywhere." While Rundstedt himself was not on the Eastern front after 1941, his position gave him more detachment of view. Moreover, the fact that he never took an optimistic view throughout, while having unique experience of high command on both fronts, gives a particular value to his opinion on the broad issue. When putting the same question to the generals who stayed in the East, I found them much more definite. All felt that Russia's offensive power could have been worn down by elastic defence—if they had only been allowed to practise it. Some gave striking examples.

Kleist cited his own experience in conducting the retreat from the Caucasus after Paulus's armies had been trapped at Stalingrad. He was promoted to field-marshal for his achievement in conducting that retreat without serious loss, and it would seem to have been better earned than many who have gained their baton for offensive successes, as is the normal rule. For it is difficult to think of any retreat in history that has extricated an army from such a dangerous position under such extraordinary difficulties—with the handicap of distance multiplied by winter, and then again by the pressure of superior forces pressing down on his flank and rear.

Relating the story of that retreat Kleist said: "Although our offensive in the Caucasus had reached its abortive end in November, 1942, when stalemate set in, Hitler insisted on our staying in that exposed forward position, deep in the mountains. At the beginning of January a serious danger to my rear flank developed from an attack which the Russians delivered from Elista westwards past the southern end of Lake Manych. This was more serious than the Russian counterattacks on my forward position, near Mozdok. But the greatest danger of all came from the Russian advance from Stalingrad, down the Don towards Rostov, far in my rear.

"When the Russians were only 70 kilometres from Rostov, and my armies were 650 kilometres east of Rostov, Hitler sent me an order that I was not to withdraw under any circumstances. That looked like a sentence of doom. On the next day, however, I received a fresh order—to retreat, and bring away everything with me in the way of equipment. That would have been difficult enough in any case, but became much more so in the depths of the Russian winter.

"The protection of my flank from Elista back to the Don had originally been entrusted to the Rumanian Army Group under Marshal Antonescu. Antonescu himself did not arrive on the scene, thank God! Instead, the sector was placed under Manstein, whose 'Army Group South' included part of the Rumanian forces. With Manstein's help, we succeeded in withdrawing through the Rostov bottleneck before the Russians could cut us off. Even so, Manstein was so hard pressed that I had to send some of my own divisions to help him in holding off the Russians who were pushing down the Don towards Rostov. The most dangerous time of the retreat was the last half of January."

Kleist emphasized how the course of this retreat, which had appeared hardly possible to achieve, showed the power of elastic defence. After his forces had got safely back to the Dnieper, they were able to launch a counter-offensive that turned the tables on the Russian advance westward from Stalingrad and the Don. This riposte recaptured Kharkov and restored the whole situation on the southern front. A long lull followed, which lasted until after mid-summer 1943.

That breathing space enabled the Germans to consolidate a firm position in the East, and to build up their strength afresh—not to its former level, but sufficient to provide a good prospect of holding the Russians at bay. But Hitler refused to listen to any advice in favour of changing to a defensive strategy. It was he, not the Russians, who took the offensive initiative in the summer. Although his effort was on a more limited scale and frontage than ever, he threw into it all the resources he had—employing seventeen armoured divisions in a converging attack on the Russians' Kursk salient. Talking of this offensive, Kleist said that he had little hope of any good resulting from it, but Kluge and Manstein who were put in charge of the pincers stroke seemed to be quite optimistic beforehand. "If it had been launched six weeks earlier it might have been a great success—though we had no longer the resources to make it decisive. But in the interval the Russians got wind of the preparations. They laid deep minefields across their front, while withdrawing their main forces farther to the rear, so that comparatively few were left in the bag that our high command had hoped to enclose."

When this last German offensive had been brought to a halt, the Russians launched theirs—as a counter-offensive. They now had ample resources to maintain the momentum, whereas the Germans in this last gamble had squandered the strength that might still have enabled them to impose a prolonged series of checks, and even produce a stalemate. Almost all the mobile reserves were exhausted. Thus the Russian advance rolled on during the autumn and winter with only short halts

—caused more by out-running its own supplies than by the Germans' counter-thrusts. The whole southern front was in a state of flux.

But on the northern front, where the German forces had been allowed to remain on the defensive, the Russian attacks repeatedly broke down in face of the tenacious and well-knit resistance. I had a striking account of this period from Heinrici, who then commanded the 4th Army on the sector from Rogachev to Orsha, astride the great highway from Moscow to Minsk. Mentioning that he had been re-reading what I had written about the trends of modern warfare, he said: "I want to tell you how strongly I agree, from experience, with your conclusions as to the superiority of defence over attack in the tactical field. The problem turns, as you remark, on the ratio of space to force. I think it may interest you to have some illustrative examples from my experience.

"After the evacuation of Smolensk, the Russians advanced to within twenty kilometres of Orsha, where the troops of the 4th Army were able to check them, after occupying a hastily prepared position that consisted of only one trench line. That autumn we there had to meet a series of strong Russian offensives, beginning in October and continuing until December. There were five successive offensives. I had ten divisions in my army to hold a sector that was 150 kilometres wide as the crow flies, but actually about 200 kilometres allowing for the irregularity of the front. The 4th Army was without any reserves, and much weakened by the losses it had suffered. But its artillery was intact—that was a vital asset.

"The main objective of the Russians was the great rail centre of Orsha—in order to cut the lateral railway from Leningrad to Kiev. With this aim they concentrated the weight of their assault on a frontage of 20 kilometres astride the main highway. In their first offensive they employed 20-22 divisions; in the second 30 divisions; and in the next three about 36 divisions apiece. Part of them were the original ones, but most of them were fresh.

"To meet this assault I used 3½ divisions to hold the 20 kilometres frontage where the attack came, leaving 6½ to hold the remainder of my very wide front. Every attack was checked. These five successive battles each lasted five or six days, but the crisis usually came about the third or fourth day, after which the attack began to peter out. The Russians did not try any large armoured drive—because no considerable gap was made in the defences. The attacks were supported by up to fifty infantry tanks, but these were always checked.

"The Russians usually made about three tries a day—the first about 9 A.M., after heavy artillery preparations; the second between 10 and 11; and the third between 2 and 3 in the afternoon. It was almost like clockwork! There was no question of the Russian troops failing to advance, until they were stopped by our fire—for they were driven forward under the compulsion of officers and commissars, marching in rear, and ready to turn their pistols on anyone who shirked. The Russian infantry were badly trained, but they attacked vigorously.

"In my opinion, there were three main factors that contributed to the success of the defence. First, I formed narrow divisional sectors, with a high ratio of force to space, on the actual frontage of the Russian assault. Secondly, I managed to form a very powerful artillery grouping, of 380 guns, to cover the threatened sector. This was controlled by a single commander, at Army Headquarters, and was able to concentrate its fire on any required point of that 20 kilometre frontage. The Russian offensives were supported by up to a thousand guns, but their fire was not so concentrated. Thirdly, the losses of the German divisions engaged—which had to be reckoned as the equivalent of about one battalion per division in each day of battle—were compensated by a system of drawing battalions from the divisions on other parts of the Army front. I always tried to have three fresh battalions—one for each of the divisions holding the battle front—ready behind this before the attack started. The other battalion of the regiment from which it was drawn would follow, together with the regimental staff, and in this way I would get complete fresh regiments incorporated in the front, and then complete fresh divisions. The temporary mixing of divisions was inevitable, and part of the price of the defensive success, but I always tried to restore their integrity as soon as possible."

In May, 1944, Heinrici was given command of the 1st Panzer Army together with the 1st Hungarian Army on the Carpathian front, and with these forces conducted the retreat to Silesia early in 1945 after the German front had collapsed in the north. In March, 1945, he was given command of the Army Group that faced the Russians' final push for Berlin. With this he fought the battle of the Oder and the battle of Berlin.

In this later stage, he said, he had further developed the defensive methods which he had already described. "When the Russians were found to be concentrating for an attack, I withdrew my troops from the first line under cover of night, to the second line—usually about 2 kilometres behind. The result was that the Russian blow hit the air, and its further attack did not have the same impetus. Of course, a necessary condition of success was to discover the actual intended day of the assault, which I sought to do by using patrols to secure prisoners. After the Russian attack had been broken, I continued to hold the second line as my new forward position, while on the sectors that had not been attacked the troops moved forward again to re-occupy the first line. This system worked very well in the battle of the Oder—the only drawback was our scanty strength, after so much had been wasted needlessly by the rigid defence of positions impossible to hold.

"I never suffered defeat during three years of defensive battles when I could base my plan on such methods—and I was proud that I never had to call on the Higher Command to spare me any of its reserves. I found self-propelled guns were of the greatest value in applying these defensive tactics.

"In the light of my experience, I consider that your conclusion that the attacker needs a three to one superiority is under the mark, rather than over it. I would say that, for success, the attacker needs six to one or seven to one against a well-knit defence that has a reasonable frontage to cover. There were times when my troops held their own against odds of 12 to 1 or even 18 to 1.

"The German defeat in the East was, in my opinion, due to one main reason—that our troops were compelled to cover immense spaces without the flexibility, in the command, that would have enabled them to concentrate on holding decisive points. Thus they lost the initiative permanently. I doubt whether we could have worn down the Russians by pure defence, but might well have been able to turn the balance by a more mobile kind of warfare, and by shortening our front so as to release forces that could be used for effective counter-strokes.

"But the army commanders were never consulted about the plan or method of defence. Guderian, when Chief of the General Staff in the last year, had no influence on Hitler. His predecessor, Zeitzler, had only a very slight influence. Earlier still, Halder's advice had been largely disregarded.

"My first experience after taking over command of the 4th Army in 1942, opened my eyes. I withdrew a small detachment from an awkward position it was holding—whereupon I received a warning, conveyed through General von Kluge, then the commander of the Army Group, that if I did anything of the sort again the least that would happen to me would be a court-martial.

"Hitler always tried to make us fight for every yard, threatening to court-martial anyone who didn't. No withdrawal was officially permitted without his approval—even a small-scale withdrawal. This principle was so hammered into the army that it was a common saying that battalion commanders were afraid 'to move a sentry from the window to the door.' These rigid methods cramped us at every turn. Time after time, forces stayed in impossible positions until they were surrounded and captured. But some of us ventured to evade his orders so far as we could."

Such evasion was only possible in a local and limited way. Tippelskirch, who succeeded Heinrici in command of the 4th Army, bore witness to the value of elastic defence, but also to the disastrous consequences of being unable to practise it to an adequate extent. "At Mogilev in March, 1944, I was commanding the 12th Corps—which consisted of three divisions. In the offensive the Russians then launched, they used ten divisions in the assault on the first day, and by the sixth day had used twenty divisions. Yet they only captured the first line, and were brought to a halt before the second. In the lull that followed I prepared a counter-stroke, delivered it by moonlight, and recovered all the ground that had been lost —with comparatively few casualties."

Tippelskirch then went on to relate what happened in the Russians' summer offensive in 1944. He took over command of the 4th Army three weeks before it opened. The army commanders on that front begged for permission to withdraw to the line of the Beresina—a long step back that would have taken the sting out of the Russian blow. But their proposals were rejected. Tippelskirch nevertheless made a short step back on his sector to the line of the Dnieper, and that sufficed to keep his front intact. But the fronts of both the armies on his right and left were ruptured, and a general collapse followed. The retreat did not stop until the Vistula had been reached, near Warsaw.

"It would have been much wiser strategy to withdraw the whole front in time. The Russians always needed a long pause for preparation after any German withdrawal, and they always lost disproportionately when attacking. A series of withdrawals by adequately large steps would have worn down the Russian strength, besides creating opportunities for counter-strokes at a time when the German forces were still strong enough to make them effective.

"Hitler had been justified in his 1941 veto on any withdrawal, but his great mistake was to repeat it in 1942 and later, when conditions were different. For after the first year the German Army was well equipped for winter fighting, and felt quite able to hold its own with the Russians under these conditions. Thus a strategic withdrawal would not have shaken its morale. Our troops were quite capable of carrying out such a manœuvre in winter. Besides economizing their own strength, it would have enabled them to stage a powerful come-back.

"The root cause of Germany's defeat was the way that her forces were wasted in fruitless efforts, and above all in fruitless resistance at the wrong time and place. That was due to Hitler. There was no strategy in our campaign."

General Dittmar contributed some interesting points to the discussion, from his wider and more detached point of view. As a military commentator he was amazingly objective in his broadcast commentaries during the war—more so perhaps than any other military critic anywhere. This was the more notable because he had to expound the situation under restrictions, and dangers, far worse than any Allied commentator had to fear. When I asked him how he was able to speak so candidly on many occasions, he told me that he owed this latitude to Fritsche, the head of radio propaganda, who alone saw his broadcasts before they were delivered. He had the feeling that Fritsche had reached an underlying disillusionment with regard to the Nazi régime, and was glad to give scope to someone who would express what he secretly felt himself. Naturally there were many protests, though Fritsche did his best to shield Dittmar. "I always felt that I was walking a tight-rope with a noose round my neck."

When I asked Dittmar whether he thought that if the Germans had adopted a strategy of elastic defence they could have worn down the Russians, he replied: "I believe we could, and the advantages of elastic defence were clear, but our military chiefs could not apply it properly because of Hitler's objections. The General Staff were not allowed to order the construction of lines in rear, or even to discuss plans in case of being driven back. They were forbidden to make any preparatory plans for a withdrawal. In 1943, however, they managed to do a little preparatory work on the quiet, by circulatting instructions in discreetly worded leaflets. These leaflets were distributed among the various armies, but without any imprint to show that they emanated from the General Staff."

I asked Dittmar whether any strategic withdrawal was attempted on the German side, prior to the launching of the great Russian offensive in July, 1943, or again before that of January, 1945. He replied: "No. Each was a case of an absolute break-through, owing to the strategy that Hitler imposed. Some of the commanders of the lower formations were shrewd enough to evade his rule that every place was to be held at all costs, and carried out short withdrawals on their own, but others clung on in strict obedience to orders, and as a result their troops were cut off and captured. The disaster in each case was due to the fundamental error of a rigidly defensive strategy. That disaster was all the worse in the case of the Russian offensive from the Vistula in January, 1945, because the reserves that had been held ready to meet the threat were taken away at the critical moment and dispatched to the relief of Budapest." They comprised three of the best-equipped armoured divisions available.

"The policy of clinging on at all costs in particular places repeatedly changed the campaign for the worse. The attempt to cement one threatened breach in the general front repeatedly caused fresh breaches. In the end that proved fatal."

XVI

THE RED ARMY

THE GERMAN GENERALS' IMPRESSIONS OF THE RED ARMY WERE interesting, and often illuminating. The best appreciation in a concise form came from Kleist: "The men were first-rate *fighters* from the start, and we owed our success simply to superior training. They became first-rate *soldiers* with experience. They fought most toughly, had amazing endurance, and could carry on without most of the things other armies regarded as necessities. The Staff were quick to learn from their early defeats, and soon became highly efficient."

Some of the other German generals disagreed, and said that the Russian infantry in general remained rather poor, tactically and technically, though the tank forces were formidable. I noted, however, that the more critical opinions came from generals who had been on the northern half of the front—which suggests that the more skilled part of the Red Army operated in the south. On the other hand, the guerrillas seem to have been more active behind the German front in the north, and by 1944 had forced the Germans there to abandon the use of all except a few of the trunk roads as supply routes. Tippelskirch, whose 4th Army was cut off on the northern Dnieper by the Russian summer offensive that year, told me that he extricated it by making a detour south-

wards towards the Pripet Marshes, after the main line of
retreat to Minsk had been blocked, moving by way of roads
which had long been abandoned because of guerrilla interference. "I found every single bridge on the route had been
broken, and had to repair them in the course of my retreat."

Talking of his four years' experience of the Northern front,
he remarked: "Our infantry lost their fear of the Russian
infantry in 1941, but they remained fearful of being taken prisoner—and sent to Siberia or worse. This fear helped to stiffen
their resistance, but it had an insidious effect as time went on,
particularly when they were compelled by Hitler's order to
remain in isolated forward positions where they were bound
eventually to be cut off."

I asked Rundstedt what he considered were the strong and
weak points of the Red Army, as he found it in 1941. His
reply was: "The Russian heavy tanks were a surprise in quality
and reliability from the outset. But the Russians proved to
have less artillery than had been expected, and their air force
did not offer serious opposition in that first campaign."

Talking more specifically of the Russian weapons Kleist said:
"Their equipment was very good even in 1941, especially the
tanks. Their artillery was excellent, and also most of the infantry weapons—their rifles were more modern than ours,
and had a more rapid rate of fire. Their T.34 tank was the
finest in the world." In my talks with Manteuffel, he emphasized that the Russians maintained their advantage in tank
design and that in the "Stalin" tank, which appeared in 1944,
they had what he considered the best tank that was seen in
battle, anywhere, up to the end of the war. British experts have
criticized the Russian tanks for lacking the refinements, and
gadgets, desirable in various operational respects—especially
for wireless control. But the German tank experts considered
that the British and Americans tended to sacrifice too much
much in the way of power and performance for these refinements.

On the equipment side Kleist said that the Russians' weakest period had been in 1942. They had not been able to make up their 1941 losses, and throughout the year were very short of artillery in particular. "They had to use mortars, brought up on lorries, to compensate their lack of artillery." But from 1943 on their equipment position became better and better. While the inpouring flow of Allied supplies was a big factor, especially in motor transport, the increasing production of the new Russian factories in the East, out of reach, accounted for even more. The tanks employed were almost entirely of their own manufacture.

A rather surprising feature of the campaign in the East was that the Russians did not make any effective use of airborne forces, although they had led the world in the development of this new arm—which had played a prominent part in their Army Manœuvres in pre-war years. I discussed this question with Student, who replied: "I often wondered why the Russians never used their parachute troops. The reason, I imagine, may have been that their training was insufficient—due to lack of practice in navigation as well as in dropping. All they did in this way was to drop agents and small parties for sabotage behind our front."

Coming to the question of leadership I asked Rundstedt which were the best of the Russian generals in his experience. He replied: "None were any good in 1941. Of Budenny, who commanded the armies facing me, a captured Russian officer aptly remarked—'He is a man with a very large moustache, but a very small brain.' But in later years there is no doubt of the improvement in their generalship. Zhukov was very good. It is interesting to recall that he first studied strategy in Germany under General von Seeckt—this was about 1921-23."

Dittmar, who in his position as the leading military commentator was best placed to gather the consensus of opinion among the German generals, said that Zhukov was regarded as outstanding. Koniev was good, a clever tactician, but not quite on the same level. "As the war went on, the Russians developed an increasingly high standard of leadership from top to bottom. One of their greatest assets was their officers' readiness to learn, and the way they studied their job." He added that the Russians could afford to make mistakes, because of their immense superiority of strength, in a way that the Germans could not.

This verdict on the Russian generals was questioned by some of their German opponents, especially those who had been on the Northern front. Broadly speaking, the run of opinion seemed to be that the top and bottom of the Russian ladder of command became the strongest sections, while the middle piece was shaky. The top rungs were filled by men who had proved themselves so able that they were allowed to exercise their own judgment, and could safely insist on doing things in their own way. The bottom rungs were filled by junior officers who, within their limited sphere, tended to develop a good tactical sense, because the incompetent soon became casualties in a field that was ruled by the hard realities of the enemy's bullets and shells. But the intermediate commanders, even more than most armies, were concerned with other factors. Their superiors' orders and judgments were more to be feared than the enemy.

In this connection one of the German army commanders on the northern front made a significant comment: "It was usually safe to encourage the Russians to attack, so long as the defence was elastically designed. The Russians were always very bull-headed in their offensive methods, repeating their attacks again and again. This was due to the way their leaders lived in fear of being considered lacking in determination if they broke off their attack."

As regards the general characteristics of the Russian soldier, Dittmar gave me an illuminating sidelight when I asked him what he considered was the Russians' chief asset. "I would put first, what might be called the soulless indifference of the troops—it was something more than fatalism. They were not quite so insensitive when things went badly for them, but normally it was difficult to make any impression on them in the way that would happen with troops of other nations. During my period of command on the Finnish front there was only one instance where Russian troops actually surrendered to my own. While that extraordinary stolidity made the Russians very difficult to conquer it was also their chief weakness in a military sense—because in the earlier campaigns it often led to them being encircled."

Dittmar added: "On Hitler's specific orders, an attempt was later made in the German Army to inculcate the same mental attitude that prevailed in the Red Army. We tried to copy the Russians in this respect, while the Russians copied us, more successfully, in tactics. The Russians could afford to train their troops in this attitude because losses mattered little to them, and the troops were accustomed to do implicitly what they were told."

Blumentritt, who was fond of discoursing philosophically and historically on all these subjects, gave me his impressions at greater length, starting with his experience in the First World War.

"In 1914-18, as a lieutenant, I fought for the first two years against the Russians, after a brief contact with the French and Belgians at Namur in August, 1914. In our very first attack on the Russian front, we quickly realized that here we were meeting esesntially different soldiers from the French and Belgian—hardly visible, entrenched with consummate skill, and resolute! We suffered considerable losses.

"In those days it was the Russian Imperial Army. Hard, but good-natured on the whole, they had the habit of setting fire on military principle to towns and villages, in East Prussia when they were forced to withdraw, just as they always did thereafter in their own country. When the red glow from the burning villages lit up the horizon at evening, we knew that the Russians were leaving. Curiously, the population did not seem to complain. That was the Russian way, and had been so for centuries.

"When I referred to the bulk of the Russian Army as good-natured, I am speaking of their European troops. The much harder Asiatic troops, the Siberian corps, were cruel in their behaviour. So, also, were the Cossacks. Eastern Germany had plenty to suffer on this score in 1914.

"Even in 1914-18 the greater hardness of war conditions in the East had its effect on our own troops. Men preferred to be sent to the Western rather than the Eastern front. In the West it was a war of material and mass-artillery—Verdun, the Somme, and so on. These factors were paramount, and very gruelling to endure, but at least we were dealing with Western adversaries. In the East there was not so much shell-fire, but the fighting was more dogged, as the human type was much harder. Night fighting, hand-to-hand fighting, fighting in the forests, were particularly fostered by the Russians. In that war there was a saying current among German soldiers: 'In the East the gallant Army is fighting; in the West the Fire Brigade is standing by.'

"It was in this war, however, that we first learnt to realize what 'Russia' really means. The opening battle in June, 1941, revealed to us for the first time the new Soviet Army. Our casualties were up to fifty per cent. The Ogpu and a women's battalion defended the old citadel at Brest-Litovsk for a week, fighting to the last, in spite of bombardment with our heaviest guns and from the air. Our troops soon learnt to know what fighting the Russians meant. The Führer and most of our highest chiefs didn't know. That caused a lot of trouble.

"The Red Army of 1941-45 was far harder than the Czar's Army, for they were fighting fanatically for an idea. That increased their doggedness, and in turn made our own troops hard, for in the East the maxim held good—'You or I.' Discipline in the Red Army was far more rigorous than in the Czar's Army. These are examples of the sort of order that we used to intercept—and they were blindly obeyed. 'Why do you fail to attack? I order you for the last time to take Strylenko, otherwise I fear for your health.' 'Why is your regiment not in the initial position for attack? Engage at once unless you want to lose your head.' In such ways we were brought to realize the inexorable character of our opponents. We had no idea in 1941 that within a few years it would be much the same with us.

"Wherever Russians have appeared in the history of war, the fight was hard, ruthless, and involved heavy losses. Where the Russian makes a stand or defends himself, he is hard to defeat, and it costs a lot of bloodshed. As a child of nature he works with the simplest expedients. As all have to obey blindly, and the Slav-Asiatic character only understands the absolute, disobedience is non-existent. The Russian commanders can make incredible demands on their men in every way —and there is no murmuring, no complaint.

"The East and the West are two worlds, and they cannot understand each other. Russia is a dumb question mark on the Sphinx. The Russians can keep their mouths shut, and their minds are closed to us."

Blumentritt's reflections touched on a point that played a part almost as great as morale. For all the generals emphasized that the Russians' greatest asset was the way they could do without normal supplies. Manteuffel, who led many tank raids deep behind their front, gave the most vivid picture—"The advance of a Russian Army is something that Westerners can't imagine. Behind the tank spearheads rolls on a vast horde, largely mounted on horses. The soldier carries a sack on his back, with dry crusts of bread and raw vegetables collected on the march from the fields and villages. The horses eat the straw from the house roofs—they get very little else. The Russians are accustomed to carry on for as long as three weeks in this primitive way, when advancing. You can't stop them, like an ordinary army, by cutting their communications, for you rarely find any supply columns to strike."

XVII

PARALYSIS IN NORMANDY

FOR BRITAIN AND THE UNITED STATES THE LANDING IN NORMANDY was the supreme venture. The story of it has been abundantly told from their points of view. It is more illuminating to follow the course of the invasion from "the other side of the hill." During the first month, the opposing Commander-in-Chief was Field-Marshal von Rundstedt, who had been in command of the Western theatre since early in 1942. He gave me his account. At the start of the second month Rundstedt was replaced by Field-Marshal von Kluge, who held the post until the collapse came. He is dead—after the collapse he swallowed a dose of poison in despair, and fear of Hitler. But General Blumentritt was Chief of Staff to both throughout this crucial campaign, and I had a very detailed account from him of events during both periods.

Under Rundstedt and Kluge in turn, the battle to check the invasion was conducted by Field-Marshal Rommel commanding Army Group "B," which stretched from Brittany to Holland. Rommel, too, is dead. But I was able to gain light on his part in the Normandy campaign from members of his staff —and get a check on each of the higher commanders' accounts from other generals who were on the scene.

Seeing the battle through the opponent's eyes is the most

dramatic way of seeing it. It is different in one important respect from "looking at it through the opposite end of the telescope." For instead of being minimized, the picture is magnified—with startling vividness.

Looking at the invasion problem from the English shore, it appeared tremendously formidable. Looking at it from the French shore, as the enemy saw it, one could better appreciate the very different feelings of those who faced the threat of invasion by Powers which held the command of the sea, and of the air. "I had over 3,000 miles of coastline to cover," Rundstedt told me, "from the Italian frontier in the south to the German frontier in the north, and only 60 divisions with which to defend it. Most of them were low-grade divisions, and some of them were skeletons."

The figure of 60 would not "go" into 3,000 miles on any strategic calculation. It spelt fifty miles per division, even without allowing for the need of reserves behind. That was an impossible proposition. In the 1914-18 war it used to be considered that 3 miles per division was the safety limit against any strong attack. The power of modern defence had increased since then at least double, perhaps treble—even so, the number of divisions available was far too small to cover the whole frontage with any degree of security.

The chances thus depended on guessing correctly where the Allies were likely to make their landing. Unlikely sections of the coastline had to be left almost defenceless in order to have any appreciable cover for the more probable stretches. Even then, these could only be held thinly if reserves were to be kept back for counter-attack at the actual points of landing within the sector—when these were clearly known.

Rundstedt and Blumentritt emphasized to me how much more difficult their problem was made by Hitler's readiness to imagine that the invasion might come anywhere on the circumference of occupied Europe, and his inclination to scout the shipping factors.

PRELUDE

I asked the Field-Marshal whether he had expected an Allied invasion of the West at any time prior to when it actually came. He replied: "I was surprised that you did not attempt an invasion in 1941 while our armies were advancing deep into Russia. But at that time I was myself on the Eastern front, and out of touch with the situation in the West. When I came there, and knew the situation better, I did not expect an early invasion, for I realized that your resources were not sufficient." Rundstedt's reference to his 1941 view would appear to bear out earlier reports that he then got on Hitler's nerves by his warnings about leaving the German rear exposed—a risk which Hitler sought to cover by sending Rundstedt to take charge in the West. Rundstedt's sphere of responsibility stretched from the Dutch-German frontier to the Franco-Italian frontier.

In answer to a further question, the Field-Marshal said he did not imagine that the landing at Dieppe, in August, 1942, portended an actual invasion. He thought it was merely an experimental attack, to test the coastal defences. When I questioned Blumentritt on the same point he gave a somewhat different answer—"I was not in the West at the time, but I heard a lot about the landing after my arrival, at the end of September, to succeed General Zeitzler as Chief of Staff there. The German Command was not sure whether it was merely a raid, or whether it might have been followed up with larger reinforcements if it had been more successful at the outset." It would seem that both Zeitzler and Keitel took a serious view of it.

Continuing his account, Rundstedt said: "I expected an invasion in 1943, once we had occupied the whole of France. For I thought you would take early advantage of this extensive stretching of the German forces in the West."

Blumentritt amplified this point: "After the Allied land-

ings in French North Africa—in November, 1942—the
Führer's order for us to advance into the unoccupied part of
France was prompted by his conviction that the Allies would
go on from Africa to invade southern France. It was reckoned that they would land on the Mediterranean coast, and
that the Vichy Government would not oppose them. The occupation took place without any great friction, and the only
casualties were caused by partisans—whose activities were
already becoming uncomfortable. Field-Marshal von Rundstedt himself went on alone ahead of his troops in order to
arrange at Vichy that the occupation should be carried out
peacefully, so as to avoid useless losses to both sides. He succeeded in that purpose."

1943—"THE YEAR OF UNCERTAINTY"

"After the fall of Tunis in May," Blumentritt said, "Hitler
became increasingly anxious about the possibility of a landing
in the south of France. In fact, that year Hitler was constantly on the jump—at one moment he expected an invasion
in Norway, at another moment in Holland, then near the
Somme, or Normandy and Brittany, in Portugal, in Spain, in
the Adriatic. His eyes were hopping all around the map.

"He was particularly concerned about the possibility of a
pincer-type invasion, with simultaneous landings in the south
of France and the Bay of Biscay. He also feared a stroke to
capture the Balearic Islands, followed by a landing at Barce-
lona and an advance from there northward into France. He
was so impressed with the risks of an Allied invasion of Spain
that he ordered strong German forces to be sent to the Pyrenees to meet it. At the same time he insisted that the German
forces must be careful to observe the strictest neutrality, and
avoid any offence to Spain.

"We soldiers, however, did not share some of his apprehensions. We thought it was unlikely that the British High Command would attempt a landing in the Bay of Biscay as it

was outside the range of air support from England. We also discounted the Spanish possibilities, for several reasons—we doubted whether the Allies would risk incurring Spain's hostility, and in any case it was unfavourable country for large-scale operations, the communications being bad, and the Pyrenees forming a barrier beyond. Moreover, we were on friendly terms with the Spanish generals along the Pyrenean frontier, and while they let us know clearly that they would resist any German invasion, they were helpful in providing us with information."

Blumentritt, however, went on to say that while the generals discounted some of the threats that worried Hitler, they thought a landing would come somewhere. "This year showed every sign of being the one for the expected invasion. Rumours grew stronger throughout 1943 that an invasion was coming. They reached us largely from foreign diplomatic sources—from the Rumanian, Hungarian, and Japanese military attachés, as well as from Vichy quarters."

It would seem that rumour was more effective than planned deception in playing on the mind of the enemy command. In one of my talks with Rundstedt, I asked him whether he thought that a cross-Channel invasion was coming in September that year—at that time we made an elaborate feint, moving large forces down to the south coast of England, and making an appearance of embarking them. He replied, with a smile: "The movements you made at that time were too obvious—it was evident that they were a bluff."

That too apparent piece of stage-play tended to relieve the anxieties of the German Command, by its indication that the Allies were putting off the attempt. Since autumn gales were about due, it meant that the German garrisons of France might count upon another winter's respite before the storm broke upon them. It was a partial relief after a long period of strained alertness.

"In brief, 1943 might be summed up as 'the year of uncertainty and insecurity,'" remarked Blumentritt. Its difficulties were increased because the Resistance movement in France had by then become very formidable, and was causing us many casualties, as well as serious strain. It had not amounted to much in 1942. It was then divided into three distinct groups—Communists, Gaullists and Giraudists. Fortunately for us, these three groups were antagonistic to one another, and often brought us information about one another's activities. But from 1943 onwards they became united—with Britain directing their operations and supplying them with arms by air."

CHANGING THE GUARD

During 1943 various alterations were made in the defence scheme to meet invasion, under the handicap of limited resources. For France had been used as a convalescent home where divisions exhausted in the Eastern campaign could recuperate and reorganize. Describing the steps, Blumentritt said: "Up to 1943 there had been fifty to sixty divisions in France which were repeatedly being replaced by badly-damaged divisions from the Russian front. This continual interchange was detrimental to a proper system of defence on the coast. So permanent coast-defence divisions were formed, with a specialized organization adapted to their particular sectors. This system had the advantage of ensuring that they were well acquainted with the sector they had to guard, and it also enabled the most economic use of the limited equipment available in the West. But it had inevitable weaknesses. The officers and men were mostly of the older classes, and their armament was on a lower scale than in the active divisions. It included a large proportion of captured French, Polish, and Yugo-Slav weapons, which fired differing kinds of ammunition—so that supplies were more liable to run out, at awkward moments, than in the case of standard weapons. Most of these divisions had only two infantry regiments, with two field batteries comprising 24 pieces in all, and one medium battery of 12 pieces. As the artillery was horse-drawn it had little mobility.

"Besides these coast-defence divisions there was the coastal artillery. But this, whether naval or military, came under the Naval Command—which was always inclined to disagree with the Army Command."

A fresh complication arose at the end of the year with Rommel's entry on the scene. He had previously been for a short time in command of the German forces that occupied Northern Italy, but in November he was appointed by Hitler to inspect and improve the coast defences from Denmark to the Spanish frontier. After dealing with those in Denmark he moved to France just before Christmas—which brought him into Rundstedt's sphere. He worked under special instructions from Hitler, yet without any clear definition about his relationship to Rundstedt. Controversy naturally developed, and the more inevitably because their ideas differed.

Blumentritt's comment was: "Soon, the armies did not know whether they were under the command of Rundstedt or Rommel, as the latter wanted his ideas on coast defence to be put into practice everywhere. To solve the problem, Rundstedt suggested that Rommel should take over executive charge of the most important sector of the front along the Channel, from the Dutch-German border to the Loire, while the Southern front from the Loire to the Alps would be entrusted to Blaskowitz—both being under Rundstedt as supreme commander. Under Rommel's Army Group "B" would be placed the troops in Holland; the 15th Army, holding from there to the Seine; and the 7th Army, from the Seine to the Loire. Blaskowitz's Army Group "G" comprised the 1st Army, covering the Bay of Biscay and the Pyrenees, and the 19th Army, covering the Mediterranean coast."

According to Rommel's staff, the proposal came from him —"as the only way of putting his ideas into execution quickly." In any case the arrangement was sanctioned, about a month after his arrival. It went some way to ease the situation, although the difference of views between Rundstedt and Rommel was not compatible with a real solution.

Speaking to me of Rommel, Rundstedt said—"He was a brave man, and a very capable commander in small operations, but not really qualified for high command." But he had no complaint of Rommel's loyalty. "When I gave an order Rommel obeyed it without making any difficulty." On the other hand, it would appear that Rundstedt was almost too scrupulous in refraining from interference in what he regarded as his subordinate's proper sphere of responsibility. Hence he hesitated to overrule Rommel on matters where his own view was basically different, and where Rommel's decisions were bound to have a far-reaching effect on his own steps.

Here I would remark that the more I saw of Rundstedt the better impression he made. That was due to indirect as well as direct evidence. His seniority might have partly explained the high respect, but not the deep affection he inspired among those who shared his captivity. He has a rather orthodox mind, not only in the operational sphere, but it is an able and sensitive mind, backed by a character that makes him outstanding. He is dignified without being arrogant, and essentially aristocratic in outlook—giving that term its best sense. He has an austere appearance that is offset by a pleasant smile and a nice gleam of humour. This frequently comes out. Walking back with him on one occasion to his cramped little room, after passing through the heavily barbed-wire gate into the inner compound, we came to the front door. I motioned him to go in first. He replied to this gesture, with a smile: "Oh, no—this is *my* house."

WHERE?

When 1944 came it was clear that the main invasion would be launched from England, because of the scale of the American forces which were being transported there. But it was more difficult to determine where the landings would be made in France. "Very little reliable news came out of England," Blumentritt told me. "All that side of the Intelligence was directed by O.K.W. under Hitler, not by us—and was carried out by a special branch of the S.D. We were dependent on them for our information.

"They gave us reports of where, broadly, the British and American forces respectively were assembled in Southern England—there were a small number of German agents in England, who reported by wireless transmitting sets what they observed. But they found out very little beyond that. We were so weak in the air that reconnaissance over England was very limited. Towards D-day, however, night-flying 'planes reported large movements of transport towards the southwest coast—which they could follow because the vehicles had their headlights on." (Presumably these were American troops, as the western half of Southern England was occupied by them.) "We also intercepted a wireless message from the British Fleet which gave us an indication that something important was about to take place in the Channel.

"Another hint came from the increased activity of the 'Resistance' in France. We captured several hundred wireless transmitters, and were able to discover the bearing of the code phrases used in communicating with England. The messages were veiled, but the broad significance was evident.

"But nothing we learnt gave us a definite clue where the invasion was actually coming. We had to depend on our own judgment in that vital respect."

Blumentritt then told me: "Our Naval Staff always insisted that the Allies would land near a big port. They anticipated an attack on Le Havre—not only because of its value as a port, but because it was the base for our midget submarines. We soldiers did not agree with their view. We doubted whether the Allies would make a direct attack on such a well-fortified place. Moreover, we had information about a big exercise carried out in southern England, where the troops had been disembarked on a flat and open coastline.

"From this we deduced that the Allies would not try to

attack a port at the outset. But we had no idea, nor any report, that they were developing artificial harbours—the Mulberries. We thought you were probably intending to lay your ships side by side, to form a bridge over which stores could be unloaded and carried ashore to the beaches."

Rundstedt said frankly: "I thought the invasion would come across the narrower part of the Channel, between Le Havre and Calais—rather than between Caen and Cherbourg. I expected the landing to take place on either side of the estuary of the Somme. I thought the first landing might take place on the west side, between Le Tréport and Le Havre, followed by a further landing between the Somme and Calais."

I asked Rundstedt his reasons for this calculation. He replied: "The Somme-Calais area seemed to us so much better, strategically, from your point of view—because it was so much closer to Germany. It was the quickest route to the Rhine. I reckoned you could get there in four days."

His reasoning suggested that his calculation was governed by a preconceived view, based on the assumption that the Allies would take what was theoretically the best line, regardless of the practical difficulties. I remarked to him that, for the same reasons, it was likely to be the most strongly defended sector—surely a good reason why the Allies were likely to avoid it.

He admitted the point but answered: "The strength of the defences was absurdly overrated. The 'Atlantic Wall' was an illusion, conjured up by propaganda—to deceive the German people as well as the Allies. It used to make me angry to read the stories about its impregnable defences. It was nonsense to describe it as a 'wall.' Hitler himself never came to visit it, and see what it really was. For that matter the only time he came to the Channel coast in the whole war was back in 1940 when he paid a visit on one occasion to Cap Gris Nez." I remarked: "And looked across at the English coast, like Napoleon?" Rundstedt nodded, with an ironical smile.

Rundstedt went on to say that another reason for his

anticipation that the invasion would come in the Somme-
Calais area was that we should be forced to attack the area
where V-weapons were located at the earliest possible moment, in order to save London from destruction. He was told
that the effect of these weapons would be much greater than
it was in reality. Hitler built excessive hopes on them, and
that affected strategic calculations.

It was Hitler, however, who guessed that the Allied landings would come in Normandy. Blumentritt revealed this.
"At the end of March O.K.W. issued instructions which
showed that Hitler expected an invasion of Normandy. From
that time onward we received repeated warnings about it,
starting with the words—'The Führer fears . . .' I don't
know what led him to that conclusion. But as a result the
91st Air-landing Division with some tank squadrons was
moved down there, and posted in reserve behind the Cherbourg Peninsula—near Carentan."

Members of Rommel's staff had told me that he likewise
anticipated that our landings would take place in Normandy,
in contrast to Rundstedt's view. I asked Rundstedt and Blumentritt about this, and they said it was correct. Rommel
came round to that view increasingly in the spring. They did
not know how far it was his own judgement, or influenced by
Hitler's repeated warnings—"Watch Normandy."

It would seem that Hitler's much derided "intuition" was
nearer the mark than the calculations of the ablest professional soldiers. They were unduly influenced by their tendency to go by what was the proper course in orthodox
strategic theory—or by a conviction that the Allied planners
were sure to do the conventional thing. The value of doing
the "unexpected" was overlooked.

In this connection, Rundstedt made a significant disclosure
in answer to one of my questions. "If the Allies had landed
in western France, near the Loire, they could have succeeded
very easily—both in establishing a large enough bridgehead,
and then driving inland. I could not have moved a single

division there to stop them." Blumentritt added: "Such a landing would have met practically no opposition. There were only three divisions covering 300 miles of coast south of the Loire, and two of them were training divisions composed of raw recruits. A company commander on that coast had to cycle all day in covering his company sector. We regarded the Loire area as too far from England for air support, and thus assumed it was unlikely the Allied Command would attempt to land there—knowing how much they were inclined to count on ensuring maximum air cover."

On the same reasoning the German Command, except Rommel, thought that a landing in Normandy was less likely than where the Channel was narrower, and air support easier. Rundstedt said, too: "We thought that any landing in Normandy would be limited to an attempt to capture Cherbourg. The American landing near here was thus less unexpected than the British landing round Caen."

THE GERMAN DISPOSITIONS

In June, 1944, there were (to be exact) 59 German divisions in the West—eight of these being in Holland and Belgium. More than half the total were coast-defence or training divisions. Of the 27 field divisions, only 10 were armoured—three of these were in the south, and one near Antwerp.

Along the 200 mile stretch of the Normandy coast, west of the Seine, stood six divisions (four of them merely coast-defence). Three of these were in the Cherbourg Peninsula, two held the forty-mile stretch between there and Caen—from the Vire to the Orne—and one was between the Orne and the Seine. Blumentritt commented: "The dispositions would more truly be described as 'coast-protection' rather than as 'defence'! As we did not anticipate that any landing would be made on the west side of the Cherbourg Peninsula, that sector was held very lightly—we even put Russian units there."

There was one armoured division in the forward area, for counter-attack. This was the 21st Panzer Division. "There were prolonged arguments," Blumentritt said, "as to where the 21st Panzer Division should be placed. Field-Marshal von Rundstedt would have preferred it to be south of St. Lo, behind the Cherbourg Peninsula. But Rommel chose to put it nearer the coast and on the other flank, close to Caen. This meant that it was too near the coast to be really available as a reserve for the sector as a whole."

Nevertheless, the presence of that division near Caen proved an important factor. But for it, the British might have captured Caen on the first day of the landing. Rommel begged in vain for a second armoured division to be at hand near the mouth of the Vire—where the Americans landed.

Here we are brought to the great controversy that vitally affected the German plans to meet the invasion. Rundstedt felt that, with forces so limited and a coastline so long, it was not possible to prevent the Allies achieving a landing. He relied, therefore, on a powerful counter-offensive to throw them out—after they had committed themselves, but before they were well established.

Rommel, on the other hand, felt that the only chance lay in defeating the invaders on the coast, before they were properly ashore. "The first twenty-four hours will be decisive," he often said to his Staff. Blumentritt, though of the opposite school, explained Rommel's reasons to me most fairly: "Rommel had found in Africa that the tanks were apt to be too far back for delivering a counter-attack at the critical moment. He also felt that if the panzer reserves were kept far back inland, as the Commander-in-Chief preferred, their move-up would be interrupted by the Allied air force." From Rommel's own Staff I learnt that he was greatly influenced by the memory of the way he had been nailed down for days on end in Africa by an air force that was not nearly so strong as what he now had to face.

But neither Rundstedt's nor Rommel's plan prevailed. Each was prevented from doing what he thought best.

"Before the Allied invasion," Rundstedt said, "I had wanted to evacuate the whole of southern France up to the Loire, and bring back the forces there to form a strong mass of manœuvre with which I could strike back at the Allies. This would have provided ten or twelve infantry divisions and three or four armoured divisions to fight a mobile battle. But Hitler would not listen to such an idea—though it was the only way in which I could hope to form a proper reserve. All the newspaper talk about 'Rundstedt's Central Army' was sheer nonsense—that Army did not exist. Worse still, I was not even allowed a free hand with the handful of armoured divisions that were available in France. I could not move one of them without Hitler's permission."

But Rommel was also narrowly restricted in applying his different idea. That was not really due to Rundstedt but to lack of reserves. He was allowed to place his divisions where he wished. As Rundstedt said to me—"While I did not like them being so near the coast, it would not have been right for me to interfere with the commander on the spot in such matters of detail—it was only Hitler who interfered in that way." But Rommel had only three armoured divisions for his whole front, from the Loire to the Scheldt—one for the Eastern, one for the Central and one for the Western sector. These had not nearly the number of tanks that a British or American armoured division possessed. It was a very light punch with which to counter a powerful invasion.

The chances were further diminished by earlier neglect to develop the coast defences. From Rommel's staff I heard of the feverish efforts he made in the Spring of 1944 to hasten the construction of under-water obstacles, bomb-proof bunkers, and mine-fields along the Normandy coast—where, he correctly judged, the invasion would come. For example, less than two million mines had been laid along the whole north coast of France in the three years before he arrived on the scene. In the few months before D-day the number was trebled —but he was aiming at over fifty million mines. It was fortunate for the invaders that there was so much more to do than could be achieved in the short time available.

Rundstedt's explanation to me was: "The lack of labour troops and material was the main handicap in developing the defences. Most of the men of the Todt labour force, who had been previously available in France, had been drawn off to Germany to repair air raid damage there. At the same time, the coast defence divisions were too widely extended—often over a forty-mile stretch—to carry out the necessary work themselves. Beyond this, there was not enough material for the job—owing to the constant interference of the Allied Air Forces, which checked both the manufacture and the movement of the necessary material."

But this does not cover the earlier neglect, in 1942 and 1943, of which Rommel complained. A deeper explanation may be that Rundstedt, a masterly exponent of mobile offensive warfare, had little belief in the value of static defences, and so gave too little attention to their construction. That is the view of Rommel's staff, and is in accord with the type of counter-offensive plan on which Rundstedt relied. It was a very natural attitude for the man who had manœuvred the French out of the Maginot Line.

The measures to meet the Allied invasion "fell between two stools"—as the result of the conflict of opinion between Rundstedt's and Rommel's ideas, multiplied by Hitler's tight hand on the reserves. It had more effect in opening the way into France than anything the Allies did to achieve surprise.

THE LANDING

"The coming of the invasion," Blumentritt remarked, "could be recognized by many signs. Increasing disorder in the interior became a serious threat, and caused us considerable loss —through ambushes and raids. There were many derail-

ments of trains that were carrying supplies and reinforcements to the front. Beyond this was the planned destruction
by air bombing of the railways in France and Western Germany—especially of the bridges across the Somme, the Seine
and the Loire. All these were pointers."

Rundstedt emphasized: "Although we had no definite report of the date of the invasion that did not matter, as we had
been expecting it any time from March onward." I asked
whether the storm that postponed the launching twenty-four
hours, and nearly compelled its cancellation, had not lulled
the defenders into a sense of security at the critical moment.
Blumentritt replied: "No, it didn't have that effect—because
we thought the Allies were sure to have the kind of vessels that
would not be affected by heavy seas. So we were always on
tenter-hooks, and just as ready at one time as another."

Rundstedt went on: "The one real surprise was the time of
day at which the landing was made—because our Naval Staff
had told us that the Allied forces would only land at high
water. A further effect of your choice of low tide, for the
landing, was that the leading troops were protected from
fire to a considerable extent by the rocks.

"The scale of the invading forces was not a surprise—in
fact, we had imagined that they would be larger, because we
had received exaggerated reports of the number of American
divisions present in England. But that over-estimate had an
indirect effect of important consequence, by making us the
more inclined to expect a second landing, in the Calais area."

Blumentritt related to me the story of D-day, from the
point of view of the German Headquarters in the West—
which was located at St. Germain, just west of Paris. (Rommel's headquarters was at La Roche Guyon, midway between
Paris and Rouen, but, as at Alamein, he was off the scene when
the blow fell, being on his way to see Hitler.)

"About 10 P.M. on June 5th we intercepted messages between the French Resistance Movement and England from
which it was deducted that the invaders were coming. Our

15th Army east of the Seine at once issued the 'Alarm,' though for some reason the 7th Army in Normandy delayed doing so until 4 A.M.[1] That was unfortunate. Soon after midnight news came that Allied parachute troops had begun dropping.

"Time was vital. The nearest available part of the general reserve was the 1st S.S. Panzer Corps, which lay north-west of Paris. But we could not move it without permission from Hitler's headquarters. As early as 4 A.M. Field-Marshal von Rundstedt telephoned them, and asked for the release of this Corps—to strengthen Rommel's punch. But Jodl, speaking for Hitler, refused to do so. He doubted whether the landings in Normandy were more than a feint, and was sure that another landing was coming east of the Seine. The 'battle' of argument went on all day until 4 P.M., when this Corps was at last released for our use.

"Then further difficulties interfered with its move. The Corps artillery had been kept on the east bank of the Seine —and the Allied Air Forces had destroyed the bridges. The Field-Marshal and I had seen some of them being smashed. The artillery thus had to make a long circuit southward by way of Paris before they could get across the Seine, and was repeatedly bombed on the march, which caused more delays. As a result two days passed before this reserve was on the scene, ready to strike."

By that time the Allied forces were well established ashore, and the chances of an early counter-stroke had faded. The armoured divisions became absorbed in the fight piecemeal, in the effort to check the invaders from spreading farther inland, instead of being used to drive them back into the sea.

I asked Rundstedt whether he had hopes of defeating the invasion at any stage after the landing. He replied: "Not after the first few days. The Allied Air Forces paralyzed all movement by day, and made it very difficult even at night. They had smashed the bridges over the Loire as well as over the

---

[1] According to 7th Army records, however, the alarm there was issued at 1.30 A.M.

Seine, shutting off the whole area. These factors greatly de-layed the concentration of reserves there—they took three or four times longer to reach the front than we had reckoned."

Rundstedt added: "Besides the interference of the Air Forces, the fire of your battleships was a main factor in hampering our counter-stroke. This was a big surprise, both in its range and effect." Blumentritt remarked that army officers who interrogated him after the war did not seem to have realized what a serious effect this naval bombardment had.

But there was still another cause of delay. Rundstedt and Blumentritt said that after about a fortnight they came to the conclusion that the expected second landing east of the Seine was not coming, but Hitler's headquarters were still con-vinced it was, and were reluctant to let them move forces westward to Normandy from the Calais area. Nor were they allowed to reshuffle their forces in Normandy as they wished. "In desperation, Field-Marshal von Rundstedt begged Hitler to come to France for a talk. He and Rommel together went to meet Hitler at Soissons, and tried to make him under-stand the situation. Although Caen and St. Lo, the two pivots of the Normandy position, were still in our hands, it was obvious they could not be held much longer. The two Field-Marshals were now in full agreement as to the only step that might save the situation short of a big retreat—which they knew Hitler would not permit. They wanted to withdraw from Caen, leave the infantry to hold the line of the Orne, and pull out the armoured divisions to refit and reorganize. Their plan was to use the latter for a powerful counter-stroke against the Americans' flank in the Cherbourg Peninsula.

"But Hitler insisted that there must be no withdrawal—'You must stay where you are.' He would not even agree to allow us any more freedom than before in moving the forces as we thought best.

"The Field-Marshal and I had come to realize more and more clearly, since the second week, that we could not drive the invading forces back into the sea. But Hitler still believed it was possible! As he would not modify his orders, the troops had to continue clinging on to their cracking line. There was no plan any longer. We were merely trying, without hope, to comply with Hitler's order that the line Caen-Avranches must be held at all costs."

While referring sympathetically to the sufferings of the troops, Blumentritt remarked: "They did not stand artillery fire as well as our troops had done in the last war. The German infantry of this war were not as good as in 1914-18. The rank and file had too many ideas of their own—they were not so disciplined and obedient. The quality of the army had suffered from its too rapid expansion, which did not allow time for a thorough disciplinary training."

The meeting with Hitler was followed by Rundstedt's removal from command—for the time being. "Field-Marshal von Rundstedt had flatly said that he could not carry on unless he had a free hand. In view of this, and of the pessimistic tone of his reports on the situation, Hitler decided to find a new commander. He wrote the Field-Marshal a letter, which was quite pleasantly worded, saying that he had come to the conclusion that, in the circumstances, it was best to make a change."

That decision of Hitler's was influenced by another piece of plain speaking on Rundstedt's part, according to Blumentritt. Keitel had rung him up to ask about the situation, and after hearing Rundstedt's gloomy report, had plaintively asked: "What shall we do?" Rundstedt pungently replied: "End the war! What else can you do?"

COLLAPSE UNDER BACK-AND-FRONT STRAIN

Field-Marshal von Kluge happened to be visiting Hitler's headquarters at that moment. He had been on the sick list for nine months recovering from the injuries sustained in a bad air crash in Russia, but Hitler had sent for him at the beginning of July in view of the precarious situation on the Eastern front. Hitler's idea was to send him back there to replace Busch, as commander of the Central Army Group, which was cracking under the strain of the Russian summer offensive that had just opened. According to Blumentritt, Kluge was actually with Hitler, when Keitel came in and told Hitler what Rundstedt had said on the telephone. Thereupon Hitler at once decided that Kluge must go to take charge in the West instead of in the East (where General Model was now promoted to replace Busch). While the decision was taken on the spur of the moment, it had long been in Hitler's mind that Kluge should be Rundstedt's deputy if the need arose.

"Field-Marshal von Kluge was a robust, aggressive type of soldier," Blumentritt remarked. "He arrived at our headquarters at St. Germain on July 6th to take up his new appointment as Commander-in-Chief in the West. At the start he was very cheerful and confident—like all newly-appointed commanders. Indeed, he was almost gay about the prospects.

"In our first talk he reproached me because we had forwarded, and endorsed, Rommel's report on the gravity of the situation in France. He said such a pessimistic report ought not to have been sent to the Führer but should have been modified by us before it was forwarded. Field-Marshal von Rundstedt was still at St. Germain at the moment—he stayed there for three days after Field-Marshal von Kluge arrived. When I told him what Field-Marshal von Kluge had said, he was rather shocked and declared emphatically: 'It was proper that such an important document should be forwarded without any alteration by a superior headquarters.'

"While Field-Marshal von Kluge clearly thought at first that the dangers of the situation had been exaggerated, his view soon changed. For he was quick to visit the front, as was his habit. While there he saw the Commander of the 7th Army, Hausser, the Commander of the 5th Panzer Army, Eberbach, and then the various corps commanders—including the 1st and 2nd S.S. Corps. All of them pointed out to him

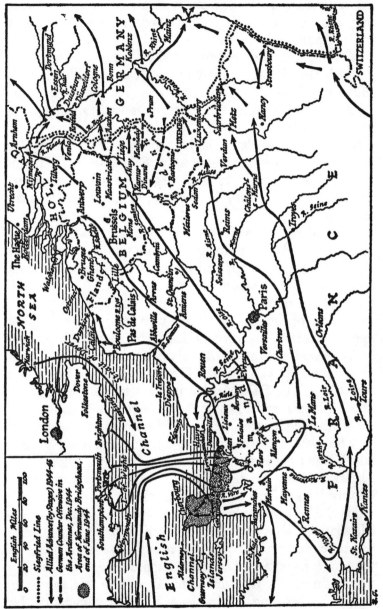

WESTERN FRONT 1944-45

the seriousness of the situation. Within a few days he became very sober and quiet. Hitler did not like the changing tone of his reports.

"On the 17th Rommel was badly injured when his car crashed, after being attacked on the road by Allied 'planes. Hitler then instructed Field-Marshal von Kluge to take charge of Army Group 'B' for the moment, as well as being Commander-in-Chief."

Then, three days later, on July 20th, came the attempt to kill Hitler at his headquarters in East Prussia. The conspirators' bomb missed its chief target, but it had terrific repercussions on the battle in the West at the critical moment there.

"Field-Marshal von Kluge was at the front that day and I was not able to get into touch with him until the evening. By that time he had already had the messages about the attempt —first that it had succeeded, and then that Hitler was still alive. The Field-Marshal told me that, more than a year before, some of the leading officers who were in the plot had approached him, and that he had received them twice, but at the second meeting he had told them that he did not want to be mixed up with the plot. He knew, however, that it was continuing. The Field-Marshal had not said anything to me about it before, and I had not been aware of the plot.

"When the Gestapo investigated the conspiracy, in the days that followed, they found documents in which Field-Marshal von Kluge's name was mentioned, so he came under grave suspicion. Then another incident made things look worse. Shortly before General Patton's break-out from Normandy, while the decisive battle at Avranches was in progress, Field-Marshal von Kluge was out of touch with his headquarters for more than twelve hours. The reason was that he had gone up to the front, and there been trapped in a heavy artillery bombardment. At the same time his wireless tender was destroyed by bombing, so that he could not communicate. He himself had to stay under cover for several hours before he

could get out and start on the long drive back to his headquarters. Meantime, we had been suffering 'bombardment'
from the rear. For the Field-Marshal's prolonged 'absence'
excited Hitler's suspicion immediately, in view of the documents that had been found. A telegram came from Hitler per-
emptorily stating 'Field-Marshal von Kluge is at once to
extricate himself from the battle area around Avranches and
conduct the battle of Normandy from the tactical headquarters of the 5th Panzer Army.' This was back near Falaise.

"The reason for this order, as I heard subsequently, was that
Hitler suspected that the Field-Marshal's purpose in going
right up to the front, was to get in touch with the Allies and
negotiate a surrender. The Field-Marshal's eventual return
did not calm Hitler. From this date onward the orders which
he sent him were worded in a brusque and even insulting
language. Field-Marshal von Kluge became very worried. He
feared that he would be arrested at any moment—and at the
same time realized more and more that he could not prove his
loyalty by any battlefield success.

"All this had a very bad effect on any chance that remained
of preventing the Allies from breaking out. In the days of
crisis Field-Marshal von Kluge gave only part of his attention
to what was happening at the front. He was looking back over
his shoulder anxiously—towards Hitler's headquarters.

"He was not the only general who was in that state of
worry for conspiracy in the plot against Hitler. Fear per-
meated and paralyzed the higher commands in the weeks
and months that followed. The influence on the generals of
July 20th is a subject that would form a book in itself."

After General Patton's break-out from Normandy, and the
collapse of the front in the West, Field-Marshal Model suddenly arrived on August 17th as the new Commander-in-
Chief. "His arrival was the first news of the change that Field-
Marshal von Kluge received—this sudden arrival of a successor
had become the customary manner of dismissal at this time
and had already happened in the case of the commanders of

the 19th and 15th Armies. At that moment Field-Marshal von Kluge was at Laroche-Guyon, the headquarters of Army Group 'B.' He stayed on there for twenty-four hours putting Field-Marshal Model in the picture.

"I went over there from St. Germain to say good-bye to him, and saw him alone. As I went in he was sitting at his table with a map in front of him. He kept tapping it at the point marked 'Avranches'—where Patton had broken through—and said to me: 'That is where I lose my reputation as a soldier.' I tried to console him, but with little effect. He walked up and down the room ruminating gloomily. He showed me the letter from the Führer, that Field-Marshal Model had brought him. It was written in quite polite terms—the Führer saying that he felt the strain of the battle was too much for the Field-Marshal and that a change was desirable. But the last sentence of the letter had an ominous note—'Field-Marshal von Kluge is to state to which part of Germany he is going.' The Field-Marshal said to me: 'I have written a letter to the Führer in which I have explained to him clearly the military position, and also other matters'—but he did not show me this letter." [1]

[1] The letter was found by the Allies in the captured German Archives. After acknowledging the order for his replacement, and remarking that the obvious reason for it was the failure to close the gap at Avranches, it went on to say—"When you receive these lines . . . I shall be no more. I cannot bear the reproach that I have sealed the fate of the West through faulty measures, and I have no means of defending myself. I draw a conclusion from that and am dispatching myself where already thousands of my comrades are. I have never feared death. Life has no more meaning for me, and I also figure on the list of war criminals who are to be delivered up." The letter then went on to a long and detailed exposition of the practical impossibility of averting the collapse at Avranches, and a mild rebuke to Hitler for not attending to the warnings he had been given both by Rommel and Kluge himself as to the critical position.

"Our appreciations were *not* dictated by pessimism but by sober knowledge of the facts. I do not know if Field-Marshal Model, who has been proved in every sphere, will still master the situation. From my heart I hope so. Should it not be so, however, and your cherished new weapons not succeed, then, my Führer, make up your mind to end the war. The German people have borne such untold suffering that it is time to put an end to this frightfulness. There

"Field-Marshal von Kluge left for home next day. On the evening of the day after his departure I had a telephone call from Metz to say that he had had a heart attack, and had died. Two days later came a medical report stating that his death was due to a cerebral hæmorrhage. Then came word that he was to have a State Funeral, and that Field-Marshal von Rundstedt had been instructed by the Führer to represent him in laying a wreath and delivering the Funeral Oration. Then came a sudden order that there was to be no State Funeral. I then heard that Field-Marshal von Kluge had taken poison, and that this had been confirmed by a post-mortem. Like other generals who had been on the Eastern front, he had carried poison capsules in case of being captured by the Russians—though many did not take them even when they were captured. He had swallowed one of these capsules in the car and was dead before he arrived in Metz. My opinion is that he committed suicide, not because of his dismissal, but because he believed he would be arrested by the Gestapo as soon as he arrived home."

While Kluge committed suicide of his own accord, Rommel was compelled to swallow a similar dose, just over a month later, while he was still convalescing from his accident. Two fellow-generals visited him, under orders from Hitler, and took him out for a drive and there confronted him with Hitler's decision that he must commit suicide or be brought to trial —with the certainty of a degrading execution. He had been more definitely implicated in the plot. A realization of the hopelessness of the situation in the West had brought him into revolt at an earlier stage. I was told by his staff that he had little confidence in the prospect even before the Allies landed and thereafter became increasingly critical of Hitler's lack of a sense of reality.

After the Allies had succeeded in establishing their bridge-

must be ways to attain this end, and above all to prevent the Reich from falling under the Bolshevist heel." The letter ended with a final tribute to Hitler's greatness and affirmation of Kluge's loyalty even in death.

head in Normandy he said to one of them: "All is over. It would be much better for us to end the war now, and live as a British dominion, than to be ruined by continuing such a hopeless struggle." Realizing that Hitler was the main obstacle to peace Rommel openly said that the only thing was to do away with him and then approach the Allies. That was a remarkable change of attitude in Hitler's favourite general. It cost Rommel his life, but it was too late to save Germany.

Talking of the general breakdown which followed Patton's break-out from the Normandy bridgehead, Blumentritt made another significant revelation. "Hitler and his staff at O.K.W. had been deluded, in postponing a withdrawal so long, by their belief that our forces would have time to get back and occupy new lines in rear, if the need arose. They counted on the British advance being deliberate, and on the Americans being clumsy. But Pétain, who was an old acquaintance of Field-Marshal Rundstedt's, had several times warned him not to underrate the speed with which the Americans could move, once they had gained experience. The event proved it. The lines in rear which O.K.W. had reckoned on holding were successively outflanked by Patton's dash before they were even occupied."

✳   ✳   ✳

After following the course of the decisive break-through as the German High Command saw it, it is worth while to supplement it by a short account of how it appeared, and felt, to the fighting commanders on the spot.

A graphic impression of the American break-through at Avranches as it looked from the German side was given me by General Elfeldt who commanded the 84th Corps, holding that sector, at the foot of the Cherbourg Peninsula. He was only sent there to take over charge just as the decisive offensive was opening. Until then he had been commanding the 47th Division, which held the Calais-Boulogne sector. "It was on the 28th July, so far as I remember, that orders came for me to go at once to Field-Marshal von Kluge's headquarters. On arrival he told me that I was to take over command of the 84th Corps from General von Choltitz. He said he did not agree with the defence policy of the latter, but did not say in what respect. The Corps, he told me, comprised the remnants of seven divisions. He also said that the 116th Panzer Division was to counter-attack westward to relieve the pressure, and would be under my command. After spending the night with the Field-Marshal I drove in the morning to Le Mans and on to the tactical headquarters of the 7th Army, which was then 10 to 15 kilometres east of Avranches. From there I was directed to my own corps headquarters. I do not remember exactly where it was, as it was hidden in the trees, away from any village. Everything was confused, and the Allied air force dominated the area. On the following day I went round my troops. They were very weak and there was no continuous front. Some of the divisions had only about three hundred infantry left, and the artillery was much depleted.

"The first order I gave was that all the troops south of the River La See, near Avranches, were to defend the south bank, while the troops from the east were to hang on where they were until the 116th Panzer Division arrived that night; they were then to join in its counter-attack. But the 116th did not arrive, as it was diverted to another danger point while on the way. On the morning of the 31st American tanks drove towards Brescy, on the River See, 15 kilometres east of Avranches. At that moment my headquarters was north of Brescy, and was nearly cut off by this flank thrust. My headquarters personnel were in the fighting line all day. Luckily the Americans were not very vigorous in their thrust here.

"In the next two days I was reinforced by two new divisions which were nearly up to strength, as well as by the 116th Panzer Division. I formed the remnants of the other seven divisions into a single one. My orders were to stop a

further break-through between Brescy and Vire, and to delay the expected American thrust south-eastwards from
Avranches, as a powerful counter-thrust was to be made by a
panzer corps, under General von Funk. This was subsequently
reinforced, to provide a counter-stroke of bigger scale, by all
the tanks that could be made available from Eberbach's 5th
Panzer Army."

Elfeldt went on to describe at length the even more precarious situation that developed, after the armoured stroke
had failed to reach Avranches, and his left flank was increasingly outflanked. He wheeled back gradually to the eastward,
and the difficulties of the withdrawal were the greater because
the armoured forces retired through his front, creating confusion. Fortunately the American pressure on his front and
immediate flanks was not too dangerous—Patton's 3rd Army
was moving on a wider circuit. "The American troops, of the
1st Army, on my front were not tactically at all clever. They
failed to seize opportunities—in particular they missed several
chances of cutting off the whole of my corps. The Allied air
force was the most serious danger.

"By the time we had got back to the Orne the whole front
had become much narrower than before, so my corps headquarters had become superfluous and was temporarily withdrawn from the line. But the following morning the Cana-
dians broke through southwards to Falaise and I was at once
ordered to form a front to check them. The available troops
were very scanty and we had no communications. The
Canadian artillery fired all day into my headquarters, but
fortunately did no damage at all although they fired about
a thousand shells. These fell all round the small house in
which I was, but no one was hurt. During the day I was able
to re-form a continuous line, but beyond my right flank I
could see the British tanks driving down the other side of the
River Dives towards Trun. Thus our line of retreat was
blocked.

"The next day I was ordered to break out *north*-eastward,

behind the backs of these armoured forces. It was soon clear that this was not possible, as the British were now there in strength. So I proposed to the army commander, General Hausser, that my troops should be placed at the disposal of General Meindl, who was commanding the parachute forces, to help the latter to break out near St. Lambert, *south*-eastward. It seemed to me that one strong thrust might have a better chance than a number of small ones. Meindl succeeded in breaking out, but when I reached St. Lambert myself next morning the gap was again closed. I tried an attack with all I had left—a couple of tanks and two hundred men. It started well but then ran into part of the 1st Polish Armoured Division. After a two-hour fight our ammunition began to run out. Then the troops which were following behind me surrendered, thus leaving me with a handful of men at the cut-off tip of the wedge. So we had to surrender in turn. The commander of this Polish division was a fine-looking man and a gentleman. He gave me his last cigarette. His division itself was in an awkward situation and had run out of water —the forces of the two sides were extraordinarily intermingled."

❋   ❋   ❋

I took the opportunity of asking Elfeldt what he thought about the German soldier in this war compared with the previous war. His views differed in some respects from those of Blumentritt (*see page* 259). "The infantry were quite as good as in 1914-18, and the artillery much better. Weapons had improved, and so had tactics. But there were other factors. In the last two years of the first war, the morale of the troops became affected by the spread of Socialistic ideas that were pacifist in trend. In this war, National Socialism had the opposite effect—it fortified their morale."

"How did discipline compare in the two wars?" "That is more difficult to answer. National Socialism made the troops more fanatical—which was both good and bad for discipline. But relations between officers and men were better than in 1914-18, and that helped discipline. The improved relationship was due partly to the new conception of discipline that was inculcated in the Reichswehr, based on the experience of 1914-18, and partly to the subsequent influence of National Socialism in diminishing the gulf between officers and men. The ordinary soldiers showed more initiative, and used their heads better in this war than they did in the last—especially when fighting on their own or in small parties." On this score Elfeldt's opinion corresponded with the judgement of British commanders, who often remarked how the German soldiers excelled their opponents when operating alone or in pairs— a verdict that was in surprising contrast to the experience of 1914-18, as well as to the continuing popular view that the Germans were no good as individualists. Since National Socialism made so strong an appeal to the herd instinct, the natural assumption was that the generation which grew up under it would show less, not more, individual initiative on the battlefield than their fathers. I asked Elfeldt if he could suggest an explanation. He said that he himself was puzzled, but added, "I think it may have been due to the kind of scout training these young soldiers had received in the 'Hitler Youth' organization."

The question how the German soldier of the two wars compared came up again, a few days later, in a discussion with Heinrici, Röhricht, and Bechtolsheim. Heinrici's view was that the German Army was better trained in the first war, but he did not consider that the discipline had been better. Röhricht and Bechtolsheim agreed, and the former added: "The Army needed a long interval between the Polish and the Western campaigns to develop its training—especially the training of the non-commissioned officers. As head of the Training Department of the General Staff, I was in close touch with this question. But morale, and discipline, were better in the later part of this war than in the later part of the first war. Between 1916 and 1918 the soldiers' morale was gradually undermined by the infiltration of Socialistic ideas, and the suggestion that they were fighting the Emperor's war, whereas this time they had and kept such extraordinary confidence in Hitler that they remained confident of victory in face of all the facts."

Heinrici and Bechtolsheim endorsed this statement of Röhricht's, who went on to say: "Nevertheless the morale of the Army was gradually weakened by the effects of overstrain, and by the tendency of the S.S. to grab the best men. On the Eastern Front the divisions never got a rest, and that became a debilitating factor."

In reply to a further question about the effect of National Socialism on the Army, Röhricht said: "It had a mixed effect. It created difficulties for us, and weakened our control, but it fostered an ardent patriotic spirit in the soldiers, which went deeper than the spirit of 1914—for this time there was no enthusiasm for war such as there had been then. That spirit had greater endurance under reverses." Heinrici agreed with Röhricht, while emphasizing that faith in a personality counted for more than the system. "The troops' tremendous confidence in Hitler was the dominant factor, whether one liked it or not."

❋   ❋   ❋

What did the German generals think of their Western opponents? They were diffident in expressing an opinion on this matter, but I gathered a few impressions in the course of our talks. In a reference to the Allied commanders, Rundstedt said: "Montgomery and Patton were the two best that I met. Field-Marshal Montgomery was very systematic." He added: "That is all right if you have sufficient forces, and sufficient time." Blumentritt made a similar comment. After paying tribute to the speed of Patton's drive, he added: "Field-Marshal Montgomery was the one general who never suffered a reverse. He moved like this"—Blumentritt took a series of very deliberate and short steps, putting his foot down heavily each time.

Giving his impression of the different qualities of the British and American troops, Blumentritt said: "The Americans attacked with zest, and had a keen sense of mobile action, but when they came under heavy artillery fire they usually fell back—even after they had made a successful penetration. By contrast, once the British had got their teeth in, and had been in a position for twenty-four hours, it proved almost impossible to shift them. To counter-attack the British always cost us very heavy losses. I had many opportunities to observe this interesting difference in the autumn of 1944, when the right half of my corps faced the British, and the left half the American."

XVIII

THE ANTI-HITLER PLOT—AS SEEN FROM H.Q. IN THE WEST

THE STORY OF THE 20TH JULY PLOT HAS BEEN TOLD FROM many angles, but not from that which has the closest bearing on the military issue. A fairly clear picture has emerged about what happened after the bomb exploded at Hitler's headquarters in East Prussia, and failed to kill him; also about the course of events in Berlin, and how the conspirators there failed to seize their momentary opportunity. To complete the picture it is important to trace what happened on that fateful day at German Headquarters in the West. I had a long account of this, and the subsequent reactions, from General Blumentritt which is worth giving in full—not only for its direct evidence, but for the atmosphere it conveys.

BLUMENTRITT'S ACCOUNT

During the early months of 1944 there were many visitors to Supreme Headquarters, Western Front, at St. Germain, and long discussions of the war-situation. A matter that was often mooted was whether the field-marshals should jointly approach Hitler and urge him to make peace.

One day, about the end of March, Field-Marshal Rommel

came to St. Germain accompanied by his Chief of Staff, General Speidel. Just before they left, Speidel said he wanted to have a word with me in private. When we had withdrawn, Speidel told me that he was speaking on Rommel's behalf and then said: "The time has come when we must tell the Führer that we cannot continue the war." It was agreed that we should broach the matter to Field-Marshal Rundstedt, and this was done. We found that he was of the same opinion. A telegram was then sent to O.K.W., asking the Führer to come to St. Germain "in view of the serious situation in France." But no reply was received.

General Speidel came to see me again about the matter, and in the course of our conversations told me that there were a number of people in Germany who were intending to tackle Hitler. He mentioned the names of Field-Marshal von Witzleben, General Beck, General Hoeppner, and Dr. Goerdeler. He also said that Field-Marshal Rommel had given him a few days leave to go to Stuttgart to discuss the matter with others there—both Speidel and Rommel came from the state of Wurtemburg, and had long known Goerdeler. But in these conversations Speidel never indicated that the assassination of Hitler was contemplated.

Nothing further developed before Field-Marshal von Kluge arrived to replace Field-Marshal von Rundstedt as Commander-in-Chief in the West—following the latter's heated telephone talk with Field-Marshal Keitel, in which he had insisted that the war ought to be brought to an end. I would add a little more about this change. Hitler knew that Field-Marshal von Rundstedt was much respected by the Army, and by the enemy. Allied propaganda broadcasts often suggested that the views of the Field-Marshal and his staff differed from those of Hitler. It was notable, too, our headquarters was never subjected to air attack. Nor was the Field-Marshal ever threatened by the French Resistance Movement—presumably, because it was known that he had always been in favour of good treatment for the French. All these things were brought to Hitler's notice, of course, in reports from his own agents. While he treated the Field-Marshal with respect—more respect than he showed other soldiers—he kept him under careful watch. Then, the Field-Marshal's emphatic advice about seeking peace provided Hitler with a suitable ground for replacing him.

Field-Marshal von Kluge arrived at St. Germain, to take over, on July 6th. On the 17th Field-Marshal Rommel was knocked out. Thereupon von Kluge moved to Rommel's headquarters at La Roche-Guyon, to conduct the battle from there, leaving me in charge at St. Germain.

JULY 20TH

The first news of the attempt on Hitler's life reached me about 3 P.M.—from Colonel Finck, the Deputy Chief of Staff, who had been transferred from the Eastern front about six weeks earlier. Colonel Finck came into my room and said: "General, the Führer is dead. A Gestapo mutiny has taken place in Berlin." I was very surprised, and asked how he had heard. Finck replied that it had come from General von Stulpnagel, the Military Governor of Paris, on the telephone.

I tried to get hold of Field-Marshal von Kluge on the telephone, at La Roche-Guyon, but was told that he was visiting the front. I then told Speidel in very guarded terms—as we were talking over the telephone—that there were serious developments, and that I would drive over myself to tell him what had happened. I left St. Germain about 4 P.M. and arrived at La Roche-Guyon about 5.30 P.M.

Field-Marshal von Kluge had just returned there. When I went into his room I saw that he had in front of him an extract from the German Radio to the effect that an attempt had been made on the life of the Führer, but that it had failed. Von Kluge told me that he had previously had two telephone messages from Germany, but without any indication of the sender's identity, which said: "The Führer is dead and you must make a decision." Von Kluge went on to say that, about a year before, Witzleben, Beck and others had come to his home to sound him about an approach to the Führer and how it should be conducted. He also said that he had made notes of these discussions.

While we were talking a telephone message from St. Germain was brought in. It said that an anonymous telegram had arrived there stating that Hitler was dead. Kluge was puzzled as to which of the statements were true, and wondered whether the Radio was merely putting out a false report. After some further discussion I put a telephone call in to General Warlimont, Jodl's deputy, at O.K.W. It was a long time before the call came through. Then the reply was merely that Warlimont was not available, as he was engaged with Keitel.

So von Kluge and I put our heads together, and discussed whom we could try next. We telephoned the Chief of the S.S. in Paris. He replied that he did not know anything beyond the radio announcement. We then telephoned General Stieff —the Chief of the Organization Department—at O.K.H. I knew Stieff well, but had no idea that he was in the inner circle of the conspiracy, as later emerged. Stieff at once asked: "Where did you get the news that the Führer was dead?" He added: "The Führer is quite well, and in good spirits"— and then rang off. We felt very uneasy about this telephone call afterwards, realizing how suspicious it must have appeared in the circumstances.

Stieff's answer and manner were so curious as to suggest a likely explanation, and I remarked to von Kluge: "This is an attempt that failed." Von Kluge then said to me that, if it had succeeded, his first step would have been to order the discharge of the V1's against England to be stopped, and that his second step would have been to get in touch with the Allied Commanders.

Von Kluge then instructed me to telephone General von Stulpnagel, and tell him to come to La Roche-Guyon. I was also to summon Field-Marshal Sperrle, commanding the Luft-waffe in the West.

General von Stulpnagel arrived first, about 7.30 P.M., ac-companied by Lieut.-Colonel Hoffacker. They sat round a table with the Field-Marshal, Speidel and I—all the circle are dead now, except Speidel and I. Von Stulpnagel began by say-ing: "May Lieut.-Colonel Hoffacker explain matters." It soon became clear that Hoffacker knew all about the attempt, and was the link between von Stulpnagel and von Witzleben. He traced how the plot had developed from an intended petition into a *putsch*—as it was realized that Hitler would not listen to argument, and that the Allies would not listen to any peace offer from Hitler. He told how von Stauffenberg had organized the actual attempt, and gave us the details.

When he had finished, von Kluge, with obvious disappoint-ment, remarked: "Well, gentlemen, the attempt has failed. Everything is over." Von Stulpnagel then exclaimed: "Field-Marshal, I thought you were acquainted with the plans. Some-thing must be *done*." Von Kluge replied: "Nothing more can be done. The Führer is still alive." I noticed that von Stulpnagel had begun to look very uncomfortable. He got up and walked out on the verandah. When he returned, he said very little.

Then Field-Marshal Sperrle arrived—and only stayed a few minutes. He refused von Kluge's invitation to remain for din-ner. I felt that Sperrle did not want to get drawn into the discussion, or be a witness of anything that transpired.

The rest of us now went in to dinner. Von Kluge seemed very vivacious and unworried in manner, whereas von Stulp-nagel was taciturn. After a while he turned to von Kluge and said: "May I speak to you privately again?" Von Kluge agreed —and said to me, "You come too." We went into a small room. Here von Stulpnagel told me that he had taken "the first precautions" before leaving Paris. Von Kluge exclaimed: "Heavens! What have you been doing?" "I gave orders for all the S.S. in Paris to be arrested"—by this he meant not the Waffen S.S., but the S.D., or Security Service.

Von Kluge exclaimed: "But you can't do that without my orders." Von Stulpnagel replied: "I tried to telephone you this afternoon but you were away from your H.Q., so I had to act on my own." Von Kluge remarked: "Well, that's your responsibility." After that, they didn't go back to finish their dinner.

Von Kluge then told me to telephone to von Stulpnagel's Chief of Staff in Paris and ask whether steps had actually been taken to arrest the S.S. This was Colonel von Linstow—who is also dead.[1] He told me that steps had been taken, adding, "And nothing can stop them." Von Kluge then said to von Stulpnagel: "Look here, the best thing you can do is to change into civilian clothes and go into hiding." He told von Stulpnagel to release all the arrested S.S. at once.

After von Stulpnagel had gone, I said to von Kluge: "We ought to do something to help him." Von Kluge pondered my suggestion and then told me to drive after von Stulpnagel, and advise him to disappear somewhere in Paris for a few days. Strictly, of course, von Kluge should have placed him under arrest.

I drove to St. Germain first. On arrival there my staff brought me fresh telegrams which had come while I had been away. One was from Field-Marshal Keitel; it said that all reports of the Führer's death were false, and all orders sent on that assumption were to be ignored. Another was from General Fromm, saying that Himmler had just taken over command of the home forces from him—Hitler no longer trusted any of the generals in Germany. A third was from Himmler—simply saying that he had taken over command of the home forces. While I was reading the telegrams a telephone call came from Admiral Krancke, the Naval C-in-C in the West—the Field-Marshal had not thought of calling him to the conference—to ask if I would drive into Paris to see him.

[1] Blumentritt's narrative was punctuated with repetitions of "tot" (dead).

About an hour after midnight I set off for Paris, where I found all the Naval H.Q. staff assembled. Admiral Krancke showed me a long telegram he had received from Field-Marshal von Witzleben, saying that the Führer was dead, and that a new government was being formed, under himself for the time being. Thereupon Krancke had telephoned O.K.W. and by chance had been put through to Admiral Doenitz, who said that it was untrue.

I then went on to the H.Q. of the Security Police. They were just coming back from prison. The first officers I saw wanted to know what had happened and why they had been arrested without any reason. Their attitude was very decent, and they showed a willingness to help in hushing things up. I asked where Obergruppenführer Oberg, the Chief of the Security Police, was at the moment. I was told that he was at a hotel, along with von Stulpnagel.

I went on there, about 2 A.M., and found what was almost like a party in progress—including Abetz, the Ambassador in Paris. Oberg took me aside into another room, and told me that he had no idea what was behind the situation, but that we must agree as to what ought to be done next. I must say that, throughout, Oberg behaved very decently, and tried to smooth things over for the sake of the Army. He suggested that the regiment that had carried out the arrests should be confined to barracks, and that the men should be told that it had been merely an exercise. But von Stulpnagel considered that it was impossible to prevent a leakage. I then conveyed von Kluge's advice to von Stulpnagel—that he should disappear. But when I got back to St. Germain I found that a message had already come from O.K.W. saying that he was to proceed to Berlin at once, to render a report.

Later in the day von Stulpnagel set off for Berlin by car, by way of Verdun and Metz. He was accompanied by one man besides the driver, as an escort in case they met French partisans. Just before Verdun was reached, he ordered the car to stop, and said that as they were just coming to the partisan area it would be a good thing for them to get out and fire their pistols at a tree, to make sure they were in working order. After that they drove on, but he stopped the car again when they came to the old Verdun battlefields—where he had fought in the previous war—and said that he would like to show them round. After going a short way he said to them: "You stop here, I'm going on alone to look at a point I know." They suggested they ought to accompany him in case of meeting partisans, but he said it was not necessary. Shortly afterwards they heard a shot. They ran forward and found him floating in a canal. He had shot himself after getting into the water—so that he would drown if the first shot did not succeed. But his attempt at suicide had not succeeded. The two men fished him out and took him to hospital. He had shot one eye out, and the other eye was so badly damaged that it had to be removed.

I heard these details subsequently from Oberg, who, feeling that von Stulpnagel was probably mixed up in the attempt on Hitler, had driven to Verdun to see von Stulpnagel in hospital, still in the hope that he might be able to keep things quiet. Von Stulpnagel, however, had refused to say anything, Oberg told me. After about a fortnight in hospital, von Stulpnagel was removed to Berlin on orders from there. He was brought to trial, condemned and hanged.

Meanwhile there was something like a panic in Paris among the Staff—as to who were suspect. Oberg received a string of telegrams to arrest various people—first, Hoffacker, then Finck; and in all about thirty or forty people, both soldiers and civilians. A few days later Oberg telephoned me to come and see him, and told me that Hoffacker had mentioned von Kluge's name in his preliminary interrogation. Oberg said that he could not believe that von Kluge was implicated.

I accompanied Oberg when he went to see von Kluge and make a report. Von Kluge told Oberg: "Carry out these interrogations as your sense of duty tells you." Oberg remarked to me that he did not like the task, but as it could not be avoided he wanted to conduct the interrogations in a gentlemanly way. So it was arranged that, as an assurance, one of the officers of my staff should be present during them. Here it is worth mentioning that neither Speidel nor I had breathed a word to anyone about the conference on the evening of July 20th.

Soon after this, von Kluge visited Rommel in hospital in Paris. On his return he told me that Rommel had expressed surprise that there had been an attempt to kill Hitler, as distinct from putting pressure on him to sue for peace.

In the days that followed I noticed that von Kluge began to look more and more worried. He often talked about himself and his own affairs. On one occasion he remarked, sombrely: "Events will take their course." Then Field-Marshal Model suddenly arrived to replace him. On his way home, as I have already related, von Kluge was found dead in the car, having swallowed a poison capsule.

Apart from the conversation we had on the evening of July 20th, von Kluge never said anything to me about a plot to tackle or overthrow Hitler. I had left von Kluge's staff in January, 1942, and had no close relations with him again until July, 1944. Colonel von Tresckow was IA[1] to von Kluge, and may have been taken more into his confidence—but he is dead.

I was in Schleswig with General Dempsey after the capitulation in May, 1945, and saw very clearly that even then the civil population was divided in their view of Hitler. One half was shocked that the German generals had taken part in the attempt to overthrow Hitler, and felt bitterly towards them in consequence—the same feeling was manifested in the Army itself. The other half complained that the generals had not turned out Hitler before.

THE AFTERMATH

After taking over command in the West, Field-Marshal Model stayed at the H.Q. of Army Group "B." Telephoning me from

[1] Head of the Operations branch.

there a day or two later, he said that he had just received a disconcerting message from the Führer's H.Q. "All *they* can talk about and think about is the 20th July, and now they want to take Speidel away, as a suspect." He had emphatically told Keitel that he could not spare the Chief of Staff at Army Group H.Q. when the situation was so critical. As a result, Speidel was left there until the first week of September. He was then relieved, and came to see me, telling me that he had been ordered to return home. On arrival there he was arrested by the Gestapo.

After General Speidel had gone, a telegram came which said that I was to be relieved by General Westphal, and was to report to the Führer's H.Q. on the 13th September. I felt somewhat depressed! On setting off, I went first to see Field-Marshal von Rundstedt at Coblenz, where he had just established his H.Q. on being recalled to take supreme command in the West. Field-Marshal von Rundstedt was very annoyed to hear that I was being taken away from my post just as he had returned to command. He at once protested to O.K.W. and asked that he might retain me as his Chief of Staff. But the answer came back that the request could not be granted. The reason given was that I had repeatedly expressed a desire for a fighting command. This did not sound very convincing in the circumstances.

I left Coblenz on the 9th September, and took the opportunity to visit my family—at Marburg—in case of what might happen. I spent Sunday, the 10th, at home. I felt a quiver every time the telephone rang or the sound of a car was heard approaching the house—and went to the window to look out.

On the 11th I took the train for Berlin. The train was held up by an air raid at Kassel, so I telephoned from there to say that I was delayed, and would thus miss the special courier train that ran nightly from Berlin to East Prussia. Continuing in the train to Berlin I had to get out at Potsdam, because of bomb damage on the line. Just as I got out of the train I suddenly heard a voice in the dark saying: "Where is General

Blumentritt?" I felt another quiver. After I had answered, an officer came up to me, accompanied by a soldier who was carrying a tommy gun. The officer addressed me politely, and said he had orders to escort me to a hotel in Berlin—the Adlon. On arrival there, the hall porter told me there was a sealed envelope awaiting me. I opened it—all that it contained was my ticket to Angerburg in East Prussia. That was rather an anti-climax. But it brought only a temporary sense of relief. I still had to wait and wonder what was in store for me at the Führer's H.Q.

The following night I caught the special train thence, arriving at Angerburg on the morning of the 13th. I was met by Field-Marshal Keitel's adjutant, who took me to Keitel's special train; here I had breakfast and left my baggage. I was told that the Führer was too tired to receive me, but that I could attend the daily conference at mid-day if I liked. I decided to do so.

In front of the house where the conference was held I found a group of generals. I went up to them and reported to General Guderian, who had become Chief of the General Staff. I noticed that he did not attempt to shake hands, while Keitel and others stood aloof. Guderian said to me, in a loud voice: "I wonder you dare to come here after what has happened in the West." I showed him the telegram ordering me to report. Then an S.S. officer arrived and said that, after all, the Führer had decided to attend the daily conference. A few minutes later we saw Hitler walking through the forest, with tired and slow steps, accompanied by an escort of five or six men.

Guderian turned to me and said, grimly: "Now you can report yourself to the Führer." But to my surprise Hitler greeted me in a pleasant manner, saying: "You've been having a very hard time in the West. I know the Allied air forces are on top and what it means. I'd like to have a talk with you after the conference."

When the conference ended Guderian said to me: "Come

and have a talk with me about the Eastern front." I replied: "It doesn't interest me in the least at the moment." I then had ten minutes' talk with Hitler, alone, and he was again very nice.

When I came out, the other generals were all waiting, and at once asked me: "What did the Führer say to you?" I replied: "He was very pleasant." Thereupon, they all became very pleasant, and Keitel invited me to have tea with him. I replied that I would like to get away that evening and go home, adding: "It's two years since I spent a leave with my wife and children." At that, Keitel said: "I don't think it is possible." I said: "But the Führer told me I could go on leave, and was then to report to Field-Marshal von Rundstedt, who would give me command of an army corps in the West." Keitel told me to wait half-an-hour. After seeing the Führer, he came back and told me I could go.

During our conversation, this time, Keitel spoke of von Kluge, and remarked that they had documentary evidence about his treasonable activities. Keitel said that they had intercepted a wireless message from some Allied H.Q., which asked to be put in touch with von Kluge. Keitel added: "And that's why he was missing so long that day near Avranches." Protesting that this suspicion was unjust, I related how von Kluge had been forced to take cover, and how he had been unable to get in touch with his own H.Q. for hours, because his wireless tender had been knocked out. But it was obvious that Keitel did not believe this explanation.

I also paid a call on Jodl before leaving. Jodl said to me, without shaking hands: "That seems to be a bad show of yours in the West." I retorted: "It might be well for you to come yourself and have a look at the situation." Jodl was surprised to hear that I was going on leave that evening.

After that I went back to Keitel's train to pick up my baggage. An orderly there gave me a bottle of claret to take away, remarking at the same time: "Where you had breakfast this morning you were sitting in the same seat where Colonel

Stieff last sat." I felt that I had had a lucky escape. Even after I reached my home at Marburg I still jumped when the telephone rang. I did not begin to feel at ease until I got back to the front, and took over command of my new corps. An underlying anxiety continued.

From then on to the end of the war many of us felt that we were under a cloud of suspicion. In March, 1945, when I was commanding the army in Holland, I received a telegram from O.K.W. telling me to report at once the whereabouts of my family. That sounded ominous—as if they might be taken as hostages. I looked at the map and saw that the American forces were approaching Marburg—being already less than sixty miles away. So I didn't send an answer to this telegram! I felt that my family would be safer with the Americans.

✼   ✼   ✼

From the night of July 20th onwards the German generals often used to discuss among themselves whether they should get in touch with the Allies—as von Kluge had thought of doing that evening, when he thought Hitler was dead. The reasons that checked them from doing so were:

(1) Their oath of loyalty to the Führer. (They now argue: "We gave our oath of loyalty to the Führer. If he is dead that is cancelled." So most of them want to believe that he is dead.)

(2) The people in Germany had not realized the truth of the situation, and would not understand any action the generals took towards making peace.

(3) The troops on the East front would reproach the West front for letting them down.

(4) The fear of going down to history as traitors to their country.

XIX

HITLER'S LAST GAMBLE—THE SECOND ARDENNES STROKE

IN THE DARK, FOGGY MORNING OF DECEMBER 16, 1944, THE German Army struck in the Ardennes. The blow came as a shock to the Allies, for some of their highest commanders had been confidently saying that the Germans would never be capable of another offensive. It soon became a greater shock, for the blow burst through the American front in the Ardennes and threatened to sever the Allied armies. Alarm spread behind the front, and was worse still in the Allied capitals. It was like a nightmare. Fears were voiced that the Germans might reach the Channel coast, and produce a second Dunkirk.

It was Hitler's last big gamble—and the rashest of all.

Everything looked very different from the German end of the telescope. The offensive was not only a long-odds chance, but an incredible muddle. The Allies spoke of it as the "Rundstedt offensive." That title acts on Rundstedt like the proverbial red rag, for his feelings about the plan were, and remain, very bitter. In reality he had nothing to do with it except in the most nominal way. Having failed to dissuade Hitler from attempting it, and feeling that it was a hopeless venture, he stood back throughout and left Field-Marshal Model to run it.

The decision was entirely Hitler's own, and so was the strategic plan. It would have been a brilliant brain-wave *if* he had still possessed the forces and resources to give it a fair chance of success in the end. That it gained a startling initial success was largely due to tactics suggested by the young General von Manteuffel—an army commander at forty-seven—who persuaded Hitler to adopt them. Hitler would never listen to the arguments of the older generals, whom he distrusted, but he had a very different attitude towards newer men and ideas. He regarded Manteuffel as one of his discoveries. He loved revolutionary ideas.

The surprise achieved at the start also owed much to the extreme secrecy in which the design had been hidden. But this was carried so far that it became more hindrance than help. It caused many of the muddles which forfeited such chance as the attack gained. But long after the plan had miscarried, Hitler insisted on pursuing the attack. He forbade any timely withdrawal. If the Allies had moved quicker, his armies might have been trapped. Even as it was they were badly hammered. The losses they suffered were fatal to the prospects of the continued defence of Germany.

It is instructive to follow the course of events through the eyes of some of the chief German commanders concerned. At the top came Rundstedt, who had been restored to his old place as Commander-in-Chief in the West early in September—when the Allies were approaching the Rhine, and Hitler needed a symbol that would rally the confidence of his shattered armies. Under Rundstedt came Model, who was not a great strategist, but who had a ruthless energy in scraping up reserves from a bare cupboard, and was one of the few generals who dared to argue with Hitler. Model committed suicide at the end of the war. Under Model came the two Panzer Army commanders, Sepp Dietrich and Manteuffel. Sepp Dietrich was an S.S. leader, formerly a rolling stone in various business jobs, who had caught Hitler's fancy by his aggressive spirit. Rundstedt regarded him as responsible for fumbling the crucial part of the offensive. Manteuffel was a professional soldier of the younger school, and an aristocrat. A man of quiet dignity, similar to Rundstedt's, he was also a dynamic exponent of new methods. Within a year he had risen from command of a panzer division to command of an Army. Besides being the designer of the tactics of the Ardennes offensive, it was his thrust that proved by far the most threatening feature. For these reasons I give the story largely in his words, checked and supplemented by evidence gathered from other sources.

Manteuffel is keenly professional enough to enjoy "fighting his battles over again," in discussion, while philosophical enough not to dwell disproportionately on how things went wrong. He has a pleasant vein of humour, too. It survived the hard conditions of the camp where the generals were then confined, as well as the strain of anxiety which all of them felt about the fate of their families, and whether they would ever see them again. That cheerless camp deep in a remote mountain valley was depressing enough, even without the barbed wire, to induce claustrophobia. Visiting it on one of the dreariest of mid-winter days, I remarked to Manteuffel that Grizedale was not a pleasing place at such a time of the year, but that it would be better in summer. He replied, with a smile, "Oh, it might be worse. I expect we shall be spending next winter on a barren island, or else in a ship anchored in mid-Atlantic."

THE PLAN

"The plan for the Ardennes offensive," Manteuffel told me, "was drawn up completely by O.K.W. and sent to us as a cut and dried 'Führer order.' The object defined was to achieve a decisive victory in the West by throwing in two panzer armies—the 6th under Dietrich, and the 5th under me. The 6th was to strike north-east, cross the Meuse between Liége and Huy, and drive for Antwerp. It had the main rôle, and main strength. My army was to advance along a more curving line, cross the Meuse between Namur and

Dinant, and push towards Brussels—to cover the flank. On the third or fourth day the 15th Army, using the specially reinforced 12th S.S. Corps under General Blumentritt, was to make a converging thrust from the north-east towards the Meuse at Maastricht—to assist the 6th Panzer Army's drive on Antwerp. The Führer's idea was that the Ardennes offensive would by then have drawn off a large part of the reserves to the help of the Americans, so that this secondary stroke, although lighter, should have a chance of success.

"The aim of the whole offensive was, by cutting off the British Army from its bases of supply, to force it to evacuate the Continent."

Hitler imagined that if he produced this second Dunkirk, Britain would virtually drop out of the war, and he would have breathing space to hold up the Russians and produce a stalemate in the East.

Rundstedt told me: "When I received this plan early in November I was staggered. Hitler had not troubled to consult me about its possibilities. It was obvious to me that the available forces were far too small for such an extremely ambitious plan. Model took the same view of it as I did. In fact, no soldier believed that the aim of reaching Antwerp was really practicable. But I knew by now it was useless to protest to Hitler about the *possibility* of anything. After consultation with Model and Manteuffel I felt that the only hope was to wean Hitler from this fantastic aim by putting forward an alternative proposal that might appeal to him, and would be more practicable. This was for a limited offensive with the aim of pinching off the Allies' salient around Aachen."

Manteuffel gave me a fuller account of their discussion and conclusions. "We were agreed in our objections to the plan. In the first place the strategic dispositions were faulty, and there would be grave risk to the flanks unless these were buttressed. Beyond that, the ammunition supplies were not sufficient for such extensive aims. Beyond that again, the Allies' air superiority would be too great a handicap in attempting such aims. Moreover, we knew that strong Allied reinforcements were available back in France, and also in England. I myself stressed the point that we must expect intervention from the airborne divisions that were ready in England. I also emphasized how the good network of roads beyond the Meuse would facilitate the Allies' counter-moves.

"We drafted a report to O.K.W. emphasizing that the forces were not adequate to deliver an offensive on the lines laid down. At the same time we suggested a modified plan. In this, the 15th Army, with a strong right flank, would deliver an attack north of Aachen, towards Maastricht. The 6th Panzer Army would attack south of Aachen, and cut in behind that place with the eventual objective of establishing a bridgehead over the Meuse in the Liége area. The main aim here was to fix the Allies' attention. The 5th Panzer Army would strike from the Eifel through the Ardennes towards Namur, with the aim of gaining a bridgehead there. The armies would then turn inward and roll up the Allied position along the Meuse. If opposition seemed to be collapsing, they could exploit their success by an advance towards Antwerp, but otherwise they could limit their risks."

The most that they really hoped, Manteuffel said, was to pinch out the American forces that had pushed beyond Aachen as far as the River Roer. But he would have preferred to wait until the Allies started a fresh offensive, and keep all the German armoured forces in hand for the delivery of a concentrated counter-stroke. Rundstedt was of the same opinion, as Blumentritt independently confirmed—"The Field-Marshal was really against any further offensive on our part. His idea was to defend the Roer and hold all the armoured divisions in readiness behind that line, as a powerful reserve for counter-attack against a break-through. He wanted to pursue a defensive strategy."

Since Hitler rejected such an idea, the only hope seemed to lie in subtly inducing him to modify his offensive design to a form that would offer a chance of moderate success without involving too heavy risks.

Manteuffel explained that the scope and direction of the

thrusts suggested was close enough to Hitler's design as to appear not so very different. In putting forward the alternative plan, they tried to increase its appeal by suggesting that, if opposition seemed to be collapsing, they could then exploit the success towards Antwerp. "On November 4, so far as I remember, this alternative plan was sent to O.K.W. for submission to Hitler. It was emphasized that we could not be ready to launch the attack before December 10—Hitler had originally fixed the date as December 1."

Manteuffel went on: "Hitler rejected this more moderate plan, and insisted on the original pattern. Meanwhile, knowing that he usually kept us waiting for an answer we had begun our own planning—but only on the narrower basis of our own proposals. All the divisions of my own 5th Panzer Army were assembled, but kept widely spaced, between Trier and Krefeld—so that spies and the civil population should have no inkling of what was intended. The troops were told that they were being got ready to meet the coming Allied attack on Cologne. Only a very limited number of staff officers were informed of the actual plan."

The 6th Panzer Army was assembled still farther back, in the area between Hanover and the Weser. Its divisions had been drawn out of the line to recuperate and be re-equipped. Curiously, Sepp Dietrich was not informed of the task that was intended for him nor consulted about the plan he would have to carry out, until much closer to the event. Most of the divisional commanders had only a few days' notice. In the case of Manteuffel's Army, the move down to the starting line was made in three nights.

THE FLAWS

This strategic camouflage helped surprise, but a heavy price was paid for the extreme internal secrecy. Commanders who were informed so late had too little time to study their problem, reconnoitre the ground, and make their preparations. As a result many things were overlooked, and numerous hitches occurred when the attack began. Hitler had worked out the plan at his headquarters in detail, with Jodl, and seemed to think that this would suffice for its fulfilment. He paid no attention to local conditions or to the individual problems of his executants. He was equally optimistic about the needs of the forces engaged.

Rundstedt remarked: "There were no adequate reinforcements, no supplies of ammunition, and although the number of armoured divisions was high, their strength in tanks was low—it was largely paper strength." (Manteuffel said that the actual number of tanks in the two panzer armies was about 800—which puts a different complexion on the Allied statement, based on the number of divisions, that this was the most powerful concentration of tanks ever seen in the war.)

The worst deficiency of all was in petrol. Manteuffel said: "Jodl had assured us there would be sufficient petrol to develop our full strength and carry our drive through. This assurance proved completely mistaken. Part of the trouble was that O.K.W. worked on a mathematical and stereotyped calculation of the amount of petrol required to move a division for a hundred kilometres. My experience in Russia had taught me that double this scale was really needed under battlefield conditions. Jodl didn't understand this.

"Taking account of the extra difficulties likely to be met in a winter battle in such difficult country as the Ardennes, I told Hitler personally that five times the standard scale of petrol supply ought to be provided. Actually, when the offensive was launched, only one and a half times the standard scale had been provided. Worse still, much of it was kept too far back, in large lorry columns on the east bank of the Rhine. Once the foggy weather cleared, and the Allied air forces came into action, its forwarding was badly interrupted."

The troops, ignorant of all these underlying weaknesses, kept a remarkable trust in Hitler and his assurances of victory. Rundstedt said: "The morale of the troops taking part was astonishingly high at the start of the offensive. 'They really believed victory was possible—unlike the higher commanders, who knew the facts."

NEW TACTICS

At the start, the chances were improved by two factors. The first was the thinness of the American defences in the Ardennes sector. The Germans had good information about this, and knew that only four divisions covered the 75-mile stretch of front. It was Hitler's keen sense of the value of the unexpected which led him to exploit this weakness, and its indication that the Allied High Command was unprepared—despite the lesson of 1940—for a large-scale German offensive in such difficult country.

The second favourable factor lay in the tactics that were adopted. These were not part of the original plan. Manteuffel told me: "When I saw Hitler's orders for the offensive I was astonished to find that these even laid down the method and timing of the attack. The artillery was to open fire at 7.30 A.M., and the infantry assault was to be launched at 11 A.M. Between these hours the Luftwaffe was to bomb headquarters and communications. The armoured divisions were not to strike until the break-through had been achieved by the infantry mass. The artillery was spread over the whole front of attack.

"This seemed to me foolish in several respects, so I immediately worked out a different method, and explained it to Model. Model agreed with it, but remarked sarcastically: 'You'd better argue it out with the Führer.' I replied: 'All right, I'll do that if you'll come with me.' So on December 2, the two of us went to see Hitler in Berlin.

"I began by saying: 'None of us knows what the weather will be on the day of the attack—are you sure the Luftwaffe can fulfil its part in face of the Allied air superiority?' I reminded Hitler of two occasions in the Vosges earlier where it had proved quite impossible for the armoured divisions to move in daylight. Then I went on: 'All our artillery will do at 7.30 is to wake the Americans—and they will then have three and a half hours to organize their counter-measures before our assault comes.' I pointed out also, that the mass of the German infantry was not so good as it had been, and was hardly capable of making such a deep penetration as was required, especially in such difficult country. For the American defences consisted of a chain of forward defence posts, with their main line of resistance well behind—and that would be harder to pierce.

"I proposed to Hitler a number of changes. The first was that the assault should be made at 5.30 A.M., under cover of darkness. Of course this would limit the targets for the artillery, but it would enable it to concentrate on a number of key targets—such as batteries, ammunition dumps, and headquarters—that had been definitely located.

"Secondly, I proposed to form one 'storm battalion' from each infantry division, composed of the most expert officers and men. (I picked the officers myself.) These 'storm battalions' were to advance in the dark at 5.30, without any covering artillery fire, and penetrate between the Americans' forward defence posts. They would avoid fighting if possible until they had penetrated deep.

"Searchlights, provided by the flak units, were to light the way for the storm troops' advance by projecting their beams on the clouds, to reflect downwards. I had been much impressed by a demonstration of this kind which I had seen shortly beforehand, and felt that it would be the key to a quick penetration before daylight." (Curiously, Manteuffel did not seem aware that the British had already developed such "artificial moonlight." And although he spoke to me of the impression made on him by a little book of mine, *The Future of Infantry,* which appeared in 1932, he had forgotten that this new development was one of the principal suggestions in that book.)

Resuming his account, Manteuffel said: "After setting forth my alternative proposals to Hitler, I argued that it was not possible to carry out the offensive in any other way if we were to have a reasonable chance of success. I emphasized: 'At 4 P.M. it will be dark. So you will only have five hours, after the assault at 11 A.M., in which to achieve the break-through. It is very doubtful if you can do it in the time.·If you adopt my idea, you will gain a further five and a half hours for the purpose. Then when darkness comes I can launch the tanks. They will advance during the night, pass through our infantry, and by dawn the next day they will be able to launch their own attack on the main position, along a cleared approach.'"

According to Manteuffel, Hitler accepted these suggestions without a murmur. That was significant. It would seem that he was willing to listen to suggestions that were made to him by a few generals in whom he had faith—Model was another —but he had an instinctive distrust of most of the senior generals, while his reliance on his own immediate staff was mingled with a realization that they lacked experience of battle conditions.

"Keitel, Jodl, and Warlimont had never been in the war. At the same time their lack of fighting experience tended to make them underrate practical difficulties, and encourage Hitler to believe that things could be done that were quite impossible. Hitler would listen to soldiers who had fighting experience, and practical ideas."

What these tactical changes did to improve the prospects of the offensive was offset, however, by a reduction of the strength that was to be put into it. For the executive commanders soon had damping news that part of the forces promised them would not be available—owing to the menacing pressure of the Russian attacks in the East. The result was that Blumentritt's converging attack on Maastricht had to be abandoned, so leaving the Allies free to bring down reserves from the north. Moreover, the 7th Army, which was to advance as flank cover to the other wing of the offensive, was left with only a few divisions—and without any tanks. Manteuffel was the more dismayed to hear this, because he had told Hitler, on the 2nd, that in his view the Americans would launch their main counter-stroke from the Sedan area towards Bastogne. "I pointed out the way that so many of the roads converged on Bastogne."

Yet the ambitious aims of the offensive were not modified. Curiously, too, Hitler and Jodl did not seem to realize the effect on the momentum of the advance. "The time of reaching the Meuse was not discussed in any detail," Manteuffel told me. "I imagined that Hitler must realize that a rapid advance would not be possible under winter conditions, and these limitations, but from what I have heard since it is clear that Hitler thought the advance could go much quicker than it did. The Meuse could not possibly have been reached on the second or third day—as Jodl expected. He and Keitel tended to encourage Hitler's optimistic illusions."

Rundstedt receded into the background after Hitler's rejection of the "smaller" plan, leaving Model and Manteuffel, who had more chance of influencing Hitler, to fight for the technical changes in the plan that were all Hitler would consider. Blumentritt bitterly remarked: "The Commander-in-Chief in the West was not, in fact, consulted any more. He was expected to carry out the offensive in a mechanical way in accordance with the Führer's operation orders—which regulated the smallest details—without being able to interfere in any way himself." Rundstedt took only a nominal part in the final conference, held on December 12th in his headquarters at Ziegenberg, near Bad Nauheim. Hitler was present, and controlled the proceedings.

THE MISSING CARD

As the start of one of my talks with Manteuffel I raised a question about the use of the airborne forces. I said that in

travelling over a large part of the Ardennes before the war
I had been struck by the fact that its possibilities for tank
movement were greater than was generally supposed, especially by the conventionally-minded French high command.
At the same time there was an obvious difficulty in the way
that the roads descended into steep valleys at the river crossings, and these might form tough obstacles if stoutly defended. It had seemed to me that the offensive answer to this
defensive problem was to drop airborne forces on these strategic defiles, and seize them ahead of the tank advance. That
was why in my commentary when the Ardennes offensive
opened I had assumed that the Germans were using their
airborne troops in this way. But it now appeared that they
did not do so. Could he, Manteuffel, tell me something about
this.

Manteuffel's reply was: "I entirely agree with your definition of the nature and problem of the Ardennes, and I think
it would have been an excellent idea to use parachute forces
in the way you suggest. It might have unlocked the door. But
I don't remember it being mooted when the plan was being
discussed, and in any case the available parachute forces were
very scanty. Our parachute forces were hampered by a shortage of transport aircraft, above all, but also by a lack of men
at the time when this offensive was launched. The dangerous
situation on the Eastern front had led Hitler to use them as
ordinary infantry, to cement breaches. Other divisions had
been drawn away to Italy and absorbed in the battle there.
The result of all these factors was that only about nine hundred
parachutists were available for the Ardennes offensive, and
they were used on the front of the 6th Panzer Army."

Manteuffel went on to talk of the neglect to make any
effective use of Germany's parachute forces after the capture
of Crete in 1941—how they had been earmarked for a stroke
against Malta or Gibraltar which never came off; how Student
had wanted to use them in Russia, and had been thwarted by
Hitler's preference for keeping them in reserve for some

special coup; and how, in the end, they had been frittered away in the rôle of ordinary ground troops instead of being employed in their own proper rôle. He concluded by saying: "In my view, there could be nothing better than a combination of panzer and parachute troops."

On this subject Thoma told me, earlier: "Guderian always worked well with Student, who trained the parachute forces, but Goering blocked proposals for combined action with the panzer forces. He always wanted to keep up the strength of the Luftwaffe, and was therefore niggardly with such air transport as he had to provide for the parachute forces."

From General Student I got details of how the parachute troops were employed in the Ardennes offensive. When the German front in France collapsed and the Allies dashed forward into Belgium, at the beginning of September, he was sent to form a fresh front in southern Holland. For this purpose he was given command of a scratch force that was imposingly named the 1st Parachute Army. It consisted of a number of depleted infantry divisions supplemented by a sprinkling of parachute units that were then in course of training under him. After the new front had been established, and the Allied advance checked, the German forces in Holland were constituted as Army Group 'H,' comprising the 1st Parachute Army and the still more newly created 25th Army. Student was given command of this army group in addition to his other function of Commander-in-Chief of the Parachute Forces.

On December 8th he was told of the intended offensive in the Ardennes and instructed to collect what he could in the way of trained parachutists in order to furnish one strong battalion. That was barely a week before the offensive was launched. The battalion comprised about 1000 men under Colonel von der Heydte, and it was sent to the sector of Sepp Dietrich's 6th Panzer Army. On getting in touch with the Luftwaffe command, von der Heydte found that more than half the crews of the aircraft allotted had no experience of parachute operations, and that necessary equipment was lacking. It was not until the 13th that he managed to see Sepp Dietrich, who said that he did not want to use parachute troops for fear that they might give the enemy a warning, but that Hitler had insisted.

The task eventually assigned to the parachute troops was, not to seize one of the awkward defiles ahead of the panzer advance, but to land on Mont Rigi near the Malmedy-Eupen-Verviers cross-roads, and create a flank block to delay Allied reinforcements from the north. Von der Heydte was ordered, despite his protests, to make the drop at night instead of at dawn, to avoid putting the enemy on the alert. But on the evening before the attack the promised transport did not arrive to take the companies to the airfields, and the drop was postponed until the next night—when the ground attack had already started. Then, only a third of the aircraft managed to reach the correct dropping zone, and the strong wind dragged the parachutes so that many of the troops were killed or injured in landing on the wooded and snow-covered heights. By this time the roads were filled with American columns streaming south, and as von der Heydte had only been able to collect a couple of hundred men he could not gain the cross-roads and establish a blocking position. For several days he harassed the roads with small raiding parties, and then, as there was no sign of Sepp Dietrich's forces arriving to relieve him, he tried to push eastward to meet them, but was captured on the way.

"This was our last parachute operation," said Student. "On D-day we had had 150,000 parachute troops, and six organized divisions. Of the total 50,000 were trained, and the rest under training. We were not able to complete their training as they were constantly committed to ground fighting, and by the time they were needed for the Ardennes offensive, five months later, only a handful were available—because they had been used up as infantry instead of being kept for their proper rôle."

The blow that gave the Allies their biggest shock since 1942 had no such weight behind it as they pictured at the time. That is now clear from the German order of battle, though Manteuffel did not emphasize it—he gave his account with marked restraint, and is the type of man who dislikes to offer excuses, however justifiable.

The offensive was launched on December 16th along a seventy-mile stretch between Monschau (south of Aachen) and Echternach (just north-west of Trier). But the 7th Army's attack on the southern sector did not really count, as it could only employ four infantry divisions. The intended main punch was delivered on a narrow front, of barely fifteen miles, by Sepp Dietrich's 6th Panzer Army, which was composed of the 1st and 2nd S.S. Panzer Corps, supplemented by the 67th Corps (of infantry). Although it had more armoured divisions than the 5th Panzer Army it was a light-weight for its purpose.

Sepp Dietrich's right-hand punch was blocked early by the Americans' tough defence of Monschau. His left-hand punch burst through and, by-passing Malmedy, gained a crossing over the Ambleve beyond Stavelot on the 18th—after a thirty-mile advance from the starting line. But it was checked in this narrow defile, and then cornered by an American counter-move. Fresh efforts failed, in face of the Americans' rising strength as reserves were hurried to the scene, and the 6th Panzer Army's attack fizzled out.

Manteuffel's 5th Panzer Army attacked on a broader front, of some thirty miles. He sketched out for me its dispositions and course. The 66th Corps (of infantry) was on his right wing, facing in the direction of St. Vith. "It was purposely put there because the obstacles were greater, and the chances of rapid progress less, than farther south." The 58th Panzer Corps was in the centre, between Prüm and Waxweiler. The 47th Panzer Corps was on the left, between Waxweiler and

Bitburg, facing the direction of Bastogne. At the start these two corps included only three armoured divisions, and despite recent reinforcement the latter only had a strength of between sixty to a hundred tanks each—one third to a half of their normal establishment. Sepp Dietrich's armoured divisions were not much stronger in tanks.

On Manteuffel's front the offensive had a good start. "My storm battalions infiltrated rapidly into the American front —like rain-drops. At 4 o'clock in the afternoon the tanks advanced, and pressed forward in the dark with the help of 'artificial moonlight.' By that time bridges had been built over the Our river. Crossing these about midnight, the armoured divisions reached the American main position, at 8 A.M., then called for artillery support, and quickly broke through.

"But Bastogne then proved a very awkward obstacle. Part of the trouble was due to the way that the 7th Army had been reduced in strength, for its task was to block the roads running up from the south to Bastogne." After crossing the Our at Dasburg, the 47th Panzer Corps had to get through another awkward defile at Clervaux on the Woltz. These obstacles, combined with winter conditions, caused delay. "Resistance tended to melt whenever the tanks arrived in force, but the difficulties of movement offset the slightness of the resistance in this early stage. When they approached Bastogne resistance increased."

On the 18th, the Germans came close to Bastogne—after an advance of nearly thirty miles from their starting line. But during the night before, General Eisenhower had placed the 82nd and 101st Airborne divisions, then near Rheims, at General Bradley's disposal. The 82nd was sent to stiffen the northern sector, while the 101st was rushed up by road to Bastogne. Meanwhile part of the 10th U. S. Armoured Division had arrived at Bastogne just in time to help a battered regiment of the 28th Division in checking the Germans' initial threat. When the 101st Airborne Division arrived on the night of the 18th, the defence of this vital road-centre was cemented. During the next two days thrusts were made against it, from front and flanks, but all were foiled.

On the 20th Manteuffel decided that no more time must be lost in trying to clear away this obstacle. "I went forward myself with the Panzer Lehr Division, led it round Bastogne, and pushed on to St. Hubert on the 21st. The 2nd Panzer Division pushed round the north side of Bastogne. To cover these by-passing advances I masked Bastogne, using the 26th Volksgrenadier Division to surround the town, with the help of a panzer grenadier regiment from the Panzer Lehr Division. The 58th Panzer Corps meanwhile pressed on through Houffalize and Laroche, after momentarily swinging north to threaten the flank of the resistance that was holding up the 66th Corps near St. Vith, and help it forward.

"Even so, the masking of Bastogne entailed a weakening of my strength for the forward drive, and thus diminished the chances of this reaching the Meuse at Dinant. Moreover, the 7th Army was still back on the Wiltz, which it had not been able to cross. The 5th Parachute Division, on its right, came through my sector and pushed forward close to one of the roads running south from Bastogne, but was not across it."

The situation was now less favourable, and potentially more dangerous than Manteuffel realized. For Allied reserves were gathering on all sides in a strength much exceeding that which the Germans had put into the offensive. Field-Marshal Montgomery had taken over temporary charge of all the forces on the north flank of the breach, and the 30th British Corps had been brought down to the Meuse, as a support to the 1st American Army. On the south flank of the breach two corps of General Patton's 3rd American Army had swung northward, and on the 22nd one of them launched a strong attack up the road from Arlon to Bastogne. Although its advance was slow, its menacing pressure caused an increasing subtraction from the forces that Manteuffel could spare for his own advance.

The days of opportunity had passed. Manteuffel's swerving thrust towards the Meuse caused alarm at Allied Headquarters, but it was too late to be really serious. According to plan, Bastogne was to have been gained on the second day, whereas it was not reached until the third, and not bypassed until the sixth day. A "small finger" of the 2nd Panzer Division came within a few miles of Dinant on the 24th, but that was the utmost limit of progress, and the finger was soon cut off.

Mud and fuel shortage had been important brakes on the advance—owing to lack of petrol only half the artillery could be brought into action. That deficiency was not compensated by air support. While the foggy weather of the opening days had favoured the German infiltration by keeping the Allied air forces on the ground, this cloak of obscurity disappeared on the 23rd, and the scanty resources of the Luftwaffe proved incapable of shielding the ground forces from a terrible pummelling. That multiplied the toll for time lost. But Hitler was also paying forfeit for the decision that had led him to place his main strength on the northern wing, with the 6th Panzer Army, where room for manœuvre was much more cramped.

In the first week, the offensive had fallen far short of what was hoped, and the quickened progress at the start of the second week was illusory—for it only amounted to a deeper intrusion between the main road-centres, which the Americans were now more firmly holding. On Christmas Eve, Manteuffel got through on the telephone direct to Hitler's headquarters, to represent the realities of the situation and to make a proposal. Speaking to Jodl, he emphasized that time was running short, that Bastogne was causing a lot of trouble, that the 7th Army was not far enough forward to cover his flank, and that he expected a massive Allied counter-stroke very soon, driving up the roads from the south. "Let me know this evening what the Führer wants. The question is whether I shall use all my strength to overcome Bastogne, or continue masking it with small forces and throw my weight towards the Meuse.

"I then pointed out that the most we could hope to do was to reach the Meuse—and gave my reasons. First, because of the delay at Bastogne. Second, because the 7th Army was too weak to bar all roads from the south. Third, because after eight days of battle the Allies were sure to be on the Meuse in strength, and it would not be possible to force a crossing in face of strong opposition. Fourth, because the 6th Panzer Army had not penetrated far, and was already held up on the line Monschau-Stavelot. Fifth, it was clear that we should have to fight a battle this side of the Meuse. For I had picked up wireless messages from the Allied Traffic Control at Huy, which was sending regular reports of the passage of reinforcements across the bridge there—we were able to decipher the code."

After that, Manteuffel made his own proposals—for a circular stroke northward on the near side of the Meuse, to trap the Allied forces that were east of the river, and sweep the bend clear. This would establish the German forces in a stronger position, which they might hope to hold. "With this aim, I urged that the whole of my army, reinforced by the O.K.W. reserves and by the 6th Panzer Army's reserves, should be concentrated south of the Ourthe, around Laroche, and then wheel round in a circuit past Marche towards Liége. I said: 'Give me these reserves, and I will take Bastogne, reach the Meuse, and swing north, so helping the 6th Panzer Army to advance.' I finished by emphasizing these points—I must have a reply that night; the O.K.W. reserves must have sufficient petrol; I would need aid support. Up till then I had only seen the enemy's aircraft!

"During the night Major Johannmeier, the Führer's adjutant, visited me and after discussion telephoned Jodl. At the end I came to the telephone myself, but Jodl said that the

Führer had not yet made a decision. All he could do for the moment was to place at my disposal one additional armoured division.

"It was not until the 26th that the rest of the reserves were given to me—and then they could not be moved. They were at a standstill for lack of petrol—stranded over a stretch of a hundred miles—just when they were needed." (The irony of this situation was that on the 19th the Germans had come within about a quarter of a mile of a huge petrol dump at Andrimont, near Stavelot, containing 2,500,000 gallons. It was a hundred times larger than the largest of the dumps they actually captured.)

I asked Manteuffel whether he felt that real success would have been possible as late as December 24th—even if he had been given the reserves immediately, and they had been provided with petrol. He replied: "I think a limited success would still have been possible—up to the Meuse, and perhaps the capture of bridgeheads beyond it." In further discussion, however, he admitted that such a belated attainment of the Meuse would have brought more disadvantage than advantage in the long run.

"We had hardly begun this new push before the Allied counter-offensive developed. I telephoned Jodl and asked him to tell the Führer that I was going to withdraw my advanced forces out of the nose of the salient we had made—to the line Laroche-Bastogne. But Hitler forbade this step back. So instead of withdrawing in time, we were driven back bit by bit under pressure of the Allied attacks, suffering needlessly heavy losses. On January 5th the situation was so serious that I feared Montgomery would cut off both our Armies. Although we managed to avoid this danger, a large part of them were sacrificed. Our losses were much heavier in this later stage than they had been earlier, owing to Hitler's policy of 'no withdrawal.' It spelt bankruptcy, because we could not afford such losses."

AFTERMATH

Manteuffel summed up the last stage of the war in two sentences: "After the Ardennes failure, Hitler started a 'corporal's war.' There were no big plans—only a multitude of piecemeal fights."

He went on: "When I saw the Ardennes offensive was blocked I wanted to carry out a general withdrawal—first to our starting line, and then to the Rhine, but Hitler would not hear of it. He chose to sacrifice the bulk of his main forces in a hopeless struggle on the West bank of the Rhine."

Rundstedt endorsed this verdict. But he also made it clear that, although the German Army's leading exponent of offensive warfare, he had never seen any point in this offensive. "Each step forward in the Ardennes offensive prolonged our flanks more dangerously deep, making them more susceptible to Allied counter-strokes." Rundstedt traced the effect, on the map, as he talked. "I wanted to stop the offensive at an early stage, when it was plain that it could not attain its aim, but Hitler furiously insisted that it must go on. It was Stalingrad No. 2."

The Ardennes offensive carried to the extreme of absurdity the military belief that "attack is the best defence." It proved the "worst defence"—wrecking Germany's chances of any further serious resistance. From that time on, the main concern of most of the German commanders seems to have been, not whether they could stop the Allies' advance, but why the Allies did not advance faster and finish the war quicker.

They were tied to their posts by Hitler's policy, and Himmler's police, but they were praying for release. Throughout the last nine months of the war they spent much of their time discussing ways and means of getting in touch with the Allies to arrange a surrender.

All to whom I talked dwelt on the effect of the Allies' "unconditional surrender" policy in prolonging the war. They told me that but for this they and their troops—the factor that was more important—would have been ready to surrender sooner, separately or collectively. "Black-listening" to the Allies' radio service was widespread. But the Allied propaganda never said anything positive about the peace conditions in the way of encouraging them to give up the struggle. Its silence on the subject was so marked that it tended to confirm what Nazi propaganda told them as to the dire fate in store for them if they surrendered. So it greatly helped the Nazis to keep the German troops and people to continue fighting—long after they were ready to give up.

X X

HITLER—AS A YOUNG GENERAL SAW HIM

IN THE COURSE OF ONE OF MY TALKS WITH MANTEUFFEL ABOUT the Ardennes offensive he gave me a military character-sketch of Hitler that differed markedly from the impression of him that the older generals conveyed. It is worth reproducing because it goes further to explain the sources of both his power and his failure.

The way in which Manteuffel attracted Hitler's notice is also illuminating. In August, 1943, he had been given command of the 7th Armoured Division—which Rommel had led in 1940. It was in Manstein's Army Group. That autumn the Russians surged over the Dnieper and captured Kiev, then rolled on rapidly west towards the Polish frontier. Manstein had no formed reserve left to meet this fresh crisis, but charged Manteuffel with the task of collecting such odd units as he could find for an improvised counter-stroke. Manteuffel broke in behind the rear of the advancing Russians, ejected them from Zhitomir junction by a night attack, and drove on north to recapture Korosten. By dividing his meagre forces into a number of small mobile groups Manteuffel created an impression out of proportion to his strength, and the sudden riposte brought the Russian advance to a halt.

After that, Manteuffel further developed this method of

294

penetrating raids that cut in between the Russian columns and struck at them from the rear. "It was handicapped by the Russians' lack of dependence on a normal system of supply—I never met any supply columns on these 'interior' raids —but I caught staff and signal centres besides striking bodies of troops in the back. These penetrating raids proved very effective in spreading confusion. Of course, for operations of this kind an armoured division must be self-contained for supplies, carrying with it what it needs, so as to be free from dependence on communications during the whole course of the operation." (It is evident that Manteuffel practised what General (then Brigadier) Hobart demonstrated with the 1st Tank Brigade in the Salisbury Plain area in 1934-35—though without convincing the British General Staff that such a form of strategy was practicable.)

Hitler was delighted with the new method, and eager to hear more about it. So he sent an invitation for Manteuffel and the commander of his tank regiment, Colonel Schultz, to spend Christmas at his headquarters near Angerburg, in East Prussia. After congratulating Manteuffel, Hitler said: "As a Christmas present, I'll give you fifty tanks."

Early in 1944 Manteuffel was given command of a specially reinforced division, the "Gross-Deutschland," and with this he was sent to different sectors to check a break-through or to release forces that had been trapped by the Russian tide of advance. In September, after he had cut a way through to the German forces that were hemmed in on the Baltic coast round Riga, he was given a big jump in promotion—to command the 5th Panzer Army, in the West.

Throughout 1944, Manteuffel saw more of Hitler than almost any other commander did, as Hitler frequently summoned him to his headquarters to discuss these emergency missions and to consult him on armoured warfare problems. This close contact enabled Manteuffel to get under the surface that terrified or mesmerized other generals.

"Hitler had a magnetic, and indeed hypnotic personality. This had a very marked effect on people who went to see him with the intention of putting forward their views on any matter. They would begin to argue their point, but would gradually find themselves succumbing to his personality, and in the end would often agree to the opposite of what they intended. For my part, having come to know Hitler well in the last stages of the war, I had learned how to keep him to the point, and maintain my own argument. I did not feel afraid of Hitler, as so many were. He often called me to his headquarters for consultation, after that Christmastide I had spent at his headquarters by invitation, following the successful stroke at Zhitomir that had attracted his attention.

"Hitler had read a lot of military literature, and was also fond of listening to military lectures. In this way, coupled with his personal experience of the last war as an ordinary soldier, he had gained a very good knowledge of the lower level of warfare—the properties of the different weapons; the effect of ground and weather; the mentality and morale of troops. He was particularly good in gauging how the troops felt. I found that I was hardly ever in disagreement with his view when discussing such matters. On the other hand he had no idea of the higher strategical and tactical combinations. He had a good grasp of how a single division moved and fought, but he did not understand how armies operated."

Manteuffel then went on to talk of how the "hedgehog" system of defence had developed, and how Hitler was led to carry it too far. "When our troops were being forced back by the Russian attacks, they were attracted, as by magnets, towards the defended localities that had been prepared in rear. Falling back on these, they found it natural to rally there, and put up a stubborn resistance. Hitler was quick to see the value of such localities, and the importance of maintaining them. But he overlooked the need of giving the sector commanders reasonable latitude to modify their dispositions, and to withdraw if necessary. He insisted on having the question submitted to him in every case. Too often, before he had made up his mind, the Russians had broken through the over-strained defence.

"He had a real flair for strategy and tactics, especially for surprise moves, but he lacked a sufficient foundation of technical knowledge to apply it properly. Moreover, he had a tendency to intoxicate himself with figures and quantities. When one was discussing a problem with him, he would repeatedly pick up the telephone, ask to be put through to some departmental chief, and ask him—'How many so and so have we got?' Then he would turn to the man who was arguing with him, quote the number, and say: 'There you are'—as if that settled the problem. He was too ready to accept paper figures, without asking if the numbers stated were available in reality. It was always the same whatever the subject might be—tanks, aircraft, rifles, shovels.

"Generally, he would ring up Speer or Buhle—who was in charge of factories. Buhle always kept a little notebook beside him, with all the figures ready for which Hitler was likely to ask, and would answer pat. But even if the numbers had actually been produced, a large part of them were still in the factories, and not with the troops. In much the same way, Goering said he would provide ten divisions of ground troops from the Luftwaffe at short notice, for the Russian front—forgetting that the officers had been trained only for air operations, and would need a lengthy fresh training before they would be fit for land operations."

I remarked to Manteuffel that the more I heard about the German side of the war the more the impression had grown that, on the one hand, Hitler had a natural flair for strategy and tactics of an original kind, while the German General Staff, on the other hand, were very competent but without much originality. I felt that, from the way many of the generals had talked, Hitler's misunderstanding of technical factors so jarred them that they tended to discount the possible value of his ideas, while he was angered by their orthodoxy and lack of receptivity. In this way, it seemed to me, that a tug-of-war had developed, instead of a good working combina-tion. Manteuffel said that he agreed completely with that definition of the situation. It summed up the trouble on the military side. "I said much the same thing to Hitler myself when I spent Christmas with him in 1943, when discussing the difference of outlook between the tank leaders and those who had grown up with the older arms. The more senior generals could not get into the mind of the fighting troops under the new conditions of warfare."

CONCLUSION

SURVEYING THE RECORD OF GERMAN LEADERSHIP IN THE WAR, and the course of operations, what are the conclusions that emerge? An utter failure on the plane of war policy, or grand strategy, is seen to be accompanied by a remarkable, though uneven, run of performance in strategy and tactics. The explanation is also of a dual nature. The older professional leaders trained under the General Staff system tended to prove highly efficient, but lacking in genius—save in the sense of "an infinite capacity for taking pains." Their immense ability carried its own limitation. They tended to conduct war more in the manner of chess than as an art, unlike the old masters of war. They were inclined to frown on fellow-professionals who had novel ideas, and were more contemptuous when such ideas came from amateurs. Most of them, also, were limited in understanding of any factors outside the military field.

Hitler was quicker to spot the value of new ideas, new weapons, and new talent. He recognized the potentialities of mobile armoured forces sooner than the General Staff did, and the way he backed Guderian, Germany's leading exponent of this new instrument, proved the most decisive factor in the opening victories. Hitler had the flair that is characteristic of genius, though accompanied by liability to make elementary mistakes, both in calculation and action. The younger soldiers he picked out and pushed on were often akin to him in these respects—especially Rommel, the most favoured military "upstart." Such men had an instinct for the unexpected and a greater sense of its incalculable value in paralyzing opponents. They brought back into warfare, in a new guise, the classical ruses and stratagems which the established military teachers of the last half-century had declared out of date and impossible to apply in modern operations. By Hitler's success in demonstrating the fallacy of orthodoxy he gained an advantage over the military hierarchy which he was quicker to exploit than to consolidate.

Sometimes the intuitive amateurs were justified by events; sometimes the mathematically calculating professionals—the latter more, naturally, in the long run. But the jealousy between them, and the way it aggravated inevitable clashes of opinion, proved more fatal to Germany than the actual errors of either side. For that, the primary responsibility lay with the established hierarchy, as it always does. The result may have been inevitable, for war is not an activity that teaches wisdom to its priests, or the quality of reconciling contrary views. In view of Hitler's policy and his temperament, he would have been very difficult to restrain in any circumstances; but the attitude of the professionals and the frequency with which his insight proved more correct than theirs made him uncontrollable. But neither side was conscious of its own limitations.

The German generals of this war were the best-finished product of their profession—anywhere. They could have been better if their outlook had been wider and their understanding deeper. But if they had become philosophers they would have ceased to be soldiers.

TABLE OF THE GERMAN HIGH COMMAND

C-IN-C OF THE COMBINED FORCES (WEHRMACHT)
1933-38 Blomberg   1938-45 $\begin{cases} \text{Hitler} \\ \text{Keitel} \end{cases}$

C-IN-C OF THE ARMY
1933-38 Fritsch   1938-41 Brauchitsch   1941-45 Hitler

CHIEF OF THE GENERAL STAFF
1933-38 Beck   1938-42 Halder   1942-44 Zeitzler
1944-45 Guderian

POSTS HELD IN THE WAR BY SOME OF THE OTHER GENERALS MENTIONED

RUNDSTEDT
Army Group South in Poland, 1939; Army Group A in West, 1939-40; Army Group South in Russia, 1941; C-in-C West, 1942 to 7/2/44 and 9/4/44 to 3/18/45

BOCK
Army Group North in Poland, 1939; Army Group B in West, 1939-40; Army Group Centre in Russia, 1941; Shelved early in 1942

LEEB
Army Group C in West, 1939-40; Army Group North in Russia, 1941; Resigned early in 1942

REICHENAU
10th Pz. Army in Poland, 1939; 6th Army in West, 1940, and in Russia, 1941; Army Group South in Russia, Dec., 1941; Died, Jan., 1942

KLUGE
4th Army in Poland, 1939; 4th Army in West, 1939-40; 4th Army in Russia, 1941; Army Group Centre in Russia, 1942-43 (Injured in air crash); C-in-C West, July-Aug., 1944; Removed and committed suicide

KLEIST
Pz. Corps in Poland, 1939; Pz. Group in West, 1940; Pz. Group in Russia, 1941; 1st Pz. Army in Russia, 1943; Army Group A in Russia, Oct., 1942-44; Shelved

MANSTEIN

Rundstedt's Chief of Staff in Poland and West, 1939-Jan., 1940; 38th Corps in West, 1940; 56th Pz. Corps in Russia, 1941; 11th Army in Russia, Sept., 1941-Nov., 1942; Army Group South in Russia, 1943; Shelved in March, 1944

ROMMEL

7th Pz. Div. in West, 1940; Africa Corps and then Pz. Army Africa, 1941-April, 1943; Army Group in N. Italy, 1943; Army Group B in West, 1944; Injured in July and compulsory suicide in Oct.

THOMA

German troops in Spain, 1936-39; Pz. Bde. in Poland, 1939; Director, Mobile Forces, General Staff, 1940; Pz. Div. & Corps in Russia, 1941-42; Africa Corps, Sept.-Nov., 1942; Captured at Alamein

MODEL

Chief of Staff, 16th Army (Busch) in West, 1940; 3rd Pz. Div. and 3rd Pz. Corps in Russia, 1941; 9th Army in Russia, 1942-43; Army Groups North, South, Centre in turn, Russia, Oct., 1943-Aug., 1944; Army Group B in West, 1944-45 (temp. C-in-C West, late Aug., 1944)

HEINRICI

12th Corps in West, 1940; 43rd Corps in Russia, 1941; 4th Army in Russia, 1942-May, 1944; 1st Pz. Army, 1944-45; Army Group West, covering Berlin, March, 1945

TIPPELSKIRCH

30th Inf. Div. in Russia, 1941-42; 12th Corps in Russia, 1943-44; 4th Army in Russia, May-July, 1944 (Injured in air crash); 14th Army in Italy, early 1945; 4th Army in E. Germany, April, 1945

MANTEUFFEL

Motor Inf. Regt. in 7th Pz. Div. (Rommel) in West, 1940, and Russia, 1941; Motor Inf. Bde. in 7th Pz. Div. in Russia, 1942; Mixed Div. in Tunisia, early 1943; 7th and G. D. Pz. Divs. in Russia, 1943-44; 5th Pz. Army in West, Sept., 1944-45

BLUMENTRITT

Rundstedt's 1A (Ops. Chief) in Poland, 1939 and in West, 1940; Chief of Staff, 4th Army (Kluge) in Russia, 1941; D.C. G. S. (Ob. Q. I.), 1942; Chief of Staff, West, Sept., 1942-Sept., 1944; Corps & Army in West, Oct., 1944-May, 1945

INDEX